MW01469506

Profiling the Fraudster

The Wiley Corporate F&A series provides information, tools, and insights to corporate professionals responsible for issues affecting the profitability of their company, from accounting and finance to internal controls and performance management.

Founded in 1807, John Wiley & Sons is the oldest independent publishing company in the United States. With offices in North America, Europe, Asia, and Australia, Wiley is globally committed to developing and marketing print and electronic products and services for our customers' professional and personal knowledge and understanding.

Profiling the Fraudster

Removing the Mask to Prevent and Detect Fraud

SIMON PADGETT

WILEY

Library of Congress Cataloging-in-Publication Data

Padgett, Simon
  Profiling the fraudster : removing the mask to prevent and detect fraud / Simon Padgett.
       pages cm. – (Wiley corporate F&A series)
    Includes bibliographical references and index.
   ISBN 978-1-118-87104-1 (hardback)
  1. Corporations–Corrupt practices. 2. White collar crimes. 3. Fraud.
4. Fraud–Prevention. 5. Fraud investigation. I. Title.
   HV6768.P33 2014
   658.4′73–dc23
                                                         2014034566

This book is dedicated to all the honest people in the world who face the uphill daily survival challenge while watching others steal their way to a luxury lifestyle. People with integrity have shaped my life and this book.

Contents

Preface

THE TYPICAL ORGANIZATION LOSES 5 PERCENT of its annual revenue to fraud. Applied to the estimated 2011 gross world product, this figure translates to a potential total fraud loss of more than $3.5 trillion worldwide, according to the Association of Certified Fraud Examiners (ACFE) *Report to the Nations, 2012*. So, put in context, fraud *is* material.

Profiling is a part of everyday life for all of us, using previous experiences to determine how we get through the day's activities. Indeed, when we approach winter months we know that we need warmer clothing. Why, because last winter told us so. When we drive through an intersection or the stoplight turns red, we know exactly what to do or how to react to the event because we have done it so many times before. More to the point, we can identify the cold of winter and the challenges we face while driving because we have seen the patterns on numerous occasions before, and our brains have analyzed the information at that time, stored the patterns of data, and drawn on the stored memory to deal with the current event. Then consider your favorite sport and trying to work out who will win. In the same way that we recall previous events, we also recall previous history of individual sports teams and individuals. Soccer players of a certain age may be in their peak, rugby players from a certain continent may win more games, and marathon runners from certain African countries are always likely to run the fastest times. This is everyday profiling of individuals based on previous experiences. If this process works in dealing with the characteristics of day-to-day activities and people we come into contact with, then why is this process of profiling not more prevalent in the fight against fraud? It can be seen that many forensic investigations do not have a formal process for either drawing from or contributing to fraud type and fraudster profiling.

Fraud profiling has the potential to serve as an aid to fraud investigations. Valuable data and information on offenders and fraud situations and scenarios is not being used as much as it should or could be by investigators in the identification of fraud in the workplace.

Occupational fraud or white-collar crime reflects a high rate of incidence and a relatively low rate of detection, making it one of the significant crime challenges of the twenty-first century. Fraud risk can be more effectively managed by integration and use of previous knowledge concerning the individual, the situational environment, and motivations driving fraud offenders. Examination of empirical research on fraud types and fraud offenders yields common characteristics such as the fact that the average fraudster, statistically, is male, is married with a degree, and has a professional relationship, usually by means of employment, with the victim organization. The fraudster is most likely to work in the accounting, finance, or procurement department—those being the gatekeeper elements of the business process—and not within the internal audit department. Currently, he or she is more likely to be working for a financial services organization, according to the Association of Certified Fraud Examiners and its 2012 *Report to the Nations on Occupational Fraud and Abuse*. Research has revealed many types of fraud offender and the circumstances in which fraud is committed. Much of this research tells us that the fraudster is the opportunistic offender with no criminal record who, out of greed, abuses a position of financial trust to commit a fraud alone or with few accomplices. An interesting finding is the fact that most fraud offenders find complex methodologies to carry out and also to hide their crimes. This has implications for prevention strategies insomuch as the traditional barriers to fraud of internal accounting controls and employment screening are no longer sufficient on their own.

So, if profiling techniques are to be added to the fraud investigator's toolbox, then we must first ask and, more important, answer some questions. How does profiling assist and add value to investigations? What key aspects of an offender profile should be included in the profiling, and are such details as marital status, age, and race really necessary, as well as fraudster background, skill, and professional qualifications? Would it be beneficial to include in such profiling the characteristics of the fraud scheme or scenario itself and the situation that lends itself to the fraud? Furthermore, should the type of victim organization be analyzed, and should this be further drilled down into as to which departments and divisions are more prone to fraud attack? Many surveys tell us that 80 to 85 percent of fraud is committed by insiders. Surely, if we knew from which departments the fraudsters emanate or, possibly more important, which vulnerable departments they try to be recruited in, then this could be a focal area for both proactive fraud risk management and reactive investigation.

We all too often focus on the control environment, and quite often human beings are fundamental to that control environment or at least key elements of it. Human beings are the weakest link. How strong is the control in a segregation of duties if the employees in the process exhibit characteristics that place their honesty and integrity in doubt? Surely, if the human element of the control environment is not considered then such controls are weak or even nonexistent. Profiling of these employees is fundamental to an effective control environment. There is no doubt, however, that a full understanding of what fraud is and which measures are best suited to combating the fraud disease is absolutely necessary before we can start to profile the fraudster or his actions.

We have to face the fact that fraud cannot be prevented. Internal controls and security systems reduce the risk, but there are no guarantees and the track record of prevention and detection is, actually, not great. Humans can be ingenious and their behavior unpredictable. Some are desperate; many are merely risk takers. Most are both. Some employees may have a lot more devious entrepreneurial spirit than we may have imagined. If fraud is committed by trusted employees who know the system, then it is quite likely that they also know how to bypass these controls, and therefore something more is required in the preventive and detective fight. Fraud profiling is the process of identifying the characteristics that the fraudster and his fraud would present or be visualized if that fraud were to happen in your organization. If you know what it looks like, you can identify or recognize it and catch it when it happens. If you catch it when it happens, it will make the next person think twice about committing fraud and will leave investigators with key indicators of the behavioral or situational patterns or footprints for the future.

Interestingly, as is the case at the time of writing, in periods of economic slowdown or recession the likelihood of employee fraud increases. Apart from the increase in financial need there is also increased psychological pressure on employees. Employees tend to not only be under greater personal financial stress currently but may also be under greater personal insecurity about their future in the organization. When close colleagues are laid off, fear and insecurity prevail psychologically. This brings about a further dimension to the profiling scenario, the fact that the economic environment should be included as a constituent part of profiling fraudsters. Put simply, human beings in a deprived part of a city in a country going through economic slowdown might be more apt to commit fraud than those earning good salaries in a country that is booming or bypassing recession. The economic environment, therefore, also needs to be included in any profiling methodology.

In summary, fraud happens. It happens in any organization that has money or assets, irrespective of profitability. Quite often it is a cause of an organization not being profitable. The fraudster is internal. Remember, 80 to

85 percent of fraud is committed by persons inside the organization, by our colleagues who are more often than not at a senior level and to whom we report and upon whom we rely to safeguard the assets of our business. We have to adopt the attitude that the fraudster is within our organization, and therefore it is only prudent that we alter the paradigm and expect that fraud will happen and adopt a preventive strategy. In order to be ahead of the curve, that strategy has to include the relatively new dimension of profiling.

In order to identify anything, you have to know what it looks like. If you don't know what it looks like, you may walk right past it without recognizing it. There are an infinite number of characteristics of fraud offenders and fraud types or scenarios, and there are an infinite variety of industries, business structures, departments, accounting systems, and so on. Like attempts to prevent fraud, there is no guarantee that a detection strategy will work all the time and identify every fraud, but research indicates that most occupational fraud is not sophisticated and, generally, not well concealed. All that is required is to identify what it would look like, and it will, more than likely, be found. Profiling is not intended to provide an absolute guarantee of fraud detection but an incremental improvement in the odds against your business becoming a victim of fraud.

So, if we can profile the following footprints attributable to the act of fraud, then we have a pretty good coverage of all likely characteristics, providing us with the greatest chance of recognizing the fraudster and the fraud act:

- The fraudster's behavioral indicators.
- The environment in which the fraud occurs, to include:
    - Victim organization type and sector.
    - Victim department.
    - Fraudster's position in department.
    - Geographical location.
    - Economic situation.
- Fraud type characteristics.
- Fraud methodology or modus operandi.
- Fraud motivators.
- Characteristics of consequences or the impact of fraud.

The process of profiling has to be made simple and understandable, yet it should be rigorous and comprehensive. Its objective is the development of a set of detection controls that will identify the characteristics of a fraudster or patterns that fraud would present if it were to occur in your business.

This book examines how profiling occupational fraudsters and their actions and characteristics can help in the proactive fight to reduce fraud risk in the organizational workplace, and it explains how to prepare a fraud profiling methodology for your organization. This book is a must-have valuable resource in your antifraud library.

Profiling the Fraudster: Removing the Mask to Prevent and Detect Fraud features:

- Detailed analysis and breakdown of profiling and its relevance in occupational fraud fighting methodologies.
- Clear insights into the mind of the fraudulent employee.
- Observations, analysis, and conclusions to guide readers through prevention and detection strategies using profiling.
- Integrated extracts from professional surveys, including the ACFE's *Report to the Nations on Occupational Fraud and Abuse* revealing statistics on cost, prevalence, patterns of fraud and fraud prevention, and what it all means.
- A step-by-step approach to using profiling and investigative psychology to manage fraud risk.
- Designing fraud profiling methodologies to suit your organization.

Acknowledgments

COMPLETION OF THIS BOOK would not have been possible without the support of many people. First, many thanks to colleagues at my current place of work who have given me the support and assistance required to enable me to carry out this research and writing and to the many colleagues and professional services firms with whom I have had the pleasure to interact throughout my career and who have provided insight, inspiration, and material. Thanks to my parents who inspired me with their endurance to my never-ending skepticism of anything put to me and to Oxford Brookes University and my MBA supervisors for their assistance and the availability of excellent resources in terms of the written and spoken word. I also wish to thank my fellow board members of the Association of Certified Fraud Examiners (ACFE), UAE chapter, for their encouragement and support and the many ACFE members as well as the ACFE in general who have allowed me to use some of their valuable information to add structure and substance to the profiling theory. I would also like to thank John Wiley & Sons and in particular Stacey Rivera, senior development editor, for their guidance and advice throughout the drafting, submission, and publishing of this book. Perhaps the biggest thanks, however, should go to the many fraudsters whom I have had the pleasure of investigating and interacting with, for supplying me with the reasons for writing this work. Last but not least, I would like to thank my family, who provided unwavering support, encouragement, patience, and silence throughout the gestation period and writing and production life cycle of the development of this book.

PART ONE

Occupational Fraud and Corruption

CHAPTER ONE

Introduction to Occupational Fraud and Corruption and Recent Trends

W HEN I STARTED WRITING THIS BOOK, I considered jumping in at the deep end and commenced rapidly making notes of the various approaches to profiling by compiling a list, based on my 20 or so years of experience in the fraud investigation field, of exactly what, when profiled, would be of use to the fraud investigator. Yes, there is the behavior of the convicted fraudster to understand as well as his modus operandi, but what about which industry type or department he is likely to work in, his likely position within the organization, the likely geographical location, economic environment, and personal circumstances? We also need to understand the profile of higher risk victim organizations and their characteristics. Anyway, I quickly realized that to fully understand the subject of profiling we first need to have a fairly good grounding in or understanding of the subject of fraud and corruption—what it is and how it affects organizations and all of us who are associated with those organizations. It is also, possibly even more so, very important to understand the types of controls that are designed, put in place, and often bypassed to enable us to manage fraud risk in organizations. After all, fraud is perpetrated by human beings as a reaction to opportunities created by weak safeguarding processes. Profiling is a further antifraud methodology to add to the stable, and it does require an understanding of how and where in the corporate environment it would best sit. After all, you would not bring in a new team member without first ensuring a good fit or put a new thoroughbred into a stable to share with other horses without first having an understanding of those neighbors and what makes them kick. So, let's have a look at the world of fraud and corruption and how, since time immemorial, we appear to be failing in our attempts to manage fraud risk in the organizational environment.

DECEPTION THROUGH BREACHING TRUST

The term *fraud* has come to encompass many forms of misconduct. Although the legal definition of fraud is very specific, for most people like you and me, antifraud professionals, regulators, the media, and the general public alike, the common use of the word is much broader and generally covers any attempt to deceive another party to gain a benefit. Expense fraud, forgery, counterfeiting, identity theft, theft of inventory by employees, manipulated financial statements, insider trading, Ponzi schemes, mortgage fraud—the range of possible fraud schemes is actually endless but at their core all involve a violation of trust. It is this violation that, perhaps even more than the resulting financial loss, makes such crimes so harmful. For businesses to operate and for commerce to flow freely, organizations must entrust their employees with resources and responsibilities. So when an employee defrauds his or her employer, the fallout is often especially harsh. The focus of this book is *occupational fraud* schemes in which an employee abuses the trust placed upon him or her by an employer for personal gain. The formal definition of *occupational fraud*, taken from the Association of Certified Fraud Examiners (ACFE) website, http://www.acfe.com/fraud-101.aspx is

> the use of one's occupation for personal enrichment through the deliberate misuse or misapplication of the employing organization's resources or assets.

While this occupational fraud category is but one facet of the vast overall fraud universe, fraud in the workplace is huge and covers a wide range of employee misconduct. It is, without doubt, a material threat faced by all organizations and their employees worldwide.

GLOBAL TRENDS IN OCCUPATIONAL FRAUD

The Association of Certified Fraud Examiners (ACFE), a leading professional body of fraud examiners, has undertaken extensive research into the costs and trends relating to occupational fraud schemes. The findings of the ACFE's initial research efforts were released in 1996 in the first *Report to the Nations on Occupational Fraud and Abuse*, with subsequent reports released in 2002, 2004, 2006, 2008, and 2010. The ACFE's 2012 *Report to the Nations on Occupational Fraud and Abuse*, now carried out every two years, provides an analysis of 1,388 fraud cases investigated worldwide by qualified fraud examiners and continues a tradition of shedding light on trends in the characteristics of fraudsters, the schemes they perpetrate, and the organizations being victimized. The ACFE findings truly reflect global trends in occupational fraud and abuse and are invaluable in keeping us abreast of the fraud disease.

The goals of these reports have been to

- Summarize the opinions of experts on the percentage of organizational revenue lost to all forms of occupational fraud and abuse.
- Categorize the ways in which occupational fraud and abuse occur.
- Examine the characteristics of the employees who commit occupational fraud and abuse.
- Determine what kinds of organizations are victims of occupational fraud and abuse.

Each version of the report has been based on detailed information about fraud cases investigated by certified fraud examiners (CFEs). Each new edition expands and modifies the analysis contained in the previous reports to reflect current issues and enhance the quality of the data that is reported. This evolution has allowed the release of increasingly meaningful information from the experiences of CFEs and the frauds that they encounter.

Fraud, like many other crimes, can be explained by the existence of the following four key drivers:

1. A supply of motivated, pressurized, or incentivized offenders.
2. The absence of capable guardians and policing, or weaknesses in control systems, opening up an opportunity.
3. Rationalization in the fraudster's mind bringing about justification for his actions in exploiting the opportunity to satisfy the motivation.
4. The availability of suitable victim organizations.

The motivation, pressure, or incentive to defraud may be as simple as financial need or greed or anything from unrealistic deadlines and performance goals to personal vices such as gambling or drugs.

The opportunity to commit and conceal fraud is really the only element over which an organization has significant control. The opportunity is an open door to solving a nonshareable problem by violating a position of trust and is generally provided through weaknesses in the internal controls. Some examples of weak internal controls include but are by no means limited to absent or inadequate procedures surrounding the following:

- Supervision and review.
- Segregation of duties.
- Management approval and delegation of authority.
- System controls.

Rationalization is a crucial component because most people need to reconcile their behavior with the commonly accepted notions of decency and trust. Some examples of justifications for their actions given by fraudsters I have met include the following:

- "I really need this money, and I'll put it back when I get my salary at the month's end."
- "I'd rather have the company on my back than the tax people."
- "Everyone else is doing it."
- "I just can't afford to lose everything I have worked for—my home, car, everything."

The availability of a suitable victim organization is an easy one. It is more often than not the fraudster's employer, with whom he has built up a relationship of trust, quite often over many years.

The ACFE 2012 *Report to the Nations on Occupational Fraud and Abuse* analyzes statistics from fraud cases investigated worldwide to gain an understanding of the characteristics of fraudsters, their schemes, and the types of organizations being targeted. Throughout the report, the statistics include comparison charts showing several years of data, which highlight the consistency of findings over time. This uniformity is among the most notable of observations from the ongoing research and indicates that the findings truly reflect global trends in occupational fraud and abuse and that the ACFE statistics represent an important core base for profiling in any organization.

 ## THE COST OF OCCUPATIONAL FRAUD AND CORRUPTION

Determining the full cost of occupational fraud is an important part of understanding the depth of and motivation for the fraud problem. News reports provide visibility to the largest cases, and most of us have heard stories of employees who have brazenly stolen from their employers. Even so, fraud is all too often treated as an anomaly in the business process rather than a common example of the risk faced by all organizations. Unfortunately, obtaining a comprehensive or exact measure of the financial impact of fraud and corruption on organizations is challenging, if not impossible. Because fraud inherently involves efforts of concealment, many fraud cases will never be detected, and of those that are, the full amount of losses might never be determined or reported. Consequently, any attempt to quantify the extent of all occupational fraud losses will be, at best, an estimate. As part of the ACFE's research in its *Report to the Nations*, each CFE who participated in the survey was asked to provide his or her best assessment of the percentage of annual revenues that the typical organization loses to fraud. The median response indicates that organizations lose an estimated 5 percent of their revenues to fraud each year. To illustrate the magnitude of this estimate, applying the percentage to the 2011 estimated gross world product of $70.28 trillion results in a projected global total fraud loss of more than $3.5 trillion. It is imperative to note that this estimate is based on the collective opinion of antifraud experts rather than on specific data or factual observations, and should thus not be interpreted as a literal calculation or extrapolation of the exact and total worldwide cost of fraud against organizations. Even with that caveat, however, the approximation provided by more than 1,000 CFEs from all over the world with a median 11 years of experience as professionals who have a firsthand view of the fight against fraud may well be the most reliable measure of the cost of occupational fraud available and certainly emphasizes the undeniable and extensive threat posed by these crimes.

Of the 1,388 individual fraud cases reported in the ACFE survey, 1,379 included information about the total dollar amount lost to fraud, as shown in Figure 1.1.

Individuals commit occupational fraud costing businesses considerable sums of money, worldwide a potential global fraud loss of more than $3.5 trillion, according to the ACFE report. The median loss, the report states, was $140,000. More than one-fifth of the frauds involved losses of at least $1 million and the frauds lasted a median of 18 months before being detected. It can be seen that any methodology that can be used to improve fraud risk management must be seriously considered.

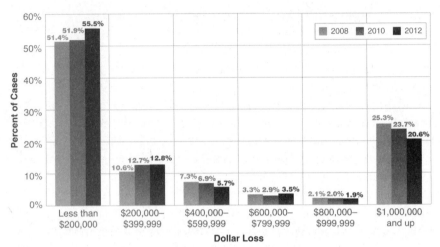

FIGURE 1.1 Distribution of Dollar Losses. *Source:* ACFE, *Report to the Nations,* 2012.

 ## TYPES OF OCCUPATIONAL FRAUD

The top three classifications or means of committing occupational fraud are *corruption, asset misappropriation,* and *fraudulent financial statements,* as depicted in Figure 1.2.

Within each classification is a myriad of types and schemes that need to be understood when considering methodology profiling. As indicated in Figure 1.3, asset misappropriation is by far the most frequent form of occupational fraud, comprising 87 percent of the cases reported; it was also the least costly form of fraud, with a median loss of $120,000.

At the lower end of the frequency spectrum are cases involving financial statement fraud. Financial statement fraud was, however, by far the most costly form of occupational fraud. Financial statement fraud schemes made up just 8 percent of the cases in the ACFE study, but caused the greatest median loss, at $1 million. Corruption schemes fell in the middle, occurring in just over one-third of reported cases and causing a median loss of $250,000, with asset misappropriation having the lowest median loss, as depicted in Figure 1.4.

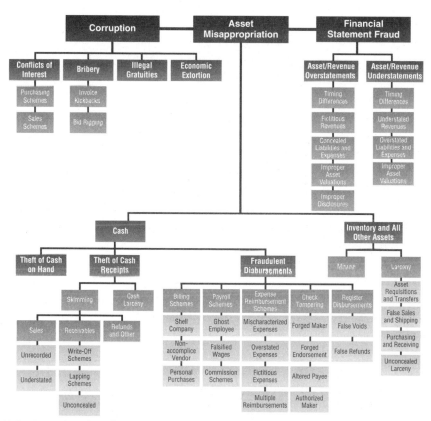

FIGURE 1.2   Classification of Occupational Fraud and Abuse.   *Source:* ACFE, *Report to the Nations*, 2012.

High-level or owner/executive perpetrators cause the greatest fraud loss to their organizations, in terms of monetary value rather than quantities of frauds. This is particularly shocking considering that the "tone at the top" is considered to be a fundamental constituent part of a sound antifraud program. In actual fact frauds committed by owners/executives were more than three times as costly as frauds committed by managers and more than nine times as costly as other employee fraud, according to the ACFE. Executive-level fraud also took much longer to detect.

The most common executive-level fraud, according to the survey, is corruption (54 percent of cases), followed by fraudulent invoicing schemes

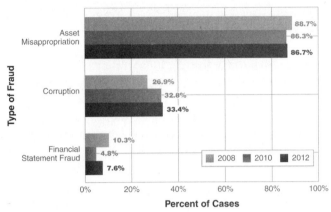

FIGURE 1.3 Occupational Frauds by Category—Frequency. *Source:* ACFE, *Report to the Nations*, 2012.

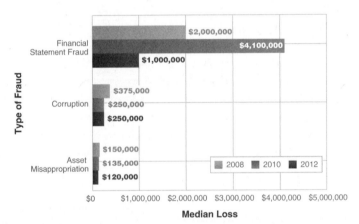

FIGURE 1.4 Occupational Fraud by Category—Median Loss. *Source:* ACFE, *Report to the Nations*, 2012.

(33 percent), expense reimbursement fraud (21 percent), and fraudulent financial statements (21 percent). Other schemes include payroll fraud, check tampering, and cash theft.

EARLY FRAUD

Business has been around for thousands of years, and the way it is run and sometimes abused can be embedded deep in the culture. Occupational fraud was defined by American criminologist Edwin H. Sutherland (1883–1950) as "a crime that involves a betrayal of trust implied in the holding of an office or other position of trust." Sutherland used the term *white-collar crime*, casting doubt on the idea that poverty breeds crime. Sutherland argued in *White Collar Crime* that members of society occupying positions of privilege and status were just as likely to commit crime as those from lower classes. Sutherland's work, it could be argued, reflects some of the earliest studies on profiling criminals.

It can be contended that rationalization of occupational crime comes from its low visibility, occurring under cover of employment, with victims often suffering without meeting perpetrators, resulting in the indirect nature of the act giving the appearance that it is victimless. Research shows, however, that occupational fraudsters display criminal thinking that parallels street-level offenders with similar behavioral traits that serve as risk factors.

Generally, fraudsters live well-ordered lives and are well respected in their communities and at work. They commit fraud in their workplace to fulfill a financial need when there is an opportunity to do so and when then can rationalize their deed (Cressey's fraud triangle, 1953). Trusted, well-paid employees risk their careers by stealing from their employers due to financial difficulties, lifestyle maintenance, anger, low loyalty, revenge, and boredom (KPMG, 2011). Occupational fraud is costlier than other crimes and affects more people (ACFE, *Report to the Nations*, 2012). It relies on deceit and concealment and often employs sophisticated technology.

Further to motive and opportunity, techniques of neutralization enable individuals to violate normative and ethical standards (Coleman, 2002). For example, by justifying theft as "borrowing," criminal activities may be deemed to be a normal way of stealing or achieving business targets. Trying to prove that a fraudster intends to permanently deprive an organization can be difficult when the fraudster has claimed that he intends to repay the amount or has already done so. Offenders may justify their behavior by claiming that they are not really hurting anyone, that everyone else is doing it, or that the activities may have been carried out that way for many years. This may be a reflection on their culture or background.

The ACFE estimates that some $3.5 trillion of fraud is happening worldwide. The National Fraud Authority in the United Kingdom publishes its Annual Fraud Indicator every year, which estimates that fraud in 2011 was costing the UK economy over £38 billion a year, equating to a shocking £765 per adult per year. This figure includes estimated undetected losses.

In the *Compliance Reporter* article "UK Fraud at Record Level" (2012), KPMG reported the actual 2011 UK fraud to be £3.5 billion. The 2011 *FraudTrack Report*, released by accountancy firm BDO, revealed a significant increase in both the number and value of reported frauds in the United Kingdom in the previous year to the highest level of fraud since the report began in 2003. In 2010, there were 372 cases of reported fraud with an average value of £3.7 million each. This had risen to 413 cases with an average value of £5 million each.

THE FIGHT AGAINST FRAUD

The nature and threat of occupational fraud is universal, according to the ACFE. Although the research in its 2012 *Report to the Nations* noted some regional differences in the methods used to commit fraud, as well as organizational approaches to preventing and detecting it, many trends and characteristics are similar regardless of where the fraud occurred. Whereas this may make writing a textbook on how to deal with fraud a little easier in that much of the approach may take a standardized approach, this is certainly not the case when we start to consider profiling. Profiling the human being cannot be a standard process with a one-size-fits-all solution. Each human being has unique characteristics and behavioral attributes, thereby giving a unique angle to what may be described as universal fraud.

Providing individuals with a means to report suspicious activity is a critical part of any antifraud program. Fraud reporting mechanisms, such as communication channels and whistleblowing hotlines, should be set up to receive tips from both internal and external sources and should ideally be externally managed, should offer anonymity and toll-free calling, and should allow confidentiality. Management should actively encourage employees to report suspicious activity, offering a reporting process free of reprisals and with the maximum protection for the whistleblower. In many jurisdictions this protection comes through the legal system with whistleblower protection embedded in local law. Interestingly, where I have worked on introducing whistleblowing mechanisms in organizations in jurisdictions where there is no legal protection for whistleblowers, I strongly advise that the organization's CEO or chairman state in his launch address as well as in his preamble in the whistleblowing policy that he personally guarantees the protection of whistleblowers and that their actions will not be detrimental to them in any way, irrespective of legal protection or its absence.

External audits should not be relied on as an organization's primary fraud detection method, says the ACFE. Such audits were the most commonly implemented control in the study; however, they detected only 3 percent of the frauds reported and they ranked poorly in limiting fraud losses. While external audits serve an important purpose and can have a strong preventive effect on potential fraud, their usefulness as a means of uncovering fraud is limited. Both internal and external auditors, however, have access to and are therefore crucial to the collection and analysis of the information and data required to set up a profiling mechanism in the organization.

Targeted fraud awareness and sensitization training for employees and managers is a critical component of an effective antifraud program and is a proven method of preventing and detecting fraud. Not only are employee tips the most common way occupational fraud is detected, but the research shows that organizations that have antifraud training programs for employees, managers, and executives experience lower losses and shorter fraud durations than organizations that do not have such programs in place. At a minimum, staff members should be sensitized as to what fraud actually is, what actions constitute fraud, how fraud harms everyone in the organization, and how to report suspected fraudulent activity.

Research continues to show that small businesses are particularly vulnerable to fraud. These organizations typically have fewer resources than their larger counterparts, which often translates to fewer and less-effective antifraud controls. In addition, because smaller businesses have fewer resources, the losses they experience tend to have a greater impact than they would in larger organizations. Managers and owners of small businesses should focus their antifraud efforts on the most cost-effective control mechanisms, such as hotlines, employee training, and setting a proper ethical tone at the top and within the organization. Additionally, assessing the specific fraud schemes that pose the greatest threat to the business can help identify those areas that merit additional investment in targeted antifraud controls. The fraud risk assessment process is invaluable in determining fraud risk exposure and is a fundamental element of fraud profiling.

 ## PROFILING AS A SOLUTION

In terms of profiling, most fraudsters exhibit behavioral traits that can serve as warning signs of their actions. These red flags, such as living beyond one's means or exhibiting excessive territorial control issues, generally will not be identified by traditional internal controls that are designed to focus on the organization's processes rather than human behavior. Managers, employees, and auditors should be educated through the training and sensitization programs on these common behavioral patterns and encouraged to consider them, particularly when noted in tandem with other anomalies, to help identify patterns that might indicate fraudulent activity.

The cost of occupational fraud, both financially and, possibly more important, to an organization's reputation, can be acutely damaging. With nearly half of victim organizations unable to recover their losses, proactive measures to prevent fraud are critical. Management should continually assess the organization's specific fraud risks and evaluate its fraud prevention programs in light of those risks. Profiling of the fraudster and his modus operandi will be a valuable addition to the fraud fighter's toolkit.

The fact that the level of reported fraud is up is worrying, but not at all surprising. When the economic climate is difficult there is even more focus on the bottom line and driving out unnecessary costs, so fraud is more likely to be uncovered. Companies should have a proactive approach to fraud protection to avoid increases in the level of fraud. Organizations need to be taking a profit-and-loss approach to fraud risk. If companies continue to take a reactive approach to preventing fraud, it will continue to rise year after year. You cannot design all fraud risk out of a business, but you can put tripwires in place.

2

Types of Occupational Fraud and Corruption

M OST OCCUPATIONAL FRAUD AND CORRUPTION SCHEMES use one or more of the following embedded techniques: abuse of power, embezzlement, misuse of business time, computer fraud, stock and equipment pilferage, and expense abuse.

- **Abuse of power**. This scheme involves making inappropriate financial decisions to benefit the employee rather than the organization. For example, the employee signs contracts with more expensive outside vendors and receives a kickback in return. Kickbacks are a form of corruption, also defined as an abuse of one's position of power.
- **Embezzlement**. One of the most common occupational frauds is the manipulation of accounting records to steal business funds. Financially astute employees may be able to devise sophisticated schemes to cover their theft. This is called misrepresentation, one of the characteristics of fraud.
- **Misuse of business time**. Employees who perform nonwork-related functions while at work are committing fraud because they are depriving the business of employee productivity during that time. The act of fraud itself is also included in this category. Alternatively, running a personal business

from the employment office constitutes theft of time, as does the time occupied by committing fraudulent activity.

- **Computer fraud**. The advent of modern technology has provided more opportunities for employees to commit computer or electronic fraud, facilitating the electronic manipulation of business funds so as to deposit them into personal or other third-party accounts. Not only do computers facilitate the fraudster's activities, but they are also essential in fraud detection.
- **Stock and equipment pilferage**. The theft of stock and capital equipment such as laptop computers, furniture, printers, and so on.
- **Expense abuse**. Disguising personal expenses as business expenses in order to steal funds.

 ## A MYRIAD OF FRAUD SCHEMES

Within the three types or classifications of corruption, asset misappropriation, and fraudulent financial statements, the list of occupational fraud types, schemes, and methodologies is endless and includes the following:

- **Theft**. The intent to permanently deprive another, usually of either assets or money.
- **Procurement fraud**. Stealing items purchased or the funds intended to pay for those purchases and covering the theft by false accounting entries.
- **Bribery**. Offering or requesting, paying or receiving anything of value with the intent to influence actions, inactions, opinions, or decisions, usually paid up front.
- **Corruption**. The abuse of a position of power to gain an advantage.
- **Embezzlement**. When a person entrusted with safeguarding an organization's money or property misappropriates it for his or her own benefit.
- **Computer sabotage**. Using a computer virus or some other highly technical method to incapacitate the business's computer system with a view to extortion.
- **Counterfeiting**. The copying or imitating of an item or document without due authority and passing the copy off as being an original.
- **Forgery**. An unauthorized change to a real or original document, which is then used to deceive in order to obtain an advantage.
- **Credit card fraud**. The unauthorized use of a credit card to obtain value and personal gain.
- **Extortion**. Illegally obtaining property from another by actual or threatened force, fear, or violence.

- **Financial statement fraud**. Reporting incorrect results or facts in the financial statements in order to deceive the reader and user. Such fraud can be committed by omission.
- **Insider trading**. Using inside, confidential, or advance information to trade in shares and obtain an advantage.
- **Intellectual property theft**. The theft and sale of cutting-edge technology by employees from their employers.
- **Kickback**. Paying an employee a portion of an inflated purchase price as a reward for facilitating the deal, usually after the event.
- **Bank fraud**. Engaging in activity where fraudulent transactions go through a bank.
- **Money laundering**. The movement of the proceeds of crime to disguise the illegal source.

It is usual, and perhaps a good time now to note, that the counterfeiting and forgery methodologies are quite often those used to hide the misrepresentation implicit in the fraud act itself and are fundamental to most forms of organizational fraud and corruption.

CYBERCRIME

Cybercrime warrants a separate discussion as a methodology or fraud type as it has specific advantages to the fraudster and corresponding challenges to the investigator, enabling the fraudster to effectively remain anonymous, thereby camouflaging his profile. The threat of cybercrime is growing, according to the Association of Chartered Certified Accountants' February 2012 edition of *Accounting and Business* international magazine. Cybercrime is now ranked as one of the top four economic crimes, after asset misappropriation, accounting fraud, and bribery and corruption, according to PricewaterhouseCoopers' (PwC) *Global Economic Crime Survey 2011*. Of the 3,877 respondents polled in 78 countries, almost half (48 percent) thought the risk of cybercrime was on the rise, with only 4 percent believing it was falling. Worryingly, stated PwC, 4 in 10 respondents said that their organization didn't have the capability to prevent and detect cybercrime.

The Internet as a Mask

Cybercrime refers to any criminal activity involving the use of a computer and a network, in particular the Internet. The computer itself can be used directly in the commissioning of a crime, or it may be the target of the crime.

The main difference between fraud in the physical world and Internet fraud is that with available data cybercriminals can commit crime at a much faster rate than conventional fraudsters, plus have the added advantage of anonymity. Unlike conventional fraudsters, Internet criminals run no risk of being apprehended in-store. This level of anonymity makes attempting and successfully conducting Internet crime far easier; it also makes dealing with Internet criminals a daunting prospect.

Cybercrime, or computer-based fraud, is the use of any dishonest misrepresentation with the intent of obtaining a benefit by deception and can be carried out by the unauthorized entry of false data; altering of data before entry; altering, destroying, suppressing, or stealing output; altering or deleting stored data; altering or misusing system tools or software packages; and altering or writing code for fraudulent purposes.

Cybercrime can range from downloading illegal music files to stealing millions of dollars from online bank accounts and also includes nonmonetary crimes, such as creating and distributing viruses or posting confidential or sensitive information on the Internet.

Perhaps the most prominent and largest form of cybercrime is identity theft, in which criminals use the Internet to steal personal information from other users to use to perpetrate frauds for their own advantage. Two of the most common methods of stealing personal information are phishing and pharming. Both of these methods lure users to fake or spoof websites that appear to be legitimate, where they are asked to enter personal information including login information such as usernames and passwords, phone numbers, addresses, credit card numbers, bank account numbers, and other information criminals can use to steal another person's identity. This personal information can then be used in a variety of Internet-based scams targeting consumers directly.

To compound the problem of Internet fraud, there are a number of opportunities that Internet-based criminals can take advantage of. For example, immediate credit has become a practical necessity for e-traders wanting to maximize web-based transactions. The result, in many cases, is that the Internet merchant makes instant credit available to online shoppers. This provides criminals with the chance to pose as a legitimate customer, obtain credit, and purchase goods online. Online banks and e-traders need to be constantly vigilant and take steps to protect themselves and their customers against this danger.

Typically, online customers are requested to provide personal details before an Internet transaction can be processed. This might include information as to their name, postal address, credit card number, e-mail address, and the product or service being ordered. As has been the experience with online banks, this is an area where web merchants can begin to combat fraud. Asking for extensive personal details helps to determine the legitimacy of an application or online order. In some cases, the person concerned should be the only one knowing the required details, and with this information provided, merchants can then build up a bigger picture of the customer. Ideally, this assessment process should be overlaid with information as to the applicant's past online activity, for example, sites last visited. Closer inspection and analysis of the data collected on application forms can provide insight into fraudulent behavior. Often, the first pattern to emerge comes from an analysis of the credit card type and card number. A strong positive correlation exists between the credit card type section on an application form being left blank and the probability of attempted fraud. Another example is where the credit card type and the credit card number do not correspond. This discrepancy can be ascertained from the credit card number, the bank identification number (BIN) being the first part of the credit card number used to identify the bank issuing the card. Where the BIN is illogical this may be an indication that the applicant is attempting to guess the correct card type. Obviously, where the card type and card BIN concur, detecting potential fraud becomes harder. In the latter example, the credit grantor would need to examine additional criteria for inconsistencies.

Interaction between call center staff and applicants offers a number of advantages. Call center staff can further review applicants and prevent frauds slipping through. With known and valued customers, a telephone call can reinforce the existing communication and marketing channels. Deepening of the customer relationship may take the form or disguise of staff using this as an opportunity to cross-sell or up-sell special offers, discounts, or club memberships. The Internet provides online fraudsters with a myriad of ways to attempt crimes, in some cases with only a minimal chance of being apprehended. Web merchants have learned to look closely at the information provided on application forms and online orders as certain patterns tend to be highly predictive of fraudulent behavior. Cybercrime increases the opportunity for anonymity, which is a major advantage to the fraudster and makes profiling of these people even more challenging.

While computers and the Internet have made our lives easier in many ways, with databases being able to handle massive amounts of data in minimal time periods, it is unfortunate that people also use these technologies to take advantage of others.

It is imperative that all stakeholders currently affected by or who potentially will be affected by occupational fraud and corruption have an understanding of the facts and implications of this serious crime. Criminologist

Edwin Sutherland coined the phrase *white-collar crime* in 1939 during a speech given to the American Sociological Society and referred to the betrayal of trust, with crime being committed by persons of high social status in the normal course of their occupation. The main features of occupational fraud and abuse were then further examined by Sutherland, revealing the fact that victims often suffer without ever meeting the perpetrators who live well-ordered lives and are well respected in the community and that these frauds are costlier than other forms of crime, affecting more people, relying on deceit and concealment, whereas other traditional crimes involve force or violence. The wide variety of occupational fraud schemes adopted result in an ever-growing threat against corporate integrity.

CHAPTER THREE

What Is Fraud and More Specifically Occupational Fraud?

THE TERM *FRAUD* HAS EVOLVED to encompass many forms of misconduct. Occupational fraud is financial crime. Financial crime generally refers to offenses that result in financial loss that do not involve violence. Occupational fraud is theft with a fountain pen rather than a gun. This classification is more convincing than that of *white-collar crime* or *organizational crime* given that people who wear white collars have been known to engage in acts of violence and that the criminal classes are not restricted to people with blue collars, and of course fraud also occurs outside of the organizational environment.

There are many definitions of *fraud* pertaining to fraud in an occupational sense.

The legal definition of fraud, from USLegal Dictionary (http://definitions .uslegal.com), is that it is *an **intentional misrepresentation** of **material existing** fact made by one person to another with knowledge of its **falsity** and for the purpose of **inducing** the other person to act, and upon which the other person relies with resulting injury or **damage**. Fraud may also be made by an **omission** or purposeful failure to state material fact.* [Emphasis added.]

Merriam-Webster's online dictionary (www.merriam-webster.com) defines fraud as *an intentional perversion of truth in order to induce another to part with something of value.*

Black's Law Dictionary defines fraud as *a knowing misrepresentation of the truth or concealment of a material fact to induce another to act* and *conduct involving bad faith, dishonesty, a lack of integrity, or moral turpitude.*

In terms of financial statement fraud, we can define fraud as *the deliberate **misrepresentation** of the financial condition of an enterprise accomplished through the **intentional** misstatement or omission of amounts or disclosures in the financial statements in order to **deceive** financial statement users.* [Emphasis added.]

The US Department of Justice states that accounting fraud involves *officers of publicly traded companies seeking to manipulate accounting data and corporate reports to make the financial soundness of their companies appear better than it is.*

Fraud is defined by the Serious Fraud Office in the United Kingdom as an act of deception intended for personal gain or to cause a loss to another party. The legal definition, as provided by the Lectric Law Library (www.lectlaw.com), is somewhat longer:

> *an intentional misrepresentation of material existing fact made by one person to another with knowledge of its falsity and for the purpose of inducing the other person to act, and upon which the other person relies with resulting injury or damage.*

Fraud may also include an omission or intentional failure to state material facts.

The fundamental difference between fraud and theft is that whereas a thief will physically steal things, a fraudster will plan his crime with more care covering his tracks with a misrepresentation or a lie. In the corporate environment this misrepresentation often manifests itself as false accounting, quite often using counterfeiting or forgery, and represents a violation of trust.

The word *forensic* in *forensic investigation* refers to the act of debate or designates a connection with, or use in, public discussion and debate or, more specifically, in a court of law.

 ## THE ASSOCIATION OF CERTIFIED FRAUD EXAMINERS' DEFINITION

Joseph T. Wells, founder and chairman of the Association of Certified Fraud Examiners (ACFE), defines *occupational fraud* in the 2012 *Report to the Nations on*

Occupational Fraud and Abuse as *"the use of one's occupation for personal enrichment through the deliberate misuse of the employing organization's resources or assets."*
The ACFE classifies fraud into six main categories:

1. **Misrepresentation of material facts.** A material false statement, with knowledge of its falsity, which is relied upon and damages are suffered.
2. **Concealment of material facts.** Knowledge of a material fact that the defendant failed to disclose with the intent to deceive the other party.
3. **Bribery.** Payment to gain a commercial or business advantage.
4. **Conflict of interest.** A situation that has the potential to undermine the impartiality of an individual because of the possibility of a clash between the individual's self-interest and professional or public interest.
5. **Theft of money and property.** Includes embezzlement, larceny, and misappropriation of trade secrets and proprietary information.
6. **Breach of fiduciary duty.** Not abiding by the duty of loyalty or the duty of care that exist in a fiduciary relationship.

THE AMERICAN INSTITUTE OF CERTIFIED PUBLIC ACCOUNTANTS' DEFINITION

The American Institute of Certified Public Accountants (AICPA) defines fraud according to the definition given by *Black's Law Dictionary*, sixth edition (1990) as *an intentional perversion of truth for the purpose of inducing another in reliance upon it to part with some valuable thing.* The AICPA further classifies fraud into internal and external fraud:

- **Internal fraud.** Activities perpetrated within the organization such as intentional misrepresentation of financial statement transactions, theft, embezzlement, or improper use of the organization's resources.
- **External fraud.** Improper use of the organization's resources perpetrated by individuals outside the organization.

STATEMENT OF AUDITING STANDARD NO. 99 DEFINITION

The AICPA also implemented Statement of Auditing Standard No. 99 (SAS 99): Consideration of Fraud in a Financial Statement Audit (2002), which assists auditors in making sure that financial statements are free of material misstatement, whether caused by error or fraud, in the audit process. Fraud is defined as *intentional misstatements or omissions of amounts or disclosures in financial statements.* Misstatements are said to arise from two distinct types of acts: fraudulent financial reporting and misappropriation of assets.

SAS 99 also identifies that in order for fraud to occur, three conditions must be present:

1. **Incentive/pressure**. A reason to commit fraud.
2. **Opportunity.** For example, ineffective controls and override of controls.
3. **Attitude/rationalization**. The ability to justify the fraud to oneself.

This is known as Cressey's fraud triangle and will be examined in more detail later.

 ## THE INSTITUTE OF INTERNAL AUDITORS DEFINITION

The Institute of Internal Auditors (IIA) describes fraud as *any illegal act characterized by deceit, concealment or violation of trust.* It further clarifies fraud and misconduct into risk categories: *financial reporting risk, operational risk,* and *compliance risk.*

For businesses to operate and commerce to flow, companies must entrust their employees with resources and responsibilities. This is known as the *agency theory* whereby managers are acting as agents for owners. With agency theory, unfortunately, comes a lack of care and risk of theft as employees abuse this position of trust. So when an employee defrauds his or her employer, the fallout is often especially harsh. This book focuses on *occupational fraud* schemes in which an employee abuses the trust placed in him or her by an employer for personal gain.

The formal definition of occupational fraud is *the use of one's occupation for personal enrichment through the deliberate misuse or misapplication of the employing organization's resources or assets.*

While this fraud category is only one small part of the overall fraud universe, occupational fraud covers a wide range of employee misconduct and activity and is a threat faced by all organizations worldwide, large or small.

In order to consider the application of profiling to the problem of occupational fraud consideration has to be given to the costs and trends and to the who, what, where, when, why, and how relating to occupational fraud schemes.

The following will be of particular interest for the development of a fraud profiling methodology:

- The opinions of experts on the amounts of organizational revenue lost to the various types of occupational fraud and abuse.
- The variety of ways in which occupational fraud and abuse occurs.
- The characteristics and behavioral patterns of employees who commit occupational fraud and abuse.
- The kind of organization that becomes a victim of occupational fraud and abuse.

Research consistently reinforces the fact that occupational fraud schemes fall into three primary categories:

1. **Asset misappropriation** schemes, in which an employee steals or misuses the organization's resources (e.g., theft of company cash, false billing schemes, or inflated expense reports).
2. **Corruption** schemes, in which an employee misuses his or her influence in a business transaction in a way that violates his or her duty to the employer in order to gain a direct or indirect benefit (e.g., schemes involving bribery or conflicts of interest).
3. **Financial statement fraud** schemes, in which an employee intentionally causes a misstatement or omission of material information in the organization's financial reports (e.g., recording fictitious revenues, understating reported expenses, or artificially inflating reported assets).

DURATION OF FRAUD SCHEMES

There is obviously great benefit in detecting fraud schemes as close to their inception as possible, including the ability to limit the financial and reputational damage caused by the crime. Analyzing the duration of the occupational frauds reported can provide insight into areas of opportunity for organizations to increase their fraud detection effectiveness. The median duration, or the amount of time from when the fraud first occurred to when it was discovered, for all cases in the ACFE 2012 study was 18 months. However, the duration of cases in each category of fraud ranged from 12 months for disbursement schemes and noncash schemes to 36 months for payroll schemes, as depicted in Figure 3.1.

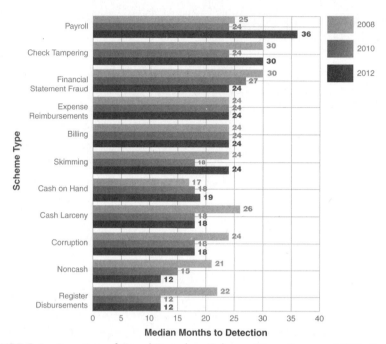

FIGURE 3.1   Duration of Fraud Based on Scheme Type. *Source:* ACFE, *Report to the Nations*, 2012.

While there may be many definitions of fraud, it basically comes down to one thing—the act of misrepresentation by breaching a position of trust. The misrepresentation in occupational fraud is somewhat facilitated by the fact that a trust relationship has already been established by way of the contract of employment and quite often the passage of time. We will see that occupational fraud is more likely where employees have been with their employer for longer periods and the passage of time has been used to build up a trust relationship.

CHAPTER FOUR

Corruption

"ORRUPTION IS THE ABUSE OF ENTRUSTED power for private gain. It hurts everyone who depends on the integrity of people in a position of authority," according to Transparency International (2013). The 2013 Corruption Perceptions Index (CPI) measures the perceived levels of *public sector corruption* around the world, focusing on bribery, kickbacks in procurement, embezzlement of funds, and the effectiveness of anticorruption efforts. Based on expert opinion, the CPI ranks countries based on how corrupt their public sector is perceived to be in countries worldwide, scoring them from 0 (highly corrupt) to 100 (very clean). Covering 177 countries, the 2013 index paints a worrying picture. While a handful perform well, not one single country gets a perfect score. More than two-thirds score less than 50.

Huguette Labelle, chair of Transparency International, says, "It is time to stop those who get away with acts of corruption. The legal loopholes and lack of political will in government facilitate both domestic and cross-border corruption, and call for our intensified efforts to combat the impunity of the corrupt."

An organization requesting contractors to propose for a lucrative contract, government launching a competitive tender, or simply a company setting up operations abroad are just a few of the areas where corruption can breed. When it does, resources are wasted, the corrupt benefit at the expense of others, and societies suffer. So, how can corruption be prevented in such scenarios? It is important that organizations develop and promote practical tools that reduce opportunities for corruption and enhance the ability of people and organizations to resist it. Proactive prevention measures range from monitoring public procurement processes to concrete guidance for organizations on avoiding extortion and curtailing bribery. Let us not forget that corruption in the public sector has a cascading effect on organizations of all shapes and sizes, both public and private.

However, it is fair to say that, in creating reliable diagnostics for measuring and mapping corruption within the Corruption Perceptions Index, Transparency International is actually profiling corruption in such a way that it is supplying the most valuable fraud prevention and profiling tools to individuals and institutions, both in the public and private sectors, in order that they can create solutions to some of the most common corruption challenges facing them. By profiling such activities, Transparency International is a major contributory factor in proactive awareness revealing the who, what, where, when, and how of corruption activities throughout the world.

The most common types of corruption are acts of bribery and kickbacks, quite often caused by conflicts of interest involving the parties to the corrupt activities.

Public outcry at corruption, blaming it on economic instability, sent shockwaves around the world in recent times, particularly in the Middle East and Northern Africa. Backgrounds may be diverse, but the message is the same: "More transparency and accountability from our leaders is needed," according to Transparency International, and "No region or country in the world is immune to the damages of corruption."

 THE GEOGRAPHY OF CORRUPTION

As shown in Figure 4.1, the majority of the 177 countries and territories assessed are in the red zone.

In the "Corruption Perceptions Index 2013," Denmark and New Zealand tie for first place with scores of 91, closely followed by Finland, Sweden, and Norway with scores of 89, 89, and 86, respectively. Afghanistan, North Korea, and Somalia make up the worst performers, scoring just 8 points each.

"This year we have seen corruption on protestors' banners be they rich or poor. Whether in a Europe hit by debt crisis or an Arab world starting a

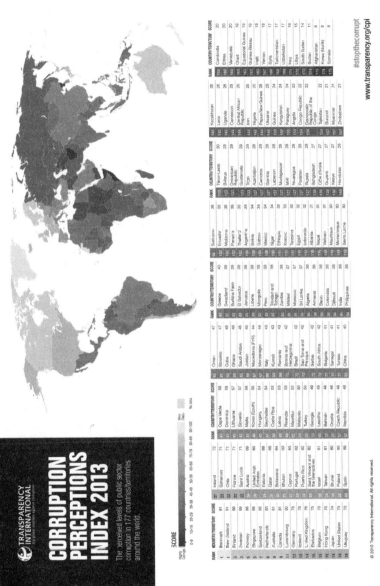

FIGURE 4.1 Corruption Perceptions Index 2013. Source: Transparency International. "Corruption Perceptions Index 2013."

new political era, leaders must heed the demands for better governance," said Huguette Labelle, chair of Transparency International.

Corruption continues to have a devastating impact on societies and individuals around the world, with more than two-thirds of countries surveyed scoring less than 50 in the latest CPI. The results of the 2013 index serve as a warning that more must be done to enable people to live their lives free from the damaging effects of corruption that are eating away at corporate integrity within the business community both directly through corrupt trading practices and through the corrupt *tone at the top*.

Despite 2013 being a year in which governments around the world passed new laws and forged fresh commitments to end corruption, people are not seeing the results with these anticorruption promises failing to materialize. Government guarantees of greater accountability are not always bringing about tangible results at the local level. Protests in Brazil recently showed public exasperation at the continuation of political scandals in spite of governmental assurances of a zero-tolerance policy on corruption. Words must be backed by action.

Some countries, such as Estonia, have seen improved CPI scores go hand in hand with efforts to combat corruption, such as the development of a new anticorruption strategy.

Other countries, however, prove that words are not enough in the fight against corruption. After recent years blighted by political scandals indicating a lack of accountability and fading public trust, Spain recently tried to remedy its corruption troubles with a new transparency law. It is certainly a step in the right direction, but the provisions do not go far enough. This missed opportunity to bring about significant legislative changes is particularly worrying given Spain's six-point drop in the CPI.

EU and Western European countries continue to perform best with an average score of 66, while Sub-Saharan African countries once again show the highest perceived levels of public sector corruption, averaging a score of only 33. But scores vary widely within each region, and with a global average of just 43, all regions have a long way to go in curbing corruption.

The Bribery Act of 2010, which came into force on July 1, 2011, places the United Kingdom among the countries with the strongest antibribery rules in the world. It not only criminalizes the payment and receipt of bribes and the bribing of a foreign official but also extends criminal liability to commercial organizations that fail to prevent bribery committed in their organizations.

Provisions on extraterritorial jurisdiction allow the Serious Fraud Office in the United Kingdom to prosecute any company, or associated person, with a UK presence, even if the company is based overseas. Commercial organizations are exonerated from criminal liability if they had adequate procedures to prevent bribery.

The European Commission's *EU Anti-Corruption Report*, released in February 2014, covers all 28 European Commission member states and provides a snapshot of the corruption situation in each member state in terms of measures in place, outstanding issues, policies in place, and areas that could be improved. The report shows that the nature and scope of corruption varies from one member state to another and that the effectiveness of anticorruption policies is quite different. It also shows that corruption deserves greater attention in all EU member states. Corruption continues to be a challenge for Europe, a phenomenon that costs the European economy around 120 billion euros per year, more than the actual budget that they are managing. EU member countries have taken many initiatives in recent years, but there is no doubt that more should be done to prevent and punish corruption. Europeans are deeply worried about corruption. According to the report, three-quarters (76 percent) of Europeans think that corruption is widespread, and more than half (56 percent) think that the level of corruption in their country has increased over the past three years. One out of 12 Europeans (8 percent) say that they have experienced or witnessed a case of corruption in the past year.

 ## THE FIGHT AGAINST CORRUPTION

A closer look at the situation in individual European countries reveals a variety of approaches to address corruption problems. Some of the suggestions are as follows:

- Strengthen accountability and integrity standards.
- Fine-tune and strengthen internal control mechanisms within public authorities.
- Strengthen asset disclosure systems.
- Improve effectiveness of policies for addressing conflicts of interest.
- Implement more effective policies to address corruption risks at local level and in specific areas or sectors vulnerable to corruption.
- Improve effectiveness of courts, prosecution services, and law enforcement bodies against corruption.
- Safeguard the independence and capacity of anticorruption agencies where such agencies are in place.

- Ensure that criminal proceedings on corruption charges concerning elected politicians are not obstructed.
- Implement effective protection mechanisms for whistleblowers.
- limit risks of foreign bribery, notably in vulnerable sectors such as defense.
- Take more determined measures to ensure transparency of lobbying.
- Develop mechanisms and policies to effectively address corruption risks related to state-owned and state-controlled companies.
- further develop e-tools to enhance transparency of public spending and decision making in public administration.

These are some of the conclusions from the first ever *EU Anti-Corruption Report*.

"Corruption undermines citizens' confidence in democratic institutions and the rule of law, it hurts the European economy and deprives States from much-needed tax revenue. Member States have done a lot in recent years to fight corruption, but today's Report shows that it is far from enough. The Report suggests what can be done, and I look forward to working with Member States to follow it up," said Cecilia Malmström, EU commissioner for home affairs.

Corruption affects all member states in many different ways, says the report. Here are some of the main corruption-related trends across the EU:

Control Mechanisms
- **Use of preventive policies** (e.g., ethical rules, awareness-raising measures, easy access to public interest information). There are large differences between member states concerning prevention of corruption. For some, effective prevention has contributed to a strong reputation of lower rates of corruption. Others have implemented preventive policies in an uneven way and with limited results.
- **External and internal control mechanisms.** In many member states, internal controls on procedures within public authorities (particularly at local level) are weak and uncoordinated.
- **Conflicts of interest.** Rules on conflicts of interest vary across the EU, and the mechanisms for checking declarations of conflicts of interest are often insufficient. Sanctions for violations of rules are rarely applied and often weak.

Prosecution and Punishment
- **Criminal law** rules making corruption a crime are largely in place, in line with the standards of the Council of Europe, UN, and EU legislation. However, EU law on corruption in the private sector has been rolled out in an uneven way.

- **The efficiency of law enforcement and prosecution** in investigating corruption varies widely across the EU. Outstanding results can be seen in some member states. In others successful prosecutions are rare and investigations lengthy.
- **Comprehensive corruption crime statistics** are missing in most member states, complicating comparison and assessment. Procedural rules, including rules on lifting immunities of politicians, obstruct corruption cases in certain member states.

Political Dimension

- **Political accountability.** Integrity in politics remains an issue for many EU states. For instance, codes of conduct within political parties or elected assemblies at central or local level are often missing or lack teeth.
- **Financing of political parties.** Although many member states have adopted stronger rules on party financing, considerable shortcomings remain. Dissuasive sanctions against illegal party funding are rarely imposed in the EU.

Risk Areas

- Within member states, corruption risks are generally higher at regional and local levels, where checks and balances and internal controls tend to be weaker, than at the central level.
- Urban development and construction, as well as health care, are sectors vulnerable to corruption in a number of member states.
- Some shortcomings exist regarding the supervision of state-owned companies, increasing their vulnerability to corruption.
- Petty corruption remains a widespread problem only in a few member states.

CORRUPTION AND THE PUBLIC PURSE

Procurement in the public sector is an area that has always been particularly vulnerable to corruption. In many countries paying bribes is seen as a normal and necessary activity and in many respects the only way to obtain goods or services in a reasonable time frame. Corruption is seen as a means of oiling the somewhat inefficient government machinery. The *EU Anti-Corruption Report* therefore has a dedicated section on public procurement, as in the EU economy as much as one-fifth of the GDP is spent every year by public entities buying goods, works, and services. The public purse certainly is an area vulnerable to corruption and warrants further examination.

Stronger integrity standards in the area of public procurement are called for in the report, and it goes on to suggest improvements in control mechanisms in a number of member states. All in all and conspicuous by its absence in this and any corruption report is any attention to detail in corruption cases with respect to detective or preventive activity along the lines of profiling of either the offenders, the modus operandi, or the cases themselves.

Corruption persists in being a pervasive force in the public sector, hurting citizens in their daily lives and in times of dire need. We have to ensure that money devoted to public sector services and infrastructure is not siphoned away into private pockets.

CULTURAL AND LEGAL INFLUENCES ON CORRUPTION

Culture can be described as the collective programming of the mind distinguishing the members of one group or category of people from another. Essentially, it is the way in which one group of people solves problems and reconciles dilemmas when compared to another group.

Diversity in how people see themselves and one another, and the varying perceptions, can lead to behavior that some may consider irrational. While an inclusive workplace makes for a creative environment, miscommunications and misunderstandings brought about by cultural differences can introduce mistrust and initiate fraudulent behavior.

Culture shapes the level of corporate integrity in a region. Employees may be mentally programmed on national culture and they may actually be very different in the workplace and not their true self. Some regions adopt a culture of sensitivity with higher privacy thresholds, resulting in underreporting with respect to fraud. I have conducted fraud investigations in such culturally sensitive regions and have been anxious to go to the newspapers and to post the successful outcome of a fraud investigation in the staff magazine or report it to the police for criminal action, only to be advised by the board to let the culprit go quietly, in fact, to pay him off and brush the whole thing under the carpet. The fact that organizations in certain cultures have allowed themselves to be stolen from is quite simply embarrassing and an issue that has to be kept quiet from the neighbors.

Likewise, some countries with particularly immature legal systems have no law against corruption. If there is no law against something, then it is legal, as is the situation in primitive or immature economies where greasing palms is the norm in order to make the machinery of business work a little faster.

In general ledgers in such countries we can regularly see pages representing expenses titled "facilitation payments" or "commissions." These are treated as normal business expenses deemed necessary for the privilege of being involved in business, and these payments are quite often tax deductible.

Proactive fraud risk management may require a shift in organizational culture to one of openness and disclosure, both characteristics of good governance but certainly a challenge in some organizations and cultures. The introduction of policies and procedures relating to fighting fraud and corruption is certainly a major cultural change in many organizational cultures, effectively planning and producing safe, well-considered outcomes. Many forward-thinking organizations treat the cultural change to one of enterprise-wide governance and fraud awareness as an extended process of learning and will adopt an incremental approach.

If you are in an economy with a culture of zero tolerance toward fraud that is backed by a sound legal system supporting the fight against fraud and corruption in a low-risk organization, in a low-risk industry, in a country where fraud and corruption is historically low, then you are not going to spend a great deal of money on fraud risk management.

I lived and worked in the Middle East for many years where incidences of fraud were relatively low compared to other regions. Yes, having the death penalty may possibly be the ultimate deterrent, but perhaps being a wealthy oil money–fueled region reduces motivational factors. Quite possibly, having a religion and culture that focus on honesty and the fact that there are many expatriate professionals policing the economy makes the region culturally less risky.

However, the laws of supply and demand are also in effect in the fraud world, and there are also some factors that need to be considered as to the reasons why fraud can and actually does happen in the Middle East. Put simply, there is lots of money to steal in the region and a culture of giving gifts. Giving prize-winning camels in exchange for contracts is seen as a thank-you rather than a bribe to influence a decision, so I am told. Locals working more than one job may clear the way for preference in tender fraud scenarios and the fact that most of the workforce is actually expatriate and not therefore influenced by the cultural and wealth reasons for not committing fraud. Indeed, fraud happens in all regions and cultures.

If we look at the world today, and in particular the United States, we see a huge increase in the detection of fraud and corruption. Enron seems to be mentioned in every fraud and corruption conference of late, along with World-Com and Tyco and many others. We all know that the U.S. financial system and, effectively, the discovery of financial statement fraud in the banking and mortgage market played a role in the cause of the worldwide economic slow-down and recession of late. This does not mean that fraud has increased in the region over the last 10 or so years, but it does mean that detection has increased. This can be attributable to antibribery and corruption initiatives that include task forces and enforcement capabilities designed to clamp down on misconduct. In particular, much detection can be attributed to the introduction of the Foreign Corrupt Practices Act, a U.S. federal law enacted in 1977 to prohibit companies from paying bribes to foreign government officials and political figures for the purpose of obtaining business. The Dodd-Frank Act of 2010 intends to award whistleblowers a reward of between 10 and 30 percent of fines levied for financial misconduct. This, along with greater whistleblower protection, has resulted in increased fraud detection. In the United Kingdom, for example, the Public Interest Disclosure Act of 1998 protects employees who blow the whistle where there are reasonable grounds that a crime of fraud has been committed.

The UK Bribery Act of 2010 makes it an offense for any UK citizen or resident to pay or receive a bribe, either directly or indirectly. The act provides for transactions that take place in the United Kingdom and abroad, and both in the public and private sectors. Companies and partnerships can also commit an offense where a bribe has been paid on their behalf by an associate. Associates include employees, agents, and other persons providing services on behalf of the corporate entity. However, it is a defense to have adequate procedures in place to prevent bribery.

In short, investigative methodology is very much dependent on cultural and legal boundaries, and any profiling methodology will also have to fit inside these parameters if it is expected to contribute in a more strategic, focused, and cost-effective way as more proactive tooling in managing fraud risk in the organization.

CHAPTER FIVE

Normative Crime Analysis and Investigative Psychology

S OCIAL NORMS GUIDE HUMAN BEHAVIOR, but the manner in which those social norms are communicated influences the optimization of the impact of normative messages in situations characterized by objectionable levels of undesirable conduct, such as fraud.

FRAUD IS NOT A NORM

Normative statements make claims about how things should or ought to be, which things are good or bad, and which actions are right or wrong. Such statements, by their nature, apply a value to doing the right thing. Normative claims are factual statements that attempt to describe reality and are supported by theories, beliefs, or propositions.

Behavioral patterns of fraudsters or potential fraudsters within an organization are therefore based on data analysis of normative and nonnormative behavior. The analysis is used to create an *acceptable use template* for the individual, the role, the function, and so on.

Normative crime analysis can also be applied to the crime of fraud and examines fraud prevention theory in the areas of what motivates an individual to commit fraud, what creates an opportunity for him to do so, and why an organization becomes a suitable victim. The fraud examiner can then consider utilizing the resultant fraudulent behavior to assist in compiling profiles and use those profiles to manage fraud risk. The fraud behavior will result in fraud indicators, otherwise known as alerts or red flags. Fraud methods or the modus operandi can also be analyzed, which are generally similar in nature for each type of fraud, for example, simple procurement fraud, where employees authorize payments to themselves or companies they have created; ghosts on the payroll; rolling; and misappropriation of accounts receivable monies by the falsification of bank reconciliations all leave similar patterns or footprints. The consequences of fraud or the systemic, business, or operational impact on an organization as a result of the fraudulent behavior can also be analyzed for profiling.

These three components of normative fraudulent behavior—motivation, opportunity, and availability of suitable victim organization—should be carefully studied or analyzed by utilizing three categories of analytics: fraud indicators, modus operandi, and consequences. This will extend the fraud theory into an analysis-led *fraud risk assessment* methodology that utilizes the process of investigation, induction (gathering of information), and deduction (analysis), thus developing fraud profiles for use in providing a focused, cost-effective response to fraud prevention and detection by organizations, increasing institutional governance.

Fraud is a particular, or specific, type of crime. It does not usually involve violence upon another person, but does create harm to organizations, which in turn can harm people, albeit not physically. Fraud can be defined as dishonest actions to steal or misrepresent or gain advantage at the expense of others by circumventing due process. The effects of fraud are widespread; companies can suffer financially and people can be disadvantaged and lose employment.

Normatively speaking, it can be stated that motivation, opportunity, and availability of a suitable target organization are the three key ingredients for fraud and that organizations can act responsibly and proactively by using them as a primary focus for assessing fraud risk. What is needed, as the fraudster gets more complex and as fraud incidence increases as do economic woes and employee need, is a more robust methodology that will identify critical areas of fraud risk within an organization and assist management in assuming their responsibility to proactively manage fraud risk.

Fraud is not a recent commercial phenomenon. History is littered with instances of misrepresentation for unlawful gain. If occupational fraud and abuse is an estimated 5 percent of revenue, an estimate of considerable concern, let's not forget that these misappropriated funds represent a much larger percentage of the bottom line. Fraud prevention traditionally attacks the problem by attending to these areas with a whole range of individual and corporate activity.

First, motivation is both personal and caused by circumstance. Organizations need to increasingly understand what motivational influences result in criminal behavior.

Second, opportunity exists because of ineffective monitoring systems, poor management, bad leadership, and rotten organizational cultures. It is internal control mechanisms on the whole that reduce fraud opportunities and minimize an organization's profile as a target. Similarly, resources and time spent on developing an ethical culture are good long-term investments in minimizing the availability of a suitable victim organization as well as motivation to offend. While greater regulation through monitoring and legislation can be encouraged to combat fraud, organizations are increasingly required to take responsibility for the management of their own exposure to fraud risk.

Opportunity usually occurs due to a breakdown in internal control processes. This happens for a variety of reasons: from operational expediency to management laziness to deliberate intent on the part of someone to defraud the organization.

Similarly, the availability of a suitable victim organization can be explained, more often than not, by the following reasons:

- Simple accidental discovery of organizational weakness, for example, an inadvertent and simple double claim on an employee's expense claim is noticed by the fraudster not to be detected, revealing a systemic flaw in internal controls.
- Longtime work experience in the organization, quite often at the managerial level, provides employees with a very good overall understanding of the parameters of internal control.

Internal controls can be breached as a consequence of management strategies being remote from the consequence, such as unworkable processes, operational expediency, lack of staff, and segregation of duty limitations.

Third, suitable victim organizations need to assume greater responsibility in managing fraud risk and must establish sound fraud prevention measures.

INVESTIGATIVE PSYCHOLOGY

Investigative psychology in this context covers aspects of psychology that are relevant to the conduct of criminal or fraud investigations. Its focus is on the way in which criminal or fraudulent activity may be examined and understood and is concerned with psychological input to the full range of issues that relate to the management, investigation, and prosecution of the crime of fraud.

Investigative psychology is the systematic, scientific study of investigative information, its retrieval, evaluation, and utilization; the actions and decisions that are based on this information; and the inferences that can be made about criminal activity, its development, differentiation, and prediction.

Investigative decision making involves the identification and selection of various options, such as possible fraud offenders or possible modus operandi that will lead to the eventual narrowing down of the search process. In order to generate possibilities and select from those possibilities, investigators must draw on some understanding of the actions of the offenders. They must have some understanding of the ways in which offenders behave against normative behavior so as to enable them to make sense of the information obtained and make decisions based on it.

There are typically three areas of psychological study that can facilitate an investigation.

First, there is the collection and evaluation of evidential information, including witness accounts and transcripts, interviews or reports from experts, and accounts or evidence from third parties. This is a task that can benefit considerably from the psychological study of human memory processes in order to assist in determining the reliability and validity of evidence.

The second set of tasks is the making of decisions and the related actions that will facilitate the investigation into the fraud. There is remarkably little study of the decision-making process during an investigation, or how those decisions are made. Yet there is clearly a limited range of actions available to investigators, constrained by the legal and accounting systems within which they operate. Any study of human decision making will reveal that there are likely to be many heuristic biases and other inefficiencies in the decision-making process. Awareness of these can lead to effective ways of overcoming them.

In order for decisions to be derived from the information available, assumptions have to be made about the importance or relevance of that information. The third set of tasks, therefore, derives from developing a basis for those assumptions at the heart of fraud investigations. These assumptions derive from an understanding of criminal behavior as well as normative activity. For appropriate conclusions to be drawn from the accounts available of the crime or fraud, it is necessary to have, at least implicitly, models of how various offenders act. These models allow the accounts of crime to be processed in order to generate possibilities for action. This process of model building and testing is, in effect, a scientific, psychological development of the informal, anecdote-based process often referred to as offender profiling.

A simple framework for these three sets of tasks that give rise to the field of investigative psychology is reflected in Figure 5.1.

Psychological knowledge and principles can be applied to fraud investigations to ensure that the correct information is collected, it can be improved and effectively validated, deception can be detected, and relevant indicators and aspects of the offender or fraud can be prioritized.

The capacity of humans to collate and organize information, so that decisions can be made on the basis of it, can be facilitated by a variety of means. One way is to provide visualizations of the material. Human beings can often see patterns between associations and within activities if they can be presented in a visual summary. Bar charts of frequencies are one example of this. Commercially available software can chart networks or sequences of associations or actions.

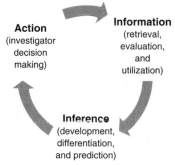

FIGURE 5.1 Investigative Psychology Cycle. *Source:* Simon Padgett, fraud and corruption training.

Decisions are also facilitated if extensive and disparate information can be described in some summary or comparative form. A further level of support to investigator decisions can be made, therefore, by identifying the salient characteristics of the information and by producing summary accounts of it. Particularly useful to the investigator will be data on the modus operandi or on fraud offenders generally. This base rate information guides the investigator toward those most salient features of fraud activity that will be most relevant to the process of deriving inferences about that particular offender.

CHAPTER SIX

The Fraud Triangle Becomes the Fraud Diamond: A Journey through the Theory

THE FRAUDSTER CAN BE A CEO, a mail room clerk, or anyone in between. While mid- and lower-level employees commit the most fraud, fraud committed by owners or executives is more than three times as costly as frauds committed by managers and more than nine times as costly as employee frauds, according to the ACFE *Report to the Nations* (2012), as depicted in Figure 6.1.

Executive-driven fraud also takes much longer to detect as, at this level, with what is quite often many years of experience, fraudulent acts can be better covered and executives may also be in a better position to deter or steer the investigation in certain directions. The fact that males commit more fraud than females is a statistic that may be distorted due to the fact that there are ordinarily more males in the workforce than females.

The advantages of understanding the fraudster's profile are obvious. It can focus one's attention in an investigation on higher risk areas, people, and situations, but, primarily, these characteristics can be used to prevent exposure to fraud risk, for example, by being a significant component in the antifraud program toolbox or by being considered by human resources departments when recruiting.

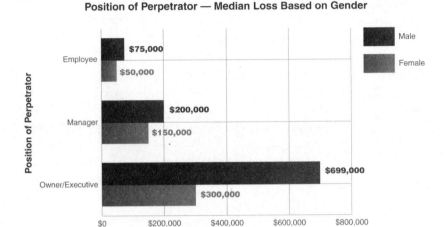

FIGURE 6.1   Position of Fraud Perpetrator. *Source:* ACFE, *Report to the Nations*, 2012.

 THE FRAUD TRIANGLE

Donald Cressey's fraud triangle, developed in the 1950s, approaches fraud theory by drawing attention to the three fundamentals required to be in existence for there to be a fraud. These three fundamentals can play a major role either by identifying frauds before they occur or by assisting in the reactive investigation process. The fraud triangle reveals that a typical fraudster will first and primarily have an *incentive or pressure*, usually financial pressure, but it could also be pressure to perform through challenging or stretched key performance indicators. The fraudster will then take advantage of an *opportunity*, usually manifesting itself as a control weakness. Finally, the fraudster will then *rationalize* his deed, by means of an attitude or mind-set that carrying out the act of fraud will resolve an immediate problem or need.

It is this third element—the rationalization or the attitude of the fraudster that represents his thought process in conceiving, planning, and carrying out the fraud act—that forms an integral part of the profiling process. After all, people are not born dishonest. They learn their traits through rationalization. Cressey's fraud triangle is shown in Figure 6.2.

We can note similarities between the fraud triangle and normative crime analysis. The availability of a suitable target organization is more often a result

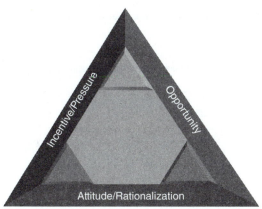

FIGURE 6.2 Cressey's Fraud Triangle. *Source:* D. Cressey, *Other People's Money*, 1953.

of the employment relationship that a fraudster has with the defrauded organization. It is also usually this employment relationship that creates the opportunity for fraud. The fraud triangle does go a stage further and explores the rationalization or attitude of the individual committing the crime.

 ## FRAUD RISK

When all three elements of Cressey's fraud triangle are present either in a situational environment or when considering an individual, one has high fraud risk. When two are present there is medium fraud risk, as depicted in Figure 6.3.

To be able to prioritize fraud risks in an effective manner, organizations should include and evaluate the human element in the fraud risk assessment process by applying the principles of Cressey's fraud triangle to the traditional risk assessment criteria of *impact* and *likelihood*, as detailed in Figure 6.4.

 ## THE THEORY SHAPING EARLY FRAUD PROFILING

Edwin H. Sutherland defined his *theory of differential association* in his book *Principles of Criminology* in 1924 by analyzing the mind of the fraudster, asserting that the excess of definitions favorable to deviance over definitions unfavorable to violation of law enforces a person to become a deviant while associating with other persons and learning such deviances from groups.

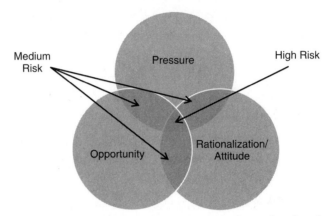

FIGURE 6.3 Fraud Risk Model. *Source:* Simon Padgett, fraud and corruption training.

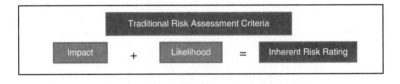

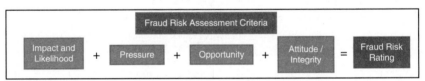

FIGURE 6.4 The Fraud Risk Assessment. *Source:* Simon Padgett, fraud and corruption training.

In Harvey Cardwell's book *The Logic and Language of Auditing for Fraud* (1960), he asserts that there are three principal factors that contribute to employees beginning to steal: the want or need for money, being aggrieved or angry with the employer, and the ability to steal.

In Gottfredson and Hirschi's *General Theory of Crime* (1990), it is stated that individuals rationally choose the behavior they wish to perform, weighing the potential pleasure of performing a behavior against the potential pain of not performing it.

In the Hollinger-Clark study (1983), 10,000 employees were surveyed with the following key results:

- One-third had committed fraud.
- Many stole because of job dissatisfaction.
- Employee perception of detection is important.
- Employee thieves exhibit other deviances like sloppy work, sick leave abuses, and so on.

Wolfe and Hermanson (2004) extended Cressey's fraud triangle to *the fraud diamond* by adding a fourth dimension, that of capability in terms of the values and personal integrity of the perpetrator. The fraud diamond is represented in Figure 6.5.

The capability of an individual to commit a fraud would include such considerations as one's function and position within the organization; his or her mind-set, confidence, and ego level; cultural issues; coercion or lying skills; and experience and stress levels. Once again, we see a move through the theory toward profiling characteristics.

The capability of an individual to commit fraud has direct links to the honesty of that person and can be further examined in terms of the *iceberg theory of dishonesty*, whereby the mind-set of a fraudster can be seen as either overt or covert, as shown in Figure 6.6.

Such overt or visual aspects of an individual's characteristics would include such considerations as his positioning in the organization and the structure of that hierarchy and how that structure is managed, the skills and technical

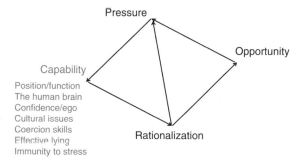

FIGURE 6.5 The Fraud Diamond. *Source:* D. Wolfe and D. Hermanson, "The Fraud Diamond: Considering the Four Elements of Fraud," *CPA Journal*, 2004.

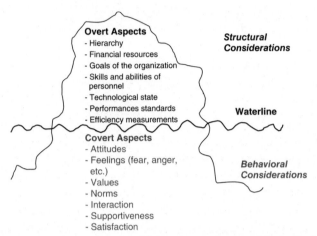

FIGURE 6.6 The Iceberg Theory of Dishonesty. *Source:* Simon Padgett, fraud and corruption training.

capabilities of the individual and those who surround him, the financial resources available to both the organization and the individual, and the goals and performance targets of both and how these are measured and managed.

Covert considerations do, however, present more challenges with respect to their examination and understanding due to the nature of human behavior and the way it can be camouflaged and hidden when necessary or required, particularly when a perpetrator is either planning a crime of fraud or being investigated following fraud. The examination of covert aspects of human behavior needs the ability to dig into the very foundations of a person's mind-set and should include analysis of such very personal and unique characteristics as personal and professional standards and norms, attitudes, values, feelings, levels and extent of personal and business interaction, social skill levels, personal satisfaction thresholds, and the very nature of the individual concerned. As the studies suggest, many of these traits are determined by the way a person is brought up and into what type of societal surroundings he or she moves in his family, work, and social life.

There is a range of incentives behind fraudulent behavior, as indicated in the fraud triangle, when discussing pressure/incentive. These motivations include but are certainly not limited to the following:

- Financial need.
- Greed.
- Gambling and other addictions.

- Revenge.
- Maintaining lifestyle.
- Jealousy.
- Financial support for business.
- Personal debt.
- Thrill seeking.
- Power dominance.

The incentive is the starting point for diverse patterns of behavior.

So, as we have now seen that incentive or motive, opportunity and availability of a suitable target organization, and rationalization or attitude are the three key ingredients for fraud, we can now see that organizations can act responsibly and proactively by using these elements as a focus for assessing their fraud risk. What is needed is a methodology that will identify critical areas of fraud risk within an organization and assist management in assuming their responsibility to proactively manage that risk. Profiling the fraudster and his modus operandi will form an integral role in this fraud risk management methodology.

PART TWO

Profiling the Fraudster

7

Using Profiling in the Fight against Crime and Occupational Fraud

R EACTION TO CRIME CAN BE generally categorized as being either reactive or proactive in nature. While it is generally acceptable that prevention is better than cure, we live in a world where budgetary and skillset constraints far too often result in the placing of more reliance on reactive crime management in the form of after-the-event investigation.

While *fraud* is defined as the unlawful and intentional making of a misrepresentation that causes actual or potential prejudice to another, *criminal investigation* is the systemic search for the truth and is primarily aimed at the positive clarification of the crime situation on the basis of objective and subjective traces. The criminal investigation is reactive and occurs following the crime event. *Crime intelligence* is intelligence used in the prevention of crime or in the conduct of investigations in order to prepare evidence for the purposes of law enforcement and the prosecution of offenders.

THE MIND OF ADOLF HITLER

The origins of profiling can be traced back to as early as the Middle Ages. During the 1880s, Thomas Bond, a medical doctor, tried to profile the personality

53

of Jack the Ripper. Bond, a police surgeon, assisted in the autopsy of one victim. Dr. Bond tried to reconstruct the murder and interpret the behavioral pattern of the offender and came up with a profile and signature personality traits of the offender to assist the police in their investigation. The profile dictated that several murders in the area had been committed by one person alone who was physically strong, composed, and daring. The unknown offender would be quiet and harmless in appearance, possibly middle-aged, and neatly attired, probably wearing a cloak to hide the bloody effects of his attacks. He would be a loner, without a real occupation, eccentric, and mentally unstable. Bond also mentioned that he believed the offender had no anatomical knowledge and could not be a surgeon or butcher.

In 1943, the U.S. Office of Strategic Services (OSS) asked Dr. Walter C. Langer, a psychoanalyst based in Boston, to develop a profile of Adolf Hitler. The OSS wanted a behavioral and psychological analysis for the construction of strategic plans, given various options. Dr. Langer used speeches, Hitler's book *Mein Kampf*, interviews with people who had known Hitler, and some 400 published works to complete his wartime report, which was eventually declassified by the OSS and published by Langer as *The Mind of Adolf Hitler* in 1972. This work contains a profile of Hitler's possible behavioral traits and his possible reactions to the idea of Germany losing World War II. Dr. Langer's profile of Hitler noted that Hitler was meticulous, conventional, and prudish about his appearance and body. He was robust and viewed himself as a standard bearer and trendsetter. He had manic phases, yet took little exercise. Langer also believed that Hitler was in reasonably good health, so that it was unlikely he would die from natural causes, but that he was deteriorating mentally. He would not try to escape to a neutral country, nor would he, in Langer's opinion, allow himself to be captured by the Allies. Hitler always walked diagonally from one corner to another when crossing a room, and he whistled a marching tune. He also had a severe fear of germs. Langer's profile also pointed out that Hitler detested the learned and the privileged, but enjoyed classical music. He showed that Hitler had strong streaks of sadism and liked circus acts that were risky and dangerous. He tended to speak in long monologues rather than have conversations. He had difficulty establishing close relationships with anyone. Since he appeared to be delusional, it was possible that his psychological structures would collapse in the face of imminent defeat. The profile went on to reveal the most likely end scenario was that he would commit suicide, although there was a possibility that he would order one of his henchmen to perform euthanasia, according to Langer.

Proactive crime management is driven by intelligence and therefore involves a broader range of enforcement stakeholders, including those who are intelligence led, investigators, professionals, and the community at large. Such intelligence is concerned not only with the methodologies for committing crime or the modus operandi but also with the evidence likely to be apparent such as spending beyond one's means, out-of-character displays of wealth, and so on. This proactive approach to crime management can be applied to the investigation of potential fraudulent activity. Fraud cases reveal a microcosm of methods used and resulting evidence from fraudulent activity. What is needed is a *fraud profiling* strategy that is focused, flexible, and cost-effective, allowing management to work as a key player in assuming responsibility for managing fraud risk and being proactive in its prevention and removal.

DEVELOPMENT OF THE PSYCHOLOGY

Profiling is all about the psychology of people and the way they behave and act. It is about the use of general or personal characteristics or behavioral patterns in attempting to understand a person or group of people to make generalizations about an individual, group, or a situation at some point in the future. Taking this to the next level, profiling is the use of these historical characteristics to determine whether a person may be engaged in illegal activity or fraud.

The recording and analysis of a person's psychological and behavioral characteristics so as to assess or predict his or her capabilities in a certain sphere or to assist in identifying categories of people or the practice or method of preparing a set of characteristics belonging to a certain class or group of people or things by which to identify individuals as belonging to such a class or group, linking them to a possible crime, is what we can refer to as *profiling*.

It can be somewhat frustrating to employers and fraud investigators looking for a quick filter that will keep financial criminals out of their organization or enable them to identify criminals who have somehow sneaked past the gatekeeper. We all want criminals to look like "them" and not like "us." If only life was that simple!

Criminologist Edwin Sutherland developed the concept of *white-collar crime* to drive a spike into theories that suggested that poverty, defective personality, or inability to delay gratification were actual causes of crime.

Those theories had provided a warm security blanket for criminologists and fraud risk managers because they implied that crime could be dealt with by eliminating poverty through social welfare or economic growth, by education, by confinement of the insane, and by sterilization of those who carry the genes for delinquency, theft, or, quite simply, failing to act like ethical employees.

If we listen to Japanese exponents of blood type psychology, a pseudo-science now embedded in Japanese popular culture and corporate recruitment, they have been claiming for some time that blue-collar criminals are predominantly of the O blood group, whereas white-collar crime involves people with A group blood type. This, of course, does not mean that all people with A group blood are fraudsters and that they need be refused access to employment. Effective profiling will involve many variants of characteristics to indicate a most likely scenario and not a definitive checkbox of yes, he is a fraudster, or no, he is not.

For example, it has been claimed that *Harry Potter* readers can be sorted into four distinct categories. *Hufflepuffs* read slowly and then reread the books. *Gryffindor* readers inhale the latest Potter in one sitting and quickly move on. *Ravenclaws* read for light entertainment, and *Slytherin* readers simply are not committed to the Potter cult. They prefer the films and may pretend to have read the books.

So, there is no stereotype or standard profile of people who perpetrate organizational fraud. The perpetrator could be a neighbor, a coworker, an entrepreneur, a professionally qualified individual or institution, or even you or me, trying to create an impression that we are not by writing and reading antifraud books. I have no doubt that fraudsters are as interested in antifraud methodologies and profiling as fraud risk managers or even more so. People involved in fraud can be recruited by ringleaders to participate in large-scale syndicated fraud rings, or they can be opportunists who try to bluff their way around the system.

So, financial crime is not restricted to the following stereotypes:

- The poor.
- People behind the cash register or front counter.
- Private sector enterprises.
- Government agencies.
- A particular gender, ethnic group, or religious faith.
- People with or without a particular type of education.
- People with addiction or abuse problems.
- People with personal problems or those undergoing a relationship melt-down.
- Those who are ugly or those of a particular blood group.

It has been claimed that people with specific attributes are more likely to engage in financial crime or specific types of financial crime. For example, women are more likely to engage in petty front-office fraud, or members of particular groups are more likely to lack ethical/religious constraints against financial temptations. In reality women, for example, appear to be underrepresented among large-scale corporate crime perpetrators because they are underrepresented in the management and executive positions at which much fraud occurs, rather than because they possess a special gene for financial probity. It has to be expected that there may be logistical reasoning behind such obtuse statistics that may not be adequately supported by accurate fraud or forensic statistics or substantiating evidence.

Bias suggesting that particular ethnic groups have a higher fraud risk due to a cultural affinity to gambling or conspicuous consumption or that perpetrators have a particular blood type is also not borne out by the statistics.

And, of course, even if a prejudice could be justified, it does not provide a foolproof tool for predicting financial crime. Excluding people from recruitment and promotion opportunities because they may be from any minority group can be an invitation for an expensive date with a discrimination law specialist for any discriminating employer.

Systematic surveillance of people who have survived the vetting process is beyond the skills and capabilities of most organizations and poses challenges for evolving privacy regimes and is inconsistent with treating people as a valued resource. After all, many of our colleagues and more of our senior executives drink, gamble, disregard marriage vows, break the law when driving, live beyond their means, or deviate from the traits taught by the very best law schools and MBA factories. Not all of them are or will become financial criminals.

Modeling can assist in developing profile mechanisms.

 ## MODELING

Fraud is a particular type of crime, quite unique in nature. It does not usually involve violence but can have devastating effects on the lives of people, organizations, countries, and the institution of governance generally. There is a need to develop a more reliable and robust predictive method for understanding, investigating, and preventing fraud as part of the contribution to ethical and effective institutional governance. Modeling is the predictive simulation of future events based on past experiences.

Predictive Modeling

Predictive modeling encompasses a variety of techniques that use the analysis of current and historical facts to make predictions about future, or otherwise unknown, events.

In fraud profiling, predictive models exploit patterns found in historical and transactional data to identify fraud risk exposure areas. Models capture relationships among many factors to allow the assessment of fraud risk or potential fraud risk associated with a particular set of conditions, guiding decision making for effective organizational fraud risk management.

Predictive analytics involves extracting information from data and using that information to predict trends and behavioral patterns for application to any type of unknown, whether in the past, present, or future—for example, in the identification of suspects after a fraud has been committed or in procurement fraud as it occurs or for general proactive fraud risk management. The core of predictive analytics relies on capturing relationships between explanatory variables and the predicted variables from past occurrences and exploiting them to predict the unknown outcome. It is important to note, however, that the accuracy and usability of results will depend greatly on the quality and depth of data analysis and the quality of assumptions.

Predictive modeling and related analytical disciplines involve rigorous data analysis, and while widely used in business for profit and cash flow predicting and budgeting, it is not necessarily so for fraud risk management and related antifraud decision making, simply because predicting human behavior is more complex than predicting financial patterns. The use of such predictive modeling has different purposes in the fraud environment, and the information gathering techniques underlying them therefore vary.

Predictive models analyze past behavior to assess how likely a person is to exhibit a specific behavior in the future and encompass models that seek out subtle data patterns for use as fraud prevention or detection models. Predictive models often perform calculations during live transactions, for example, to evaluate the fraud risk of a given transaction, in order to guide a decision. With advancements in computing speed, modeling systems have become capable of simulating human behavior or reactions to given factors, stimuli, or scenarios, also known as *avatar analytics*.

Descriptive Modeling

Descriptive models quantify relationships in data in a way that is often used to classify customers or prospects into groups. Unlike predictive models that focus on predicting a single individual's behavior, descriptive models identify many different relationships between data sets. Descriptive models do not rank the data by their likelihood of resulting in a particular action the way predictive models do. Instead, descriptive models can be used, for example, to categorize individuals or modus operandi into fraud types. Descriptive modeling tools can be utilized to simulate large data sets and make predictions.

MODELING IN FRAUD DETECTION

Predictive modeling can help weed out potential fraudsters and reduce a business's exposure to fraud risk. It can also be used to identify high-risk fraud candidates in the recruitment process. This approach can be used, for example, to detect fraud in the procurement process of an international chain with multiple branches. Each location can be scored using, for example, 10 predictors. The 10 scores are then weighted to give one final overall fraud risk score for each location. The same scoring approach could be used to identify high-risk departments and potentially fraudulent or questionable vendors. A reasonably complex model can be used to identify fraudulent monthly reports submitted to the head office by the branches indicated earlier.

Tax authorities throughout the world use predictive analytics to mine tax returns and identify potential tax fraud.

Recent advancements in information technology have also introduced predictive behavioral analysis for web fraud or cybercrime detection. This type of solution utilizes heuristics in order to study normal web user behavior and detect anomalies indicating fraud or fraud attempts.

Decision models describe the relationships between all the elements of known data in order to predict the results of decisions involving many variables. These models can be used in optimization, maximizing certain outcomes while minimizing others. Decision models are generally used to develop decision logic or a set of rules that will produce the desired action for every circumstance or varying types of fraud.

The approaches and techniques used to conduct predictive analytics can broadly be grouped into regression techniques and machine learning techniques.

Regression models are the mainstay of predictive analytics. The focus lies on establishing a mathematical equation as a model to represent the interactions between the different variables in consideration. Depending on the situation, there is a wide variety of models that can be applied while performing predictive analytics. The linear regression model analyzes the relationship between the response or dependent variable and a set of independent or predictor variables. This relationship is expressed as an equation that predicts the response variable as a linear function of the parameters. These parameters are adjusted so that a measure of fit is optimized.

A three-stage modeling methodology has been proposed: model identification, estimation, and validation. The identification stage involves identifying if the series is stable, checking for the presence of seasonality in the data by examining plots of the series, autocorrelation, and partial autocorrelation functions. In the estimation stage, models are estimated using nonlinear time series or maximum likelihood estimation procedures. Finally, the validation stage involves diagnostic checking such as plotting the residuals to detect outliers and evidence of model fit.

Understanding modeling as the predictive simulation of future events based on past experiences forms a grounding for the study of *criminal and fraud offender profiling*.

CHAPTER EIGHT

Criminal and Fraud Offender Profiling

C RIMINAL OFFENDER PROFILING IS A METHOD of collating various pieces of information and data or intelligence relating to a crime or crime offender. This intelligence is then formulated into a profile that can be used to model future criminals and fraudsters and fraud events as part of an organization's effective antifraud management program. It is used to understand why and how the crime was committed and will assist with establishing the most likely offender at future crime scenes. The creation of an investigative profile would include data that is gathered on an offender, such as passport or identity number, address, criminal record, vehicles owned, employment records, academic qualifications, cell phone records, and bank statements.

 ## THE CRIMINAL MIND-SET

Criminal profiling is used by the police and other law enforcement agencies as a tried and proven method to solve crimes. It is a method that is employed particularly for violent crimes, such as murder, abductions, and assaults. Also known as offender profiling, it involves studying the tendencies, characteristics, and mind-set of a criminal in order to ascertain his or her identity or that of like-minded individuals. Criminal investigators will also analyze the crime scene to figure out the nature, characteristics, and modus operandi of the crime. This information can be used to supplement a criminal profile.

Almost any piece of forensic or crime scene evidence, no matter how small, can be used during criminal profiling, along with victim profile information and characteristics.

Criminal profiling is an effective tool in helping law enforcement investigators narrow down the list of suspects for a crime or in creating an outline of their possible characteristics. This compiled information can be further used to determine patterns in behavior, from where the criminal originates, or where a future crime might be committed.

So, criminal offender profiling is a behavioral and investigative tool that is intended to help investigators to accurately predict and profile the characteristics of unknown criminal subjects or offenders. Criminal offender profiling is also known as criminal profiling, criminal personality profiling, behavioral profiling, or criminal investigative analysis. Geographic profiling may be another method to profile an offender. The three main goals of criminal offender profiling are to provide:

1. A behavioral, social, and psychological assessment of the offender.
2. A psychological evaluation of any evidence.
3. Suggestions and strategies for the interviewing process.

There are three main approaches to criminal offender profiling:

1. The geographical approach analyzes the patterns with regard to timing and location of the crime scene, in order to determine where the offender lives and works.
2. The investigative psychology approach focuses on the use of psychological theories of analysis to determine the characteristics of the offender by looking at the presented offending behavior and style of offense.
3. The typological approach looks at the specific characteristics of the crime scene in order to categorize the offender according to various typical or normative characteristics.

Procedural steps in generating a criminal offender profile may be summarized as follows:

1. A thorough analysis of the type and nature of the criminal act is made, and it is then compared with the types of people who have committed similar crimes in the past.

2. An in-depth analysis of the actual crime scene is made.
3. The victim's background, lifestyle, and activities are analyzed to look for possible reasons and connections.
4. The possible factors for the motivation of the crime are determined and analyzed.
5. The description of the possible offender is developed, founded on the detected characteristics, which can be compared with previous cases.

Offender profiling is a method of identifying the perpetrator of a crime based on an analysis of the nature of the offense and the manner in which it was committed. Various aspects of the criminal's personality makeup are determined from his or her choices before, during, and after the crime. This information is combined with other relevant details and physical evidence and then compared with the characteristics of known personality types to develop a practical working description of the offender.

Psychological profiling may be described as a method of suspect identification that seeks to identify a person's mental, emotional, and personality characteristics as manifested by evidence left at the crime scene. An offender's signature is the unique similarities in each of his or her offenses.

The process of criminal profiling involves a number of steps. First, all relevant information is gathered about the crime, including all evidence collected by the police. The next step is to apply this information to important questions such as where and when did the crime occur, what was the primary motive, what type of violence was used, and what risks did the criminal take?

As patterns start to emerge from the evidence, these questions can be more easily answered. The personality or character of the criminal can be determined by breaking down the behavior into four phases:

1. Premeditation: The suspect's thoughts and plans before the crime occurred.
2. Modus operandi: How the crime was committed, identifying any unique elements.
3. Disposal of or hiding any evidence.
4. Postcrime actions.

With this information and some now answered questions, the profile can be compiled to include features such as sex, age, ethnicity, educational background, psychological state, and religion.

Criminal profiling is far from a perfect science, and it does have some drawbacks. It relies heavily on stereotyping in that assumptions are made based on a small amount of information. Incorrect criminal profiles can be created by unclear evidence, faulty logic, or broad stereotyping. For this reason, criminal profiling remains controversial, and professionals continue to look for ways to more accurately categorize criminal suspects.

INVESTIGATIVE PSYCHOLOGY

Investigative psychology is the term given to a recently developed area of applied psychology that attempts to describe the actions of offenders and to develop an understanding of crime. This understanding can then help solve crimes and contribute to prosecution and defense procedures. It brings together issues in the retrieval of investigative information, the drawing of inferences about that information, and the ways in which investigator decision making can be supported.

Advocates of investigative psychology stress that the results of scientific psychology can contribute to many aspects of civilian and criminal investigation, including the full range of crimes from burglary to fraud, not just those extreme crimes of violence that have an obvious psychological or psychopathic component.

The contribution to investigations draws on the extent to which an offender displays various tested characteristics as well as contributing to procedures for enhancing the processes by which interviews are carried out or information is put before the courts. One aim of investigative psychology is to determine behaviorally important and empirically supported information regarding the consistency and variability of the behavior of many different types of offenders. Although to date most studies have been of violent crimes, there is a growing body of research on fraud.

Investigative psychology units, with teams of psychologists, have been incorporated into police forces throughout the world for some time and usually find themselves being based within the forensic units.

FRAUD OFFENDER PROFILING

The ACFE states that a fraud suspect might not be easy to pick out of a crowd; however, it goes on to say that its research helps identify certain common traits and red flags. This, in its basic form, is actually profiling. Conducting surveys is a sound methodology for providing data to organizations to enable them to understand and predict fraud.

The Typical Fraudster

KPMG's 2011 "Analysis of Global Patterns of Fraud" is research that is based on 348 actual fraud investigations conducted by KPMG firms in 69 countries and reveals the following about the typical fraudster:

- Is predominantly male.
- Is 36 to 45 years old.
- Commits fraud against his own employer.
- Works in the finance function or in a finance-related role.
- Holds a senior management position.
- Has been employed by the company for more than 10 years.
- Works in collusion with another perpetrator.

They also discovered that the overriding motivation for fraud is personal greed, followed by pressures on individuals to reach tough profit and budget targets. The survey emphasizes how weakening control structures result in opportunities to commit fraud.

Offender profiling is the identification of actual or potential offenders on the basis of behavioral or other attributes. This profiling may be carried out by retrospectively identifying an offender after a crime has taken place, as has been the case in countless Hollywood movies. Alternatively, it may be predictive in nature by attempting to identify and thereby inhibit potential criminals. Predictive profiling of financial criminals has not really advanced much beyond crude recruitment-level vetting and inferences from an individual's sweaty palms or nervous demeanor and has, therefore, been largely ineffective and will remain so in future if we do not get a grip on profiling methodology. We are simply not very good at prognostics when dealing with the human being. Financial crime is carried out by people "just like us" who don't have the tell-tale signs of a fraudster or a tattooed F for *fraud* on their forehead. It is also because there are uncertainties about who is committing financial crimes and in particular who is not being caught or simply not being prosecuted and why they are committing those crimes.

The process of building a profile is of extreme value because it encourages thought about the risk and opportunity associated with human actions and interactions, rather than through provision of a template against which you are forced to adopt a best-fit approach in order to match suspects.

No One-Size-Fits-All Solution

Applying demographics to fraud profiling is disillusionary for anyone who believes that we can usefully filter all financial criminals through a simple set of sieves or that we can rely on a one-size-fits-all explanation of what makes those people tick, or steal. Experience suggests instead that major organizations, although susceptible to significant reputational and monetary loss, have often failed to use the filters readily at their disposal.

Sometimes we disregard the signals because we don't know how to separate signal from noise; it is possible to have too much data, or maybe the data or information looks like an IT exam, not a tool for financial crime forensics. We disregard the data because it does not match our preconceptions, for example, the potential criminal has charm galore, as do many sociopaths, went to the right school, wears a nice suit, has an honest face, rides a Harley but has no tattoos, doesn't blink when telling lies, has an appetite for risk, and entered the premises and his job with what appeared to be a great curriculum vitae (CV).

In practice, we also often reward people for exhibiting the warning signs, such as aggression, greed, and impatience, after they have managed to exceed forecast profit targets. Did anyone actually question that the good-looking profits should possibly have been even higher than stated? Risk management involves thinking about those signs in a context of motivation and opportunity rather than concentrating on isolated personality traits such as decisiveness or diligence.

So, the challenges faced by financial crime profilers are many but certainly include the following:

- Financial crimes are often easier to detect in retrospect than to forecast.
- Financial crimes involve a somewhat unknown interaction between incentive, opportunity, and rationalization.
- There is no typical financial criminal (i.e., one whose appearance or activity provides a useful template for sorting sheep from wolves or wolves from sheep).

It can be said that the primary reason for criminal or fraud offender profiling is to understand by whom, why, and how the crime was committed. There are various types of offender profiles and it is important to differentiate among them. Profiles can be compiled from past frauds and from convicted fraudsters where their details become a part of an offender profile for use in proactive fraud risk management and also to assist in later investigations. There is offender profiling where the offender in a current fraud is unknown, but his or her identity can be deduced from the clues left behind at the scene of the crime. There is also the profiling of an offender who has been identified and arrested in connection with a current fraud, and evidence is required in order to present to the court.

All too often it can be seen that, although investigators collect various pieces of information about an offender during the investigation, they do not compile any formal offender profile using this information. Valuable information on offenders is therefore not being used for profiling purposes by investigators, particularly in the identification of offenders in future fraud investigations.

The various phases of an investigation include the collection and collation of available crime intelligence as well as the profiling and tracing of the suspect. The profiling of offenders is neither the solution to crime nor the alternative to investigation, but an aid in building up a database for the purposes of crime intelligence, which can assist in identifying and tracing offenders. It is important for investigators to understand the nature and use of offender profiles and also to understand the methodology through the theory and research behind offender profiling techniques.

PROFILING CHALLENGES

There are plenty of skeptics when it comes to abilities to predict the future. People are influenced by their environment in innumerable ways, and the extent of the influence certainly varies from person to person. Trying to understand what people will do, how they will do it, and when they will do it next assumes that all the influential variables can be known and measured accurately. Environments change even more quickly than the people themselves do, particularly in the world of business. Everything from the weather to their relationship with their mother can change the way that people think and act. All of those variables are unpredictable. How they will impact on a person is even less predictable. If put in the exact same situation tomorrow that they are in today, individuals may make a completely different decision. This means that a statistical prediction is only valid in sterile laboratory conditions, which cannot relate to the reality of the corporate or human environment.

We face the fact, inconvenient as it is, that a specific *identikit* profile of a financial criminal or fraudster may not actually be achievable. Reliance on stereotypes may be comforting but may not give us a true picture of criminal activity and may therefore inhibit our profiling capabilities. This we have to accept.

The problem is that there is no single type of financial crime and therefore no single type of financial criminal. In particular, therefore, it is not possible to produce an image that is of great assistance in forecasting and thereby preventing most financial crimes.

Effective profiling is an attempt to bridge a substantial forensic gap.

We know that financial crime occurs. Some of it gets detected. Some of it gets reported. Some of the reported crimes are successfully prosecuted. Much financial crime, although analysts always disagree about how much, does not get reported. This underreporting may be because organizations are worried about the fallout from reputational damage. Criticism by shareholders and watchdogs carries with it potential increased regulatory costs and often damaging unpleasant comments in the *Wall Street Journal*. The varying cultures across the globe can also create environments of underreporting. If fraud is not reported, it might not be visible, and if it is not visible, how can it be assessed, measured, and attacked?

Fraud awareness levels in many organizations may be limited. There may be budgetary constraints and the resultant lack of skillset for regular training or communication or there may be cultural sensitivities to the word *fraud*. In the United Arab Emirates there are cultural sensitivities to privacy. In effect, this means that it is deemed embarrassing to admit that you have been stolen from. People, customers, the market generally, and close neighbors and family may see this as a weakness. KPMG's 2011 "Analysis of Global Patterns of Fraud" reveals that only 46 percent of fraud cases were disclosed internally, with India being the least transparent, with 88 percent of cases not being disclosed and discussed internally, and the most transparent countries being Australia, New Zealand, and South Africa. Organizations generally do not like to make figures on fraud publicly available unless required to do so by local law or unless it is material and disclosure is necessary under accounting standards or rules. According to KPMG, information with regard to 77 percent of investigations did not reach the public domain. These figures suggest that countries are not really coming to the table on transparency surrounding fraud and corruption awareness levels in their organizations. This is a limitation to bringing about a culture of zero tolerance toward these acts and to setting a positive tone at the top and will always be an inhibitor to fraud profiling (see Figure 8.1).

There are often questions to be asked about whether data collection is comprehensive. Figures often do not match up. This should not be surprising when

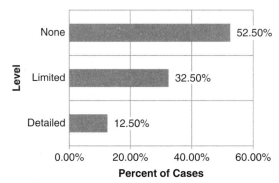

FIGURE 8.1 Internal Communication on Fraud. *Source:* KPMG, "Analysis of Global Patterns of Fraud," 2011.

there are definitional disagreements and extrapolations from small population samples in the investigatory process.

Generally speaking, we do not know how or to what extent organizations are profiling their potential employees and associates, current employees and contacts, or customers. This information is not usually made available by organizations and will only be touched upon in fraud surveys carried out occasionally. It is thus extremely difficult to assess the effectiveness of profiling. Did fraudsters ever get through the door, and if they did, were they deterred from committing fraud through an overt and seamless financial control framework? Were they caught at an early stage, detected after an initial incident rather than after systemic misbehavior? Did they exhibit warning signs, and were those signs recognized? All questions for which a standard survey or question-and-answer list is simply not possible.

Problematic CVs are often the entry point for fraud in any organization from simply inventing qualifications and academic background and supporting them with fake certificates to a fictional story of employment history and salary levels. The acceptance of bits of paper at face value is akin to accepting human beings at face value, somewhat surprising when identity theft is just a few mouse clicks away.

Much of what we know about the motivation for fraud comes from the criminals themselves. This is actually bad news as criminals lie before, during, and after the offense. Criminals also boast and exaggerate about their activities and find excuses or rationalization for their deeds. Some say that so do their lawyers, who are effectively paid large fees to find loopholes in evidence or the way it was gathered. This is a big problem if one is hoping for reliable sourcing of information to compile an identikit for forecasting future crimes of fraud.

We also need to be aware that much financial crime in the private sector goes unreported, particularly in certain cultures, in order to prevent individual embarrassment or preserve corporate reputations. I have spent many years investigating fraud and conducting profiling in the Middle East, where the local culture is one of sensitivity and privacy. There is, therefore, a culture of underreporting in an environment wherein washing your dirty laundry in public is simply not done.

Motivation is as diverse as the crimes and getting to the bottom of it is not an easy task.

The answer, therefore, or at least part of it, is to develop a process for building up a profile, rather than provide a template into which data can be dropped, water added, and stirred.

So, we have to accept that there are no comprehensive, culturally independent profiling mechanisms for identification of potential and active financial criminals, as there is no single type of financial crime and no single type of financial criminal.

Furthermore, the motivations of financial criminals vary from a simple need to resolve a financial pressure to a complex mixture of greed, resentment, financial need, and the joy of playing a power game.

Interestingly, organizations are misplacing their trust in pseudo-scientific integrity profiling and other such recruitment mechanisms, from batteries of psychological tests to handwriting analysis or the configuration of an individual's earlobes. Much of this is of dubious value because it is founded on problematic cultural assumptions or because it fails to differentiate between acceptable leadership and looting attributes.

The ultimate conclusion is that public and private sector organizations have been burned because they did not come to grips with the many challenges presented by profiling, or they either chose to disregard warning signs or simply failed to conduct basic verification work when those warning signs did manifest themselves.

CHAPTER NINE

Behavioral Warning Signs or Red Flags

THE AVERAGE FRAUDSTER IS MALE, has worked in the organization for many years in a senior position, and is considered trustworthy. Most are over 40. What, however, are the behavioral warning signs that should not only be picked up on but acted upon immediately and not ignored?

A fraud warning sign or red flag is an event or set of circumstances that should alert an organization to the presence of risk. In seeking to identify fraudulent behavior within an organization, much attention has historically been focused on these fraud indicators that are loosely termed *red flags*, *fraud alerts*, and *personal indicators*.

Fraud can best be explained by the following four factors or drivers:

1. A supply of motivated, pressurized, or incentivized offenders.
2. The availability of suitable target organizations.
3. The absence of capable guardians or a control system, opening up an opportunity.
4. Rationalization in the fraudster's mind bringing about justification for his or her actions.

The motivation, pressure, or incentive to defraud may be as simple as financial need or greed, or anything from unrealistic deadlines and performance goals to the financial demands of personal vices such as gambling or drugs.

The availability of a suitable target organization is an easy one. It is more often than not the fraudster's employer with whom he has built up a relationship of trust, quite often over many years. This trust has usually been so powerful that the employee has probably worked his way up to a relatively senior management position in the organization.

The opportunity to commit and conceal fraud is the only element over which an organization has real significant control. The opportunity is an open door to solving a non-shareable problem by violating a position of trust and is generally provided through weaknesses in the internal controls. Some examples of weak internal controls include, but are by no means limited to, absent or inadequate procedures surrounding

- Supervision and review.
- Segregation of duties.
- Management approval and delegation of authority.
- System controls.

Rationalization is a crucial component in the fraud process because most people need to reconcile their behavior with the commonly accepted notions of decency and trust. They know that they have deviated from normative or expected actions and behaviors, and they need to justify this in their own minds and also quite often to those close to them. Some examples of justifications for fraudulent actions include the following:

- "I need it more than the other person."
- "I'm borrowing and will pay it back later."
- "Everybody else is doing it."
- "The organization is big enough and it won't miss the money."
- "Nobody will get hurt."
- "The losses are insured so what's the problem?"
- "I really need this money and I'll put it back when I get my paycheck."
- "I'd rather have the company on my back than the IRS."
- "I just can't afford to lose everything—my home, car, everything."
- "I have worked for this organization for 20 years and look how they have treated me."

HOW RED FLAGS HELP US DISCOVER FRAUD

Red flags are sets of circumstances that are unusual in nature and vary from normal activity. They represent a signal that something is out of the ordinary and may need to be investigated further. Of course, we should remember that red flags do not always indicate guilt or innocence but merely provide possible warning signs of fraud.

The American Institute of Certified Public Accountants SAS 99: Consideration of Fraud in a Financial Statement Audit highlights the importance of fraud detection in a financial audit. This statement requires the auditor to specifically assess the risk of material misstatement due to fraud, and it provides auditors with operational guidance on considering fraud when conducting a financial statement audit.

MANAGEMENT RED FLAGS

It is management's responsibility to manage fraud risk in any organization. The following may represent red flags indicating that such protective actions are not being adequately carried out by management. They could also indicate that fraud may be being committed by the very people who are challenged with reducing it:

- Management's reluctance to provide information to auditors.
- Managers engage in frequent disputes with auditors.
- Management decisions are dominated by an individual or small group.
- Managers display significant disrespect for regulatory bodies.
- Weak internal control environment, including the following:
  - Poor internal controls.
  - Management override of internal controls.
  - Collusion between employees and between employees and third parties.
- Accounting personnel are lax or inexperienced in their duties.
- Decentralization without adequate monitoring.
- Excessive number of bank accounts.
- Frequent changes in bank accounts.
- Frequent changes in external auditors.
- Company assets sold below market value.
- Significant downsizing in a healthy market.

- Continuous rollover of loans.
- Excessive number of year-end transactions.
- High employee turnover rate.
- Unexpected overdrafts or declines in cash balances.
- Refusal by company or division to use serial numbered, sequentially controlled documents.
- Compensation program that is out of sync with the market.
- Financial transactions that just do not make sense.
- Service contracts resulting in no product or productivity.
- Photocopied or missing documents.
- Little supporting documentation for adjusting entries.
- Incomplete or untimely bank reconciliations.
- Increased customer complaints.
- Write-offs of inventory, receivables, or cash shortages with little or no attempt to determine the cause.
- Unrealistic performance expectations and continually missing targets.
- Frequent use of sole-source procurement contracts.
- Rumors of conflicts of interest.

CHANGES IN EMPLOYEE BEHAVIOR REPRESENTING RED FLAGS

The following employee behavioral changes are examples of red flags for fraud:

- Borrowing money from coworkers.
- Creditors or collectors appearing at the workplace.
- Gambling beyond the ability to stand the loss.
- Excessive drinking or other self-destructive personal habits.
- Easily annoyed at reasonable questioning.
- Providing unreasonable responses to questions.
- Refusing vacations or promotions (for fear of detection).
- Bragging about significant new purchases.
- Carrying unusually large sums of money.
- Rewriting records under the guise of neatness in presentation.

FRAUDSTERS LIVING BEYOND THEIR MEANS EXHIBIT KEY RED FLAGS

In many cases of fraud, perpetrators openly live beyond their means. Fraudsters have large egos, and many like to show off. Fraud carried out to bring about lifestyle changes is often committed by trusted employees whom management think they know so well. It is important to be on the lookout for employee lifestyle issues that may represent red flags indicating fraud risk. Some fraudsters are secretive in the way that they carry out their activities. In these situations, the lifestyle changes may not be so obvious. They do not want to be caught and will stash stolen funds and be extremely careful with their spending. Other aspiring fraudsters want to use, enjoy, share, and show off their fraudulently gained wealth, and what they spend their money on is quite often very obvious. They will enter into a dialogue of lies and deceit to convince all around them that the wealth was generated from legitimate sources, much in the same way that money launderers do. Explanations given by active fraudsters of new-found wealth may include such stories as

- I won the lottery.
- My husband/wife just got a great promotion.
- I have some investments that have been doing really well.
- A wealthy aunt has passed away and left us quite a nice little nest egg.
- I finally decided to get rid of some property that has been in the family for years.

As well as excessive lifestyles, abusive lifestyles such as those involving personal addictions can create financial problems for employees. Someone who is dependent on drugs, alcohol, gambling, or other addictions typically experiences a slowly tightening noose of financial pressures with the only way to satisfy such pressure being theft or fraud. Desperation fuels monetary needs, and the need arises to borrow funds to ease the financial dilemma. Employees with addiction problems may be tough to spot. Many people with addictions can function at fairly high or normal levels of behavior during work hours. The following represents indicators to look out for:

- Frequent unplanned absenteeism.
- Regular ill health or shaky appearance.
- Regularly making and breaking promises and commitments.
- Series of creative explanations.
- High level of self-absorption.
- Inconsistent or illogical behavior.
- Forgetfulness or memory loss.
- Family problems.
- Minor grievances or levels of deception.

Financial pressures are faced by most people at some period of time. For a number of reasons, often beyond their control, employees may find themselves in financially stressful situations due to a variety of factors. These may include

- Medical bills.
- School fees.
- Family responsibilities.
- A spouse losing a job.
- Divorce.
- Debt requirements.
- Maintaining a current lifestyle.
- Car/house repairs.

These financial pressures often form the basis of the motivation for commencing fraudulent activity. As resolving financial problems of employees is not a core activity of most employing organizations, it is left to antifraud programs to do what they can in terms of identifying red flags.

 ## RED FLAGS IN THE ACCOUNTING SYSTEM

Fraud red flags can be indicative of the way that an organization and its accounting systems are structured or set up and the policies and procedures that are or are not in place. Those very systems of control create opportunities for fraud as employees become familiar with operations, and they begin to understand which accounts and activities are unmonitored, which areas of the company are poorly supervised, and what size of transactions are surrounded by added scrutiny. In order to reduce the opportunity for accounting fraud, there has to be increased oversight, consistent monitoring of employee activities, division of duties or tasks, and adequate punishment of those who violate the systems of control in the accounting system.

Red Flags in Cash/Accounts Receivable

Since cash in hand or in the bank accounts is the asset most often misappropriated, investigators and auditors should pay close attention to any warning signs. Cash can be misappropriated from amounts received from customers or debtors through fictitious expenses. Petty cash can be abused, or exaggerated sales and receivables can form an integral part of a financial statement fraud. Some examples of red flags include

- Excessive number of void transactions, discounts, and returns.
- Unauthorized bank accounts.
- Sudden or unusual activity in dormant banking accounts.
- Discrepancies between bank deposits and posting.
- Abnormal number of expense items, supplies, or reimbursements to the employee.
- Presence of employee checks in petty cash.
- Excessive or unjustified cash transactions.
- Large number of write-offs on receivable accounts.
- Bank accounts not being reconciled on a timely basis.

Red Flags in Payroll

Red flags that show up in payroll are generally worthy of looking into. Although payroll is usually an automated function, it is a vulnerable area, especially if collusion is involved. Ghosts on the payroll have been a favorite pastime of fraudsters since people started to be paid wages. Some warning signs might include

- Budget variations for payroll by cost center.
- No or infrequent payroll reconciliations.
- Inconsistent overtime hours for a cost center.
- Overtime charged during a slack period.
- Overtime charged for employees who normally would not have overtime wages.
- Employees with duplicate Social Security numbers, names, and addresses.
- Employees with few or no payroll deductions.

Red Flags in Purchasing/Inventory

Extracting money from the system by introducing fictitious purchases or stealing stock can reveal the following red flags:

- Increasing number of complaints about products or services.
- Increase in inventory purchased but no increase in sales.
- Abnormal inventory shrinkage.
- Lack of physical security over assets/inventory.
- Charges without shipping documents.
- Payments to vendors who are not on an approved vendor list.
- High volume of purchases from new vendors.

- Purchases that bypass the normal procedures.
- Vendors without physical addresses.
- Vendor addresses matching employee addresses.
- Excess inventory and inventory that is slow to turnover.
- Purchasing agents who pick up vendor payments rather than having them mailed.

BEHAVIORAL CHARACTERISTICS AS RED FLAGS TO FRAUD

Once a red flag is identified, action must be taken to determine the potential impact and materiality associated with the warning sign. Evaluating the red flag may be accomplished by financial analysis, observation, or any control weakness technique that tests the level, extent, and risk of any apparent weakness. It may well be that the red flags that have no financial or reputational impact may not require a change in procedure. A red flag is only a warning that something is or could be wrong. If fraud is suspected or discovered upon examination, then an investigation is usually the next step. If it is just an error, then steps should be taken to correct the error and a control procedure put in place or follow-up initiated to prevent it from occurring again.

Red flags or fraud alerts are behavioral clues that may be picked up by managers, colleagues, internal auditors, and subordinates that suggest that an employee or colleague may be engaging in some form of fraudulent or improper conduct. They are those unusual occasions and suspicious instances associated with actions, documentation, administration procedures, or the general way business is done. These alerts are valuable because they put watchdogs on guard that something is amiss. Personal indicators of red flags are the private matters of an individual's life that might provide a motivation to commit fraud and could include the following:

- Significant personal or family problems such as health issues, divorce, or death of a loved one.
- Financial problems.
- Failure to take or rarely takes annual leave.
- Refuses or does not aspire to be promoted, giving no explanation.
- Domination of specific activities.
- Possessiveness about custody of records or office space.
- High personal debt.

- Does not willingly produce records or information.
- Prone to poor or underperformance.
- Unreliable.
- Shifts blame and responsibility.
- Extensive gambling.
- Excessive use of alcohol or drugs.
- Surrounded by favorites, or people who do not challenge.
- High turnover in administration support staff.
- Close relationships with customers and suppliers.
- Customers and suppliers will only deal with this employee.
- Excessive lifestyle.
- Cuts corners or bends rules.

Let's have a quick drill down into some of these characteristics. The *rarely takes annual leave* behavioral characteristic interests me. Historically this has always been in the list because fraudsters fear that they might be discovered while away from the action. Perhaps the customer will call in and ask why he has not been given a formal receipt, or the supplier will query why his statement says that he has been paid when he has not, or the auditors may do a surprise cash count or asset reconciliation. Yes, these may well be good reasons for not taking leave, but I actually believe that there is a more realistic reason for the fraudster not taking leave or not taking long leave. This reasoning comes from the mouths of several fraudsters whom I have had the pleasure of interviewing after their events. Fraudsters are constantly carrying out calculations in their heads. They have to in order to keep on top of their activities. The cost of an annual holiday or vacation is now becoming expensive to them because it is not merely the cost of flights and hotels, but is also the cost of the loss of opportunity to steal during the time period that he or she is sitting on a beach somewhere. The holiday may cost $1,000, but the opportunity loss of the missed fraud may have a cost of $100,000 or more. The fraudster, hence, does not like to take holidays. It is as simple as that.

Poor performance or unreliability by an employee can also be an indicator of fraudulent behavior as the efforts of these individuals are often more focused on their personal gains than on the job that they are paid to do. I have kicked off many a fraud investigation with a quick review of personnel records to draw attention to those employees who have notes on file of issues that relate to poor performance. Not reaching targets, poor time keeping, or disciplinary action for anything that equates to questionable integrity can all be indicators of an individual with characteristics for inclusion in profiling. I have even seen, believe it or not, disciplinary action for fraud and theft on an employee's record. He was given a final warning and severe reprimand but was kept on due to him being the top salesman. This, to me, brought this person, his activities, and his department into the spotlight in terms of my radar for fraud profiling. I do wonder, to this day, to what extent his sales figures, which earned him the top achiever award, could be relied upon as being true and fair and whether they had been audited.

Fraudsters have to surround themselves with colleagues who will not challenge any of their suspicious activity and who will make their lives of crime easier in the workplace. We often see the fraudster as a dominant individual whom others fear. However, it is also possible that he or she befriends such work colleagues to such an extent that they would just never suspect such a nice, honest person could do such a thing. Either of these extremes can be a clue to a fraudulent profile. Some time ago we put a purchasing manager in jail for procurement fraud. At a debriefing meeting, the head of human resources explained that he had noticed that the particular manager had a very high turnover in his secretarial assistant position. In fact, his secretary was changed on average every seven months. This is a clear indicator of someone who does not want a subordinate to get too close and start noticing things going amiss. I would also imagine that one or two of them had accumulated some suspicions and may have even drawn these to their boss's attention, thereby sealing their fate.

Close relationships in the sales function can reap positive results in increased sales and getting to know the vendors can perhaps result in suppliers giving greater discounts, but how close is too close, in terms of increased fraud risk? Where people's livelihoods are at stake and cash is involved, there is scope for bribery and kickbacks in order to buy better deals. My response to this has always been the word *transparency*. If an employee has a relationship, perhaps a close relationship, and he has nothing to hide, then he should disclose the relationship in the organization's conflict of interest declaration. If the risk manager wishes to move that employee from that client or customer project or from any decision-making responsibility, then so be it. In my opinion, if something is not disclosed, there may be a hidden agenda. I once investigated a case of suspicious activity in a construction project, following allegations that one of the project managers had a very close relationship with a contractor on the project and was living a lavish lifestyle since embarking on this particular project. Yes, he was suddenly gifted an Aston Martin, and yes, his personal residence was suddenly surrounded by beautiful palm trees the same week that 200 palm trees were delivered on the project, but no action was taken against this gentleman because on examining his conflict of interest declaration and the register of gifts received, he had disclosed everything, right down to the lunches shared with suppliers. The fact of the matter in this case was that this was a project valued in the hundreds of millions and this project manager consistently used his social skills and friendly nature to get the best deals and costs on the project. He was good for business and he was transparent in what he was doing. The car was registered in the name of the project, and the grounds of the house, on which the trees were planted, were owned by the same project.

Fraudsters are inherently dishonest and will break rules in all areas of their lives. It may be speeding on the highway or parking in disabled parking or even taking the maximum number of sick days allowed each year. These infringements are carried out by people who cannot follow simple rules in exchange for personal gain. These rule breakers are not necessarily fraudsters but they have the capability to commit fraud, and each case of what could be termed minor misdemeanors warrants further analysis or investigation. If we can obtain information on such infringements, then we have information for profiling that will enable the fraud investigator to target his efforts and examination in higher risk areas of the business.

Rarely is fraud a one-off act. With financial statement fraud, for example, fraudsters will make multiple transactions or correct entries to cover their tracks. In KPMG's survey, 91 percent of fraudsters were repeatedly fraudulent. Repeated and long-running fraudulent activity should leave many red flags over a period of time. An effective profile of these red flags could save the organization from significant loss due to fraud. According to the report, 56 percent of cases were preceded by red flags. However, such red flags were acted upon in only 6 percent of the cases. Organizations are failing to identify and react to these warning signs in a timely fashion. Ignored red flags enable fraudsters to carry out and to continue their activity (see Figure 9.1).

There is a particular skill required in recognizing warning signs such as irregular, inconsistent, or odd circumstances in the work life of others within an organization. This is more than suspicion. It is the ability to relate work behavior to a possible cause in private life, to see irregular patterns within events and procedures, and to identify potential causal links to statements and actions. These skills have long been used in psychology and counseling in dealing with projection and displacement.

If we were to look, for example, at the various aspects of procurement fraud, we could then analyze the possible behavioral warning signs in terms of incentive and motivation, opportunity and availability of a suitable target,

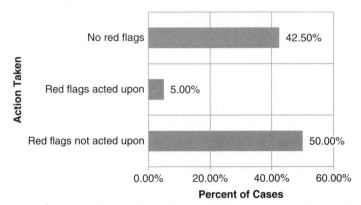

FIGURE 9.1 Actions Taken on Identified Red Flags. *Source:* KPMG, "Analysis of Global Patterns of Fraud," 2011.

and attitude or rationalization to provide a fraud profile of use to investigative procedures and the process of managing fraud risk.

The classic example of procurement fraud is where an employee conspires with an outside supplier to defraud the employer in a variety of ways. Usually the employee receives some type of kickback, remuneration, bribe, gift, or other benefits in exchange for assistance in any the following activities:

- Inflating and approving contract prices and invoices above market or fair prices or for work not performed or for inferior quality.
- Collusion to fix pricing.
- Collusion to rig the bid or tender process.

Another common form of procurement or tender fraud is when an employee establishes a dummy company or supplier account in the company's systems and then works to steal from the employer using fraudulent contracts, invoices, and/or payments.

Conflict of interest is a frequent cause and at the same time method of carrying out procurement fraud. Any input into the procurement or tender process by a party with vested interests in the outcome creates a conflict of interest situation. Conflicts can be actual, perceived, or potential. These conflicts are most common during the following phases of the tender process:

- **Strategy development phase.** Where inadequate or biased supplier market research limits sourcing options in favor of particular products or suppliers.

- **Solicitation phase.** Development of specifications or requirements that could favor a particular product or supplier.
- **Bid preparation phase.** Giving any preferential or prejudicial treatment, or undue advantage of information.
- **Receiving of bids.** Improperly securing bids, exposing them to risk of tampering/modification.
- **Evaluation phase.** Deliberately manipulating evaluation criteria or scores.
- **Contract management phase.** Acting in the best interests of the supplier, not those of the procuring entity.

An employee who has a conflict of interest may defraud the procurement or tender process by any of the following means:

- **Collusion between company employees and suppliers.** This could involve kickbacks or bribes, resulting in the internal personnel manipulating the process by restricting competition.
- **Nongenuine competition.** Different suppliers in the bidding process have the same owners or are otherwise associated.
- **Unfair advantage to individual suppliers.** Information is not disclosed consistently to all potential suppliers during the solicitation process or inside information is disclosed to a potential supplier or existing vendor.
- **Circumventing thresholds.** This would include the thresholds for undertaking formal solicitations and for review by procurement review or tender committees. These requirements can be bypassed when splitting orders and estimating costs below real costs to bring in low value contracts that are later adjusted.
- **Improper hospitality, gifts, and inducements.** Hospitality and gifts should be disclosed in line with the organization's code of conduct.
- **Cost/labor overcharging.** These are schemes by suppliers on cost-plus contracts to fraudulently inflate the contractual cost and/or amount of labor or materials.
- **Defective parts.** A known defect in design, specification, material, manufacturing, and workmanship can be overlooked in return for a bribe from the supplier.
- **Product substitution.** The introduction of counterfeit and/or substandard material and other forms of unauthorized product substitution into the procurement system.
- **Price fixing and bid rigging.** Bid rigging is any activity to suppress and eliminate competition on contracts. Price fixing and bid rigging is an

agreement where, in response to a call or request for bids or tenders, one or more bidders agree not to submit a bid, or two or more bidders agree to submit bids that have been prearranged among themselves. Profits will be shared.

In terms of motivation, the procurement employee, or anyone else committing the fraud for that matter, uses a wish for a change in lifestyle or to purchase that Ferrari as his motivator. He is dealing with contracts worth millions on a daily basis, and one of his suppliers will play on the motivating factors by dangling any carrots he can to get the deal at a good price. The opportunity is presented by a weak procurement process that is heavily reliant on the employees themselves declaring their own conflicts or potential conflicts of interest by the annual conflict of interest or gift declarations, as required by the organization's code of conduct. The target proves suitable and available simply because this is where the employee works, where he is every day, and where he has worked for such a length of time that he understands how to bypass the controls. He is also relied upon to perform his duties and is trusted by those around him and to whom he reports. Perhaps the fact that the employee is reluctant to take leave, works long hours, and carries out duties in the evenings and weekends allows him to plan his acts while alone, thereby creating opportunities. The lack of fraud awareness training and weaknesses in segregation of duties and authority-level controls also create opportunities.

What this procurement fraud example reveals is that motivated people will create opportunities and identify available suitable targets and that they will even manipulate the situation to do this. Furthermore, they will work inside the existing parameters of the fraud risk management environment and will not let those parameters inhibit them from fulfilling their objective.

The lesson for management is that there is a need to be aware of the warning signs that fraudulent indicators can manifest. It is incumbent upon senior management to recognize this proactive approach as an important part of their responsibility in attending to organizational and system vulnerability and managing fraud risk accordingly.

CHAPTER TEN

Motivation and Opportunity as Key Indicators

ALTHOUGH IT IS GENERALLY ACCEPTED that employee dishonesty is a serious issue and costs many organizations a lot of money and possibly reputational damage, the causes have for some time attracted relatively little research and attention. From almost every aspect, technology has made fraud deeper, more complex, and more expensive. Criminologists have looked at fraud causes from many angles, but most have focused on the need for money and opportunity. The motivation for fraud is deeper than this and forms the backbone to profiling.

Today's criminologists explain fraud in terms of three factors: a supply of motivated potential offenders, the availability of suitable target organizations, and the absence of effective control systems.

 ## THE MOTIVATION

There are various discussions surrounding why offenders are motivated. Are we all potential offenders, only on the straight and narrow because the internal controls are solid, the external watchdogs have sharp teeth, or the targets are insufficiently cash rich?

Reasons for offending may be topped by debt and greed, but boredom, retaliation, getting back at the boss or the organization, weak life structure, and being blackmailed have also been given by convicted fraudsters as justifications, with many stating that a culture of corruption in their organization had fueled their offending. Others felt that they had been poorly treated or not supported by their employer. Sometimes low wages or perceived low wages or not having received a bonus is the reason, and employees see theft as taking what is actually theirs and as payback. Many explain that it was easy for them to commit their offenses with little or no fraud prevention strategies in place, creating easy opportunities. Often offenders abuse the position of trust that they hold within the organization. Historically, this position of trust was associated with positions of seniority; however, of late, delegation of authority and autonomy have created opportunities for those lower down the ranks, particularly where supervision and monitoring are at a low level.

The philosophy of trust is one that requires further debate. Length of time with the employer is relevant to fraud occurrence and its magnitude, as the longer a person is in his position, the more he builds up a rapport and commitment to the organization and the greater the level of trust. Donald Cressey found that a major cause of theft was offenders having what he referred to as non-shareable problems that, he said, preceded the criminal violation of financial trust. Taking this further, Cressey realized that those who steal are able to do so by abusing a position of trust and are only able to steal larger amounts because they are in a position of trust in the first place. This creates a large problem for organizations because in order to function, they have to place employees in positions to safeguard the assets, and the larger and more valuable the asset, the larger the degree of trust involved. The owner has to trust the custodian. This is known as the *agency theory*, whereby managers act as agents to safeguard assets that are not actually theirs. It is, unfortunately, a human trait that one does not look after or preserve someone else's assets as one would do if they were their own.

Generally speaking, the noncriminologists among us will look at motivation from the perspective of the desire to increase personal wealth, threat of loss of wealth or financial status in the community, sense of superiority, or an expression of power. We also see differentiation between offenders with low self-control who commit fraud when an opportunity arises, those who engage in financial crime for ego gratification rather than for the financial wealth, and those who commit crimes to satisfy current and immediate personal situations in their lives such as threat of bankruptcy or to keep a demanding partner in bling or flashy cars.

It is interesting to examine financial crime demographics in terms of offenders who plan their activity and those with less premeditation. That is a useful differentiation from the perspective of compliance and control because financial crime is not always a strategic, sustained, carefully calculated activity. The statistics appear to suggest that many financial offenders, particularly those dealing with small sums, do not plan to commit a crime and to thereafter commit further crimes. Most do not have prior convictions for financial offenses or, for that matter, nonfinancial crimes.

There is no doubt that an element of cost/benefit analysis or risk and reward comparison is adopted by fraudsters in considering whether to perpetrate their crime. However, the impulsivity or psychopathology may have been taken to an extreme, with claims that organizational white-collar crime can be predicted by gender, with males having higher rates than females, lower behavioral self-control, higher social desirability requirements, and other traits that one may relate to greed.

We can examine the case of Raffaello Follieri, who was recently sentenced to 54 months in prison after pleading guilty to 14 counts of wire fraud, money laundering, and conspiracy in what has been dubbed the Vati-con scandal. Follieri was accused of misappropriating a $50 million investment from a billionaire that was meant to buy up Roman Catholic churches in the United States. Prosecutors accused him of raising millions by claiming that special Vatican connections allowed him to buy church properties at below market prices and redevelop them for socially responsible purposes. In reality he had no special rights but was simply competing against other bidders. He used investors' money to finance a lavish lifestyle, including a $37,000 a month apartment, dinner with celebrities, expensive watches, and designer clothing. Follieri claimed, "I didn't start off with the intention of deceiving anyone. I started off with good intentions to run an honorable business and make everyone proud of me." His lawyer portrayed him as a well-intentioned businessman whose miscalculations had spun out of control, a "fundamentally good person with a generous spirit." The assistant U.S. attorney, however, took a differing view, characterizing Follieri as a sophisticated swindler who had lured investors into something resembling a Ponzi scheme by recurrently and repeatedly misrepresenting his background and expertise. "It is not clear to me that investors would ever have given him a dime if they knew the truth," he said.

We need to resolve some uncertainties by abandoning a one-size-fits-all profiling methodology in favor of profiles that acknowledge a diverse spectrum of motivations, the significance of the availability of opportunity, and the interaction of motivation with rationalization, as depicted in Figure 10.1.

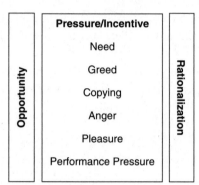

FIGURE 10.1 The Motivation Model. *Source:* Simon Padgett, fraud and corruption training.

When applying our minds to a motivation model and very much in line with Cressey's fraud triangle, one has to consider the pressure/incentive, opportunity, and rationalization of the thought process of the perpetrator and analyze the identifying factors applicable to each. Offenders use rationalization to excuse their actions or indeed justify them as an acceptable aspect of employment and to detract attention from the wrongdoing. The rationalization is the cornerstone to taking advantage of an opportunity to feed a financial pressure. Some offenders seem to truly believe that they have done no wrong or persuade others, including the courts at a later date, that they have such a belief. Interestingly, when this thought process or activity is carried out by executives, we call it confidence, charismatic leadership, and good financial risk management and reward it as such.

Need

Organizations may be able to control or try to control their own environments and cultures, but they are certainly subject to outside influences on employees such as mounting personal financial pressures on a daily basis and specifically in times of economic slowdown and particularly during the global financial crisis of late. Formerly honest and trustworthy employees affected by adversity in their personal circumstances may be more tempted to commit fraud when they see an opportunity within the workplace. So, the first motivation, one that has preoccupied social theorists for at least a millennium, is need. Some people engage in financial crime because they have to. Some people steal in order to feed themselves and their dependents, or to keep a roof over their heads, or a roof in a nicer suburb, perhaps one with more trees and less crime! Some people engage in financial crime because they have school or medical fees to pay, need to keep their business afloat, keep the bank away from the door, or pay for gambling or drug habits rather than tawdry tales of defrauded money blown on sports cars and champagne.

Some of those motivations may be detected by data mining, but others are unlikely to appear on the radar. Obtaining data on need-based crime is problematic. Need is generated by the human mind and the level of need is subjective. How does a criminologist or forensic investigator determine a fraudster's level of need at a particular point in time? Where it is claimed that gambling drives financial crime, a solution, it may be stated, may be that restricting gambling reduces fraud. The statistics, however, do not demonstrate a clear causal link. Few gamblers engage in financial crime.

What we might say is that gambling, particularly compulsive gambling and for large stakes, may be a warning sign. Unfortunately, it is a sign that cannot be relied upon.

Greed

Need turns to greed. Yes, once the need is satisfied it becomes difficult to stop. The benefits exceed the costs or the pleasure exceeds the pain, particularly as time goes by without being caught or losing in this lucrative game. In fact, the act of fraud becomes an addiction in itself over time.

We cannot forget greed. People engage in fraud to buy more toys, a crate of Bollinger, a new Ferrari or the servicing of the Ferrari, the house on the coast, or a week in Vegas.

Greed, like need, is a slippery concept. In terms of basic survival, no one truly needs five cars or a million-dollar holiday home, and a Seiko will tell the time just as efficiently as a Rolex, often better if one forgets to regularly rotate the wrist. Kids have been deprived of going to private schools and have survived to tell the tale. Greed and need are subjective and, once again, problematic concepts to the investigator.

Understanding the depth and extent of greed is a task for moralists and psychologists. Greed is problematic because it is encouraged by our financial culture: "Greed is good," as entrepreneur Gordon Gekko, the fictional character in the 1987 film *Wall Street*, famously said. In the real world we constantly reward chief executives for bigger, faster, stronger, flashier achievements in the financial Olympics.

Copying

Some people engage in financial crime out of emulation or the simulation or copying of another fraud or fraudster to either equal or surpass it or them. We would all secretly like the lifestyle of a fraudster. Many aim to emulate the cash inflow. Others see the generation of wealth from an activity that is deemed to be easier than getting up and going to work at 8 a.m. for 50 years as something that needs to be copied.

It is a matter of showing that the fraudster is the best at what he does, the wizard who can walk through firewalls and harvest financial gain and is further influenced by media coverage bringing about an amount of recognition and fame.

Data on copycat frauds is limited, problematic, and not reliable.

Anger

Several studies of the 419 e-mail, or advance fee scam, revealed that West Africans justify their activity as a righteous attack on those nasty, fat, white colonialists who infringed on their land and stole their oil and gas. The Nigerian 419 scam, named after the section of the country's penal code of which it is a breach, is a part of a growing fraud industry, said to be the country's third-largest income generator, after oil and gas production. The anger is obviously huge and widespread.

Much small-scale financial crime appears to have been driven by resentment with employees compensating themselves by taking what they thought they deserved to either compensate for rewards given to other employees or to inflict a punishment on the hand that did not feed them. Anger or retaliation is a particularly common motive in times of economic slowdown, where pay increases and bonuses have been replaced by offers of salary cuts to keep but not guarantee one's job.

Helping yourself also appears where employees believe that the organization is breaking the law or mistreating customers and suppliers, particularly where statements on corporate ethics are not being followed. Organizations with a healthy corporate culture do not necessarily attract the environmentally, socially conscious angry fraudster.

Pleasure

Believe it or not, some financial criminals are not particularly interested in money. They get their buzz from the activity, not the outcome.

Ferdinand Demara Jr., known as the Great Impostor, masqueraded as many people, from monks to surgeons to prison wardens. He was the subject of a movie, *The Great Impostor*, in which he was played by Tony Curtis and explained his motivation as "rascality, pure rascality." Ironically, he also spent time as a doctor of applied psychology. He did not know why he did it, but it felt good, he said. Other offenders, such as fraudster Frank Abagnale, re-created in the movie *Catch Me If You Can* in 2002, have spoken of the high that comes from achievement, particularly an achievement involving evasion or subversion of authority.

Where the fraudster is not driven by a particular incentive to steal to buy more toys or pay off the medical fees is a problem because most prevention assumes some rationality and a relationship between risk and reward.

We assume that financial criminals will not engage in crime purely for pleasure, although many observers of entrepreneurs are quite comfortable with the notion that people build businesses because they enjoy building. In this case, playing the game is what's important, not how many toys you have accumulated.

Performance Pressure

Attempts to conceal losses or poor performance, possibly due to stretched targets or budget constraints, are sometimes motivators of fraud. Employees will cook the books to enhance their bonuses or even to simply safeguard against loss of employment. If an employee has to make sales of 12 widgets during a year and by the year end he has only managed 10, then, depending on the performance culture of the organization, he may well be concerned about not receiving that bonus and promotion or pay raise. In worst-case scenarios, he may well fear being replaced, so what can he do? He could bring in two or three sales from January next year into December by simply changing the delivery dates on the dispatch documentation. Falsifying cut-off dates on year-end accruals is financial statement fraud and is in this case motivated by strict key performance indicator (KPI) measures.

Nick Leeson is a former derivatives broker whose fraudulent, unauthorized speculative trading caused the spectacular collapse of Barings Bank, the United Kingdom's oldest investment bank, for which he received a substantial prison sentence. Leeson started his fraud by covering up trivial losses in order to save face, ensure that his annual bonus was secured, or just keep his job. It snowballed from there, and he found it easy to break a few more rules in the belief that losses can be turned around, on paper at least.

Misjudgment

Some financial crime happens because opportunity beckons, and the offenders do not think that they will get caught. Sometimes they are right. Sometimes they are wrong. Either way, it is somewhat unsurprising in a culture that rewards risk taking.

One U.S. government official, for example, recently sent $1.2 million to 419 scammers in the belief that he would soon be richly rewarded. Alas, it was only public money rather than his own savings.

 ## THE OPPORTUNITY

The opportunity for employees to commit fraud is effectively created when they are entrusted with access to assets and information that allows them to both commit the fraud and conceal what they have done. Employees are often given access to records and valuable assets in the ordinary course of their jobs, allowing them, usually quite easily, to commit fraud. In recent times and with automation, employees have become responsible for a wider range of assets and procedural functions, effectively giving them more access as well as more control over functional areas of organizations. In terms of controlling and limiting any opportunities to defraud organizations, access should be limited to only those systems, processes, information, and assets that are truly necessary for an employee to complete his or her duties.

Opportunity, sometimes referred to as perceived opportunity, is the second leg of the fraud triangle and represents the access point by means of which the crime can be committed. Fraudsters must be able to see a way (a perceived opportunity) of abusing a position of trust that will satisfy a financial problem with a low perceived risk of being discovered, so they not only have to be able to steal funds, but they have to be able to do it in such a way that they will likely not be caught and the crime itself will not be detected. For example, if an employee has access to blank checks, he may see a perceived opportunity to forge one of the checks made payable to himself. However, that check might well be spotted during the bank reconciliation process and fraud would be uncovered. In this case, even though there is an opportunity to steal the funds, there is no opportunity to steal them in secret. But suppose the same employee also reconciles the company's bank statement. This would enable him to write the check payable to himself, and then when the bank statement arrives, he can destroy the fraudulent check and create a reconciling entry on the reconciliation. The lack of segregation of duties in the process has created an opportunity to commit the fraud and for the fraud to be hidden.

Budgets have always been tight but in recessionary times and particularly lately with increasing economic hardship caused by a worldwide slowdown, so many organizations are faced with having less money to do more with. All too often it is the governance and control environments that take the first hit in cost cutting, without due consideration for fraud risk management. It is no wonder that opportunities for fraud are appearing and increasing.

According to KPMG's 2011 "Analysis of Global Patterns of Fraud," one in seven frauds is now discovered by chance. This places question marks over the effectiveness of internal controls and more seriously, management's capabilities for detecting and preventing fraud. There are an infinite number of opportunities or gaps in controls and processes as there are an infinite number of ways to circumvent these controls. This makes plugging all the gaps virtually impossible. In effect, exposing opportunities is left, to a great extent, to whistleblowing. In the survey just over half of frauds were detected by whistleblowing.

Fraudsters can take advantage of opportunities or gaps in defenses by exploiting the control gaps, blatant dishonesty, or collusion.

CHAPTER ELEVEN

Profiling Individual Behavior and Characteristics of a Fraudster

N O MATTER HOW WELL-RUN an organization may be or how close-knit the employees are, no organization is immune from fraud. Organizational fraud, misappropriation of assets, and financial statement fraud are not new problems, but they still need to be closely monitored. Managers of organizations experiencing fraud are often shocked to learn that the fraud was perpetrated by a trusted employee of the business. It is important to ensure that safeguards are in place protecting the firm's assets and reputation, irrespective of the level of confidence and trust that managers may have in their employees.

According to the ACFE, in 81 percent of cases, the fraudster displayed one or more behavioral red flags that are often associated with fraudulent conduct; the most commonly observed behavioral warning signs are as follows:

- Living beyond one's means (36 percent of cases).
- Having financial difficulties (27 percent).
- Unusually close association with vendors or customers (19 percent).
- Excessive control issues (18 percent).

Typically, a fraudster is someone who is greedy and deceitful by nature. However, many fraudsters work within entities for several years without committing any fraud before a motivational factor such as financial worries, job dissatisfaction, aggressive targets, or simply the opening up of an opportunity tips the balance.

According to KPMG's 2011 analysis of 348 cases across 69 countries, red flags that could have signaled trouble were missed in more than half of cases. It was found that 56 percent of the frauds had exhibited one or more red flags that should have brought management attention to the issue but that only 10 percent of those cases had been acted upon. "Knowing the common traits of a fraudster can help employers be better prepared to prevent damaging incidents from happening in their organizations," said KPMG.

KPMG identified the typical fraudster as being a senior employee known as an aggressive workaholic; someone who seems stressed, yet rarely takes vacations, declines promotions, and zealously protects his business unit from outside scrutiny while personally handling choice vendors. This employee may be up to something devious. The average fraud, according to KPMG, included the following characteristics or red flags:

- A 36- to 45-year-old male in a senior management role in the finance unit or in a finance-related function.
- An employee for more than 10 years who usually would work in collusion with another individual.
- A business unit that thrives despite competitors struggling with declining sales and/or profits.
- Excessive pressure on senior managers and employees to achieve unusually tough profit targets and business goals.
- Persistent rumors or indications of personal bad habits, addictions, or vices, possibly with a lifestyle that seems excessive for the person's income or apparently personally overextended in his finances.
- Complex or unusual agreements and payment methods occur between the business and certain suppliers/customers.
- The business may have multiple banking arrangements rather than one clear provider; a possible attempt to reduce transparency over its finances.
- The business consistently pushes the limits and boundaries regarding matters of financial judgment or accounting treatment.
- Excessive secrecy about a function, its operations, and its financial results, and the unit is not forthcoming with answers or supporting information to internal inquiries.
- Increased profitability fails to lead to increased cash flows.

- Employee volatility and being melodramatic, arrogant, and confrontational with threatening or aggressive behavior when challenged.
- Performance or skills of new employees do not necessarily reflect past experiences detailed on résumés.
- Unreliability and being prone to mistakes and poor performance, with a tendency to cut corners and bend the rules, but makes attempts to shift blame and responsibility for errors.
- Being unhappy, apparently stressed, and under pressure, while bullying and intimidating colleagues.
- Being surrounded by favorites, or people who do not challenge the fraudster, and micromanaging some employees while keeping others at arm's length.
- Being the only person vendors/suppliers will deal with and also possibly accepting generous gifts or entertainment that are excessive or contrary to corporate rules.
- Being self-interested and concerned with one's own agenda and having opportunities to manipulate personal pay and rewards.

Depending on which statistics one looks at, less than 10 percent of fraud perpetrators have prior criminal convictions; those who commit fraud are largely first-time offenders, even though the average fraud perpetrator is older than 40 years of age. Additionally, fraudsters generally exhibit one of two behavioral traits, either living beyond their apparent means or experiencing financial difficulties. They may also, of course, be trusted employees of the organization. Profiling the behavioral characteristics of a fraudster involves delving down into the individual's attributes or profiles such as age and gender of human beings.

PERPETRATOR'S GENDER

As revealed by the ACFE's 2012 report, males tend to account for roughly two-thirds of all fraud cases, as depicted in Figure 11.1.

The ratio of male to female fraudsters varies greatly depending on the region. Europe, Asia, Africa, and Latin America/Caribbean each saw males account for 75 percent or more of frauds. Conversely, Canada and the United States had the lowest rates of male fraudsters. Interestingly, Canada, in fact, reported more frauds committed by females than males, at 52 percent, as depicted in Figure 11.2.

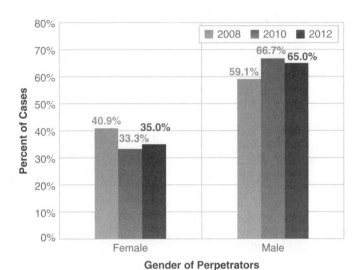

FIGURE 11.1 Gender of Perpetrator—Frequency. *Source:* ACFE, *Report to the Nations*, 2012.

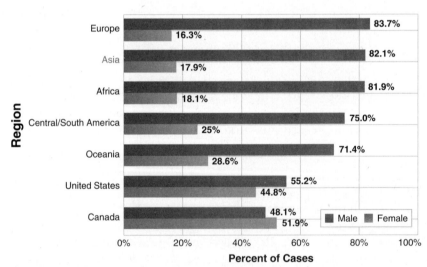

FIGURE 11.2 Gender of Perpetrator—Regions. *Source:* ACFE, *Report to the Nations*, 2012.

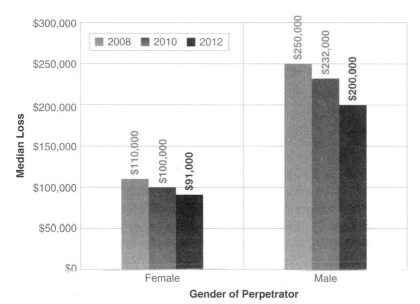

FIGURE 11.3 Gender of Perpetrator—Median Loss. *Source:* ACFE, *Report to the Nations*, 2012.

This disparity does not appear to be based solely on males occupying higher levels of authority than females. In Figures 11.3 and 11.4, losses by gender based on the perpetrators' levels of authority were compared. Males caused significantly higher losses at every level.

While men were found to be more likely perpetrators of detected fraud, 87 percent in KPMG's 2011 report, this might simply be due to there being more men in the workplace and, in particular, to the underrepresentation of women in senior management roles.

PERPETRATOR'S AGE

As shown in Figures 11.5 and 11.6, the distribution of fraudsters based on their age fell roughly along a bell-shaped curve and was fairly consistent from 2010 to 2012. Approximately 54 percent of all fraudsters were between the ages of 31 and 45. Fraud losses, however, tended to rise with the age of the perpetrator. Although this upward trend was not nearly as dramatic in 2012 as in the 2010 study, there are still incremental increases for each advancing age

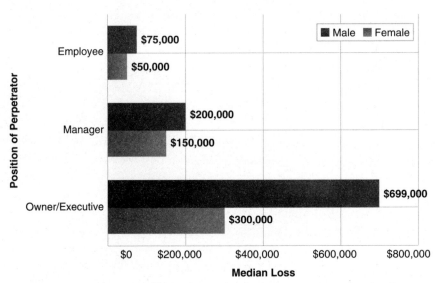

FIGURE 11.4 Position of Perpetrator—Median Loss Based on Gender. *Source:* ACFE, *Report to the Nations*, 2012.

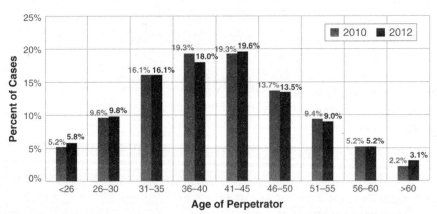

FIGURE 11.5 Age of Perpetrator—Frequency. *Source:* ACFE, *Report to the Nations*, 2012.

range, punctuated by an unexpected outlier in the 51–55 year range, where the median loss rose to $600,000, nearly two-and-a-half times higher than the median loss in any other age range.

According to KPMG's 2011 survey, the typical fraudster is between the ages of 36 and 45, and this group represents 41 percent of all fraud cases, closely

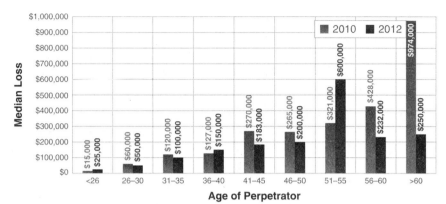

FIGURE 11.6 Age of Perpetrator—Median Loss. *Source:* ACFE, *Report to the Nations,* 2012.

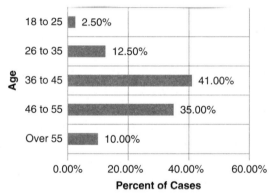

FIGURE 11.7 Age of Fraudster. *Source:* KPMG, "Analysis of Global Patterns of Fraud," 2011.

followed by a group accounting for 35 percent of fraudsters, who were between 46 and 55 years old, as depicted in Figure 11.7.

 PERPETRATOR'S TENURE

Time at the organization, or length of tenure, is also another area that can provide clues as to who may be more inclined to commit fraud. Tenure has a strong correlation with fraud losses. Individuals who have worked at an organization for a longer period of time will often have gained more trust from their

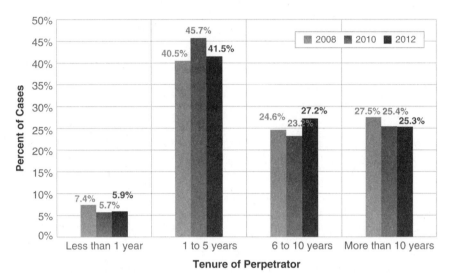

FIGURE 11.8 Tenure of Perpetrator—Frequency. *Source:* ACFE, *Report to the Nations*, 2012.

supervisors and coworkers, which can result in less scrutiny over their duties. Their experience can also give them a better understanding of the organization's internal controls, which enables them to more successfully carry out and conceal their fraud schemes. Approximately 42 percent of occupational fraudsters had between one and five years of tenure at their organizations. Meanwhile fewer than 6 percent of perpetrators committed fraud within the first year on the job, as depicted in Figure 11.8.

As previously noted, occupational fraud losses tend to rise based on the length of time the perpetrator works for the victim organization. We can see that fraudsters with more than 10 years of tenure caused a median loss of $229,000, as depicted in Figure 11.9. This was more than double the median loss caused by perpetrators who had been with the company for 1 to 5 years, and nearly 10 times greater than the median loss caused by fraudsters with less than 1 year of tenure.

According to KPMG's survey, 60 percent of fraudsters worked at the organization for more than 5 years before fraud was detected and 33 percent worked there for more than 10 years, as depicted in Figure 11.10.

Drilling down into the data it can be seen that fraudsters usually work for their organization for over 5 years or over 10 years before committing their deeds, so we can say that employees, more than likely, do not join their

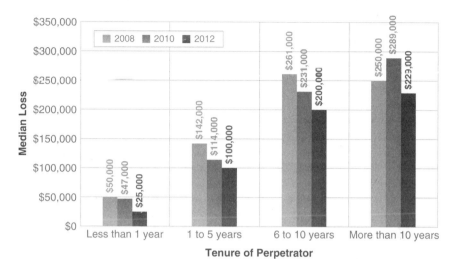

FIGURE 11.9 Tenure of Perpetrator—Median Loss. *Source:* ACFE, *Report to the Nations*, 2012.

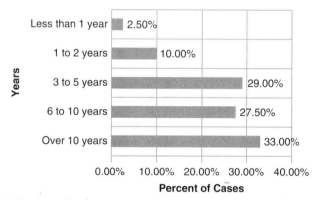

FIGURE 11.10 Length of Tenure. *Source:* KPMG, "Analysis of Global Patterns of Fraud," 2011.

organization specifically to commit fraud. It is probably a motivational driver that has arisen more recently that prompts the fraud upon stumbling across an opportunity. The all too common financial need, change in circumstances, or pressure to meet targets may influence the decision to steal once the employee has gained the trust of his employer and been given several clear audit reports.

PERPETRATOR'S EDUCATION LEVEL

Figures 11.11 and 11.12 show the distribution of fraudsters based on their education level. Approximately 54 percent of fraud perpetrators had a college degree or higher. This was similar to the distribution noted in 2010, when 52 percent of perpetrators had college or postgraduate degrees.

Historically, many studies have found that fraudsters with higher levels of education tend to cause greater losses. Smarter fraudsters equal smarter and more lucrative frauds. One would generally expect more highly educated individuals to have greater levels of authority within their employing organizations, which is probably the most significant reason for this correlation. Individuals with higher education might also possess better technical ability to engineer fraud schemes. In the 2012 data, losses rose in direct correlation to education levels. Individuals with postgraduate degrees caused $300,000 in median losses, compared to $200,000 for those with bachelor's degrees. Those with a high school diploma or less caused a median loss of $75,000, as depicted in Figure 11.12.

Many organizational managers are taken aback when they learn that a longtime, trusted employee has committed fraud. It's a common event, unfortunately, that few organizations have prepared for or even envisioned. However, one often forgotten characteristic all fraudsters possess is humanity. It is

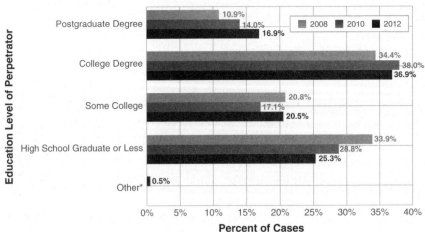

*"Other" category was not included in the prior years' reports.

FIGURE 11.11 Education of Perpetrator—Frequency. *Source:* ACFE, *Report to the Nations*, 2012.

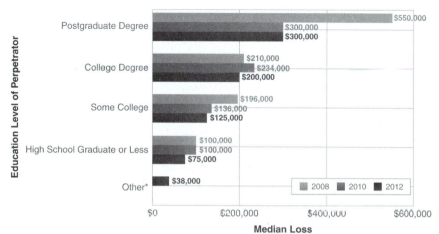

FIGURE 11.12   Education of Perpetrator—Median Loss. *Source:* ACFE, *Report to the Nations,* 2012.

important to remember that individuals who commit fraud are not necessarily bad people. Even the most honest person can turn to fraud if, for instance, he cannot afford treatments for his wife's terminal illness or food for his children. For these reasons, as well as others, it is important for firms to have internal controls in place that preclude the opportunity for fraud, minimizing this causal factor so that the risk of fraud is significantly decreased. One element of control in this situation would be to have employee support specialists within the HR department who can be consulted by those employees who are facing personal and often quite embarrassing problems.

Many studies have been carried out to analyze certain characteristics of fraudsters who have carried out acts of fraud and have been charged with such offenses. By profiling this information in a relevant and methodical way it can be used to profile and identify potential future fraud events and, more important individuals who may commit such offenses.

As Woody Guthrie, the American folk singer, said in 1939, "Some will rob you with a six-gun and some with a fountain pen." In the movies robbers are conveniently characterized with five o'clock shadows, wear black ski masks, and carry big bags marked "swag." The reality is actually more complex. The perpetrators of financial crime can and do look just like you and me.

The ACFE *Report to the Nations* (2012) surmises that 94 percent of fraudsters in the study had no previous fraud convictions and that the most common behavioral red flags were living beyond one's means (36 percent of cases) and experiencing financial difficulties (27 percent of cases). Some may question, therefore, the validity of the use of such profiles if so many fraudsters are first-time offenders. It is fair to surmise, however, that the profiling of previous offender characteristics will play a significant role in identifying even these first-time offenders. The evidence suggests that the characteristics of those first-time offenders follow the characteristics of those of previously charged fraudsters. They, after all, will exhibit characteristics of dishonesty and lying. It is also fair to note that not all fraud offenders are caught, and therefore to say that 85 percent of offenders have no previous prosecution does not mean that they have never committed acts of fraud previously.

Physiognomy (from the Greek word *physis* meaning "nature" and *gnomon* meaning "judge" or "interpreter") is the assessment of a person's character or personality from his or her outer appearance, especially the face. Ancient Greek mathematician, astronomer, and scientist Pythagoras, believed by some to be the originator of physiognomics, once rejected a prospective follower named Cylon because, to Pythagoras, his appearance, particularly his facial appearance, indicated that he was of bad character.

Lombroso was an Italian criminologist and founder of the Italian school of positivist criminology. Lombroso rejected the established classical school, which held that crime was a characteristic trait of human nature. Instead, using concepts drawn from physiognomy, Lombroso's theory of anthropological criminology essentially stated that criminality was inherited and that someone who was born a criminal could be identified by physical defects. He thought that financial criminals could be detected by looking at the shape of their skull and that if an investigator had a pair of calipers and the right sort of training, the fraudster could be identified among employees. Indeed, the Nazis during their financial management of the war machine relied on the science of nose and earlobe shapes to identify those with lower integrity.

Others more plausibly relied on reputation, assuming that past action is a reliable indicator of future behavior and that reports by colleagues and ex-employers about past integrity will truly reveal the future inner man.

Fear of litigation is reducing the reliability of written references as indicators of character, although people continue to rely on such documents, which may or may not have been sighted by the ostensible referee. Reputation is not what it used to be. Fraud has now crept into the referencing side of the fraud risk assurance process, and I have come across many a good reference that had actually been purchased. On one occasion I had the pleasure of telephoning a reference, and the suspect employee who had given me the reference details actually answered the phone … with his own name!

Enthusiastic HR departments are using psychometrics and technologies such as magnetic resonance imaging for senior positions or for those positions linked to safeguarding assets in the belief that the cerebral activity of financial criminals may be identifiably different from that of normal people. First, I would ask, who are normal people? And, second, it is difficult to envisage executives or finance and procurement staff taking a whirl though an MRI machine on day one of their employment.

Key behavioral red flags, according to the ACFE, include the following:

- Unusually close association with vendor or customer (19 percent).
- Control issues and unwillingness to share duties (18 percent).
- Wheeler-dealer attitude (15 percent).
- Divorce/family problems (15 percent).
- Irritability, suspiciousness, or defensiveness (13 percent).
- Addiction problems (8 percent).
- Refusal to take vacations (7 percent).

Some general characteristics one might find in a profile of someone likely to commit fraud within an organization may include the following:

- Three quarters of frauds are committed by men.
- They are intelligent, typically college educated, and feel challenged by computer vulnerability, being bored with their job.
- They are egotistical, feeling worth more than their position indicates.
- They are risk takers, not afraid to fail.
- They are rule breakers, forever taking shortcuts.
- They are often those who feel abused by the employer, either underpaid, overworked, unrecognized, or not being promoted.
- They are hard workers, usually arriving for work early and leaving late, and do not like to take holidays, thus creating an image of being an unlikely fraud candidate. In actuality this time is being utilized to perpetrate the fraud, and any time off for holidays is both expensive in terms of lost fraud opportunity and risky in terms of being discovered.
- They are stressed, often from an event with a financial consequence. This could be a divorce, illness, gambling, or drug dependencies or just the annual private school fee invoice arriving.

- Often they are high spenders, living beyond their means. If an employee's lifestyle spend exceeds his pay, this could indicate a fraud candidate.
- Most are married with demanding wives who provide the incentive through a constant need for jewelry and expensive handbags.
- Many are members of management, being nine times more likely to commit fraud than nonmanagement employees.
- Many are pressured to meet unrealistic financial expectations. The only way to do this is often to falsify sales or window-dress the numbers.

Most occupational fraudsters' crimes are motivated at least in part by some kind of financial pressure. In addition, while committing a fraud, an individual will frequently display certain behavioral traits associated with stress or a fear of being caught. These behavioral red flags can often be a warning sign that fraud is occurring, so it is important to identify and examine the frequency with which fraudsters display various behavioral red flags. The ACFE compiled a list of 16 common red flags for its 2012 report, and survey respondents were asked which, if any, of these traits had been exhibited by the fraudsters before the schemes identified were detected. In 81 percent of all cases reported, the perpetrator had displayed at least one behavioral red flag, and within these cases, multiple red flags were frequently observed. The fraudster living beyond his or her means (36 percent), experiencing financial difficulties (27 percent), having an unusually close association with vendors or customers (19 percent), and displaying excessive control issues (18 percent) were the four most commonly cited red flags in 2012, just as they were in the previous 2010 study. The consistency of the distribution of red flags from year to year is particularly noticeable. Despite the fact that the group of perpetrators analyzed in the 2012 study was completely different from the perpetrators included in the 2010 and 2008 studies, each group seems to have collectively displayed behavioral red flags in similar proportions. One other interesting point about the data is that the rate at which financial difficulties were cited as a behavioral flag has decreased nearly 7 percent from the 2008 study. This is particularly unexpected, as the studies focus on frauds that were investigated in the two years prior to each survey, and the cases that were reported in the 2008 study would have been investigated in 2006 and 2007, prior to the onset of the global financial crisis in 2007–2008. Yet financial difficulties were cited as a red flag more often in the 2008 survey than in either the 2010 or 2012 surveys, both of which included cases that occurred during the peak of the global crisis. Other behavioral red flags identified in the 2012 study and also represented in the earlier studies were the occurrence of divorce/family problems; having a wheeler-dealer attitude;

the existence of irritability, suspiciousness or defensiveness, addiction problems, and past employment-related problems; complaining about inadequate pay; refusing to take vacations; and the existence of excessive pressure from within the organization, past legal problems, complaints about lack of authority, excessive family/peer pressure for success, and instability in life circumstances.

BEHAVIORAL RED FLAGS BASED ON PERPETRATOR'S POSITION

The ACFE *Report to the Nations* (2012) also analyzed behavioral red flags based on the perpetrator's position or level of authority. The ACFE found that there are varying motivations and pressures that affect fraudsters at different levels within an organization. For example, owners/executives are much more likely than employees or managers to experience excessive pressure to perform from within the organization. Employees, conversely, are relatively unlikely to exhibit these red flags but are much more likely than executives to be motivated by financial difficulties. It can, however, be seen from the study that across the three perpetrator positions of employee, manager, and owner/executive, living beyond one's means, being in financial difficulties, and having unusually close associations with vendors and customers are again the three most common behavioral red flags, closely followed by control issues/unwillingness to share duties, divorce or family problems, and having a wheeler-dealer attitude. Having a wheeler-dealer attitude is, interestingly, much higher within the owner/executive category (25 percent of cases) than in the manager category (17 percent) or employee category (8 percent), due, one could surmise, to the increased opportunities to be so at that level.

BEHAVIORAL RED FLAGS BASED ON SCHEME TYPE

The ACFE *Report to the Nations* (2012) also analyzed behavioral red flags based on the type of fraud that was committed: asset misappropriation, corruption, or financial statement fraud. Perpetrators of fraud categorized as asset misappropriation left behind behavioral red flags of living beyond one's means (38 percent), having financial difficulties (29 percent), and having control issues or being unwilling to share duties (18 percent). Fraudsters who engaged in corruption exhibited unusually close associations with vendors or customers in 41 percent of cases, a much higher rate than for the other scheme categories and the highest in the study. These perpetrators also frequently were living beyond their means (39 percent) and displayed serious control issues or an unwillingness to share their professional duties (24 percent). Individuals engaged in financial statement fraud were much more likely than other fraudsters to face excessive pressure to perform from within their organizations (20 percent), but they were less likely to be living beyond their means (33 percent) or experiencing financial difficulties (22 percent). Once again, financial statement fraud scheme types are perhaps more often perpetrated by those with access to such opportunities in the organization, ordinarily at a more senior level and, as such, would perhaps not be in the same degree of financial difficulty as lower level employee perpetrators.

 ## BEHAVIORAL RED FLAGS BASED ON DEPARTMENT

The ACFE *Report to the Nations* (2012) analyzed the behavioral red flags of perpetrators based on which department within the organization the fraud occurred. This data is particularly useful in assisting organizations in the fraud risk assessment process in particular departments, creating focus on those more common behavioral red flags within those departments and organizational functions where fraud risk is more likely, particularly when considered in light of the data on different fraud schemes and the position of the perpetrator.

The vast majority (77 percent) of all frauds in the 2012 study were committed by individuals working in one of six departments: accounting, operations, sales, executive/upper management, customer service, and purchasing. It can be seen from the study that within accounting and operational departments, the most common behavioral red flags were living beyond one's means, having financial difficulties, and having control issues or being unwilling to share duties. The operational department also saw high levels of unusually close associations with vendors and customers. This behavioral red flag can be expected within such a department considering the relationships possibly necessary to operate. The sales department also exhibited living beyond one's means and having financial difficulties as the most common behavioral red flags but at lower levels than accounting and operational departments. Similar to the operational department, the sales department also saw high levels of unusually close associations with vendors and customers, again, possibly due to the need to interact at customer level. Within executive/upper management the most common behavioral red flags were living beyond one's means (this was the highest in the study of red flags by department, at 49 percent), wheeler-dealer attitude, and control issues or unwillingness to share duties. The most common behavioral red flags in the customer service department were, once again, living beyond one's means and having financial difficulties but at lower levels than other departments. The purchasing department had expected high levels of red flags due to unusually close associations with vendors and customers, perhaps understandable due to the possible need to deal with suppliers.

Knowing which red flags are most prevalent in each department or organizational function or with respect to varying offender types will be invaluable in building a fraud profiling methodology for any organization as part of its fraud risk management process.

CHAPTER TWELVE

Profiling the Fraudster's Position and Department

F RAUD WILL MOST LIKELY OCCUR in organizations where highly people-oriented processes are used to control and monitor the flow of funds, particularly cash. While people are the key element of any organization, it is essential that organizations do not overlook the fact that employees are human and that care must be taken not to provide them with unfair or excessive temptation. If you leave a piece of steak on the kitchen table and instruct a dog not to touch it, I think we all know what happens when we leave the room. While we may not view it as such, many of us break the law multiple times each day just in commuting in our cars. Speeding is illegal, but many of us commit this act frequently, giving the following justifications or rationalizations:

1. We are often pressed for time. This is the motive.
2. Most cars are powerful enough to break the speed limit. This is the opportunity.
3. We feel it is justified to reach our destination earlier and the perceived penalty is low. This is the rationalization.

If, however, our cars were electronically programmed not to exceed the speed limit, the ability to break the law would not exist, in much the same way that it is essential that organizations remove the opportunity for fraud from people-oriented processes to ensure that frauds cannot occur or at least are limited.

Participants in the ACFE's 2012 report were asked to supply several pieces of demographic information about the fraud perpetrators, including level of authority, age, gender, tenure with the victim organization, education level, department, criminal and employment history, and behavioral red flags that were exhibited prior to detection of the frauds. This information was used to identify common characteristics among fraud perpetrators, which can be helpful in assessing relative levels of risk within various areas of an organization and in highlighting traits and behaviors that might be consistent with fraudulent activities. One of the most interesting findings in the data is how consistent the results tend to be from year to year, which indicates that many findings regarding the perpetrators might reflect general trends over time among all occupational fraudsters.

 ## PERPETRATOR'S POSITION

Figure 12.1 shows the distribution of fraudsters based on three broad levels of authority: employee, manager, and owner/executive. Approximately 42 percent of fraudsters were employees, 38 percent were managers, and 18 percent were owner/executives.

As shown in Figure 12.2, there is a strong correlation between the fraudster's level of authority and the losses resulting from the fraud. Owner/executives caused losses approximately three times higher than managers, and managers in turn caused losses approximately three times higher than employees. This result was expected given that higher levels of authority generally mean a perpetrator has greater access to an organization's assets and is better positioned to override antifraud controls.

More than three-quarters of the frauds in the study were committed by individuals from six departments: accounting, operations, sales, executive/upper management, customer service, and purchasing.

Frauds committed by managers and owner/executives generally lasted for two years before they were detected. This was twice as long as the median employee scheme, and it likely reflects the fact that perpetrators with higher levels of authority are typically in a better position to override controls or

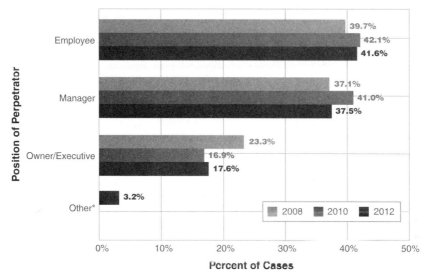

*"Other" category was not included in the prior years' reports.

FIGURE 12.1 Position of Perpetrator—Frequency. *Source:* ACFE, *Report to the Nations,* 2012.

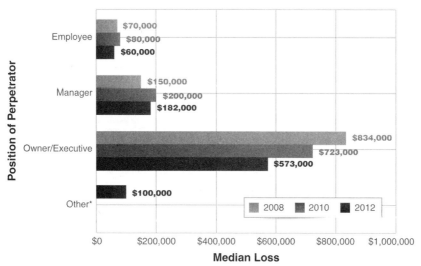

*"Other" category was not included in the prior years' reports.

FIGURE 12.2 Position of Perpetrator—Median Loss. *Source:* ACFE, *Report to the Nations,* 2012.

Position	Median Months to Detect
Employee	12
Manager	24
Owner/Executive	24
Other	10

FIGURE 12.3 Duration of Fraud Based on Position. *Source:* ACFE, *Report to the Nations*, 2012.

conceal their misconduct. It might also reflect reluctance on the part of employees and antifraud personnel to lodge complaints about or investigate those with higher levels of authority, effectively, their bosses. For this reason, an anonymous reporting channel could prove to be effective. Figure 12.3 shows the median months to detection for each level of position.

The ACFE *Report to the Nations* (2012) also studied the median loss and distribution of perpetrators based on position of authority for each region. It is particularly striking from the study that, within the position categories used—employee, manager, owner/executive, and other—generally speaking, while owner/executives may represent a lower number of cases, the owner/executive losses tended to be much larger. Geographically, Asia was by far the region with the highest median loss in the owner/executive category, with median losses of $4 million. In all but one of the regions, between 77 and 86 percent of frauds were committed by employees and managers, despite owner/executive losses tending to be much larger. The one exception was Canada, where owner/executive losses were lower than those caused by managers. However, it should be noted that there was a small sample of only eight owner/executive cases reported in Canada, which may have had an impact on the reliability of the loss figure. Interestingly, losses in the United States and Canada were lower than in other regions, particularly among owner/executives. This correlation could be the result of truly lower losses caused by U.S. and Canadian executives, or it might simply reflect the fact that U.S. and Canadian certified fraud examiners tended to investigate less costly executive malfeasance than their counterparts in other regions.

Interestingly, the longer a perpetrator has worked for an organization, the higher the fraud losses tend to be. Perpetrators with more than 10 years of experience at the victim organization caused a median loss of $229,000. By comparison, the median loss caused by perpetrators who committed fraud in their first year on the job was only $25,000.

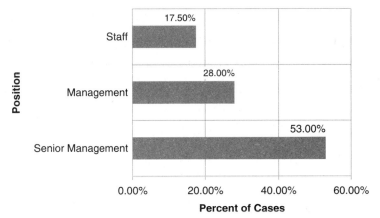

FIGURE 12.4 Position within the Organization. *Source:* KPMG, "Analysis of Global Patterns of Fraud," 2011.

An interesting point that is also visible in the KPMG 2011 "Analysis of Global Patterns of Fraud" is that the employees most entrusted with a company's sensitive information and who have the ability to override controls are statistically more likely to become perpetrators. Once again, this leads us to senior management. Fifty-three percent of frauds in the survey were committed by senior management (see Figure 12.4).

 PERPETRATOR'S DEPARTMENT

The six most common departments in which fraud perpetrators worked were accounting, operations, sales, executive/upper management, customer service, and purchasing. Collectively, these six departments accounted for 77 percent of all cases reported, as Figure 12.5 illustrates.

Not surprisingly, schemes committed by those who were in the executive/upper management suite caused the largest median loss at $500,000, while customer service cases resulted in the lowest median loss of $30,000. Schemes committed by those in the accounting department ranked fifth on median loss, at $183,000, but this department accounted for 22 percent of all reported cases, far more than any other category, as depicted in Figure 12.6.

The ACFE study examined the distribution of cases based on the perpetrator's department for each region. The top six departments, as noted previously (accounting, operations, sales, owner/executive, customer service, and purchasing) accounted for between 69 percent and 81 percent of the cases in

*"Other" category was not included in the 2010 report.

FIGURE 12.5 Department of Perpetrator—Frequency. *Source:* ACFE, *Report to the Nations,* 2012.

every region. It is immediately apparent from the study that the accounting department features either at the top or very close to the top of each region's case frequency results and actually represents the highest number of cases of all departments in any region, at 26 percent of cases, in the United States. This is understandable, considering the fact that accounting departments are more often than not given the unenviable task of gatekeeper, challenged with the job of safeguarding the assets. This, along with the fact that organizational assets, including the contents of bank accounts and cash, are controlled and managed within accounting functions, makes it a primary target for fraud and represents the most popular opportunity in terms of departments. Additionally, operations and sales departments feature high up the rankings as particularly

Department	Number of Cases	Percentage	Median Loss
Executive/Upper Management	159	11.9%	$500,000
Finance	49	3.7%	$250,000
Board of Directors	19	1.4%	$220,000
Purchasing	76	5.7%	$200,000
Accounting	293	22.0%	$183,000
Legal	8	0.6%	$180,000
Marketing/Public Relations	14	1.1%	$165,000
Manufacturing and Production	25	1.9%	$160,000
Human Resources	16	1.2%	$121,000
Research and Development	9	0.7%	$100,000
Information Technology	27	2.0%	$100,000
Other	79	5.9%	$100,000
Operations	232	17.4%	$100,000
Sales	170	12.8%	$90,000
Warehousing/Inventory	56	4.2%	$67,000
Internal Audit	8	0.6%	$32,000
Customer Service	92	6.9%	$30,000

FIGURE 12.6 Department of Perpetrator—Median Loss. *Source:* ACFE, *Report to the Nations,* 2012.

fraud-prone departments across most regions, perhaps because of the pressure in these departments to perform and the potential for interaction with external parties, which could result in the manipulation of transactions for personal gain. Owner/executives also features quite high in most regions as being particularly fraud prone. Again, these individuals ordinarily have higher level access to assets or can commit financial statement fraud by justifying their actions or bypassing internal controls and being challenged with lower levels of scrutiny or questioning. Internal audit, legal and research, and development departments are the areas of organizations least likely to house fraud across the various regions covered, according to the survey. These are the departments with lower levels of access to assets and bank accounts. My opinion is that internal audit and legal departments, in particular, include professionals who have ordinarily spent many years studying to obtain professional qualifications and are probably among the best paid employees in the organization in relatively senior positions. They do not have the same financial pressures and motives to commit fraud as other employees, and they have the most to lose.

The ACFE study also examined the most common schemes committed within each department. Corruption was the most common scheme throughout the department study, with the highest being in the purchasing department (68 percent of cases) and in the owner/executive function (54 percent). Corruption was the most common scheme in every department except accounting, where billing fraud (31 percent) and check tampering (30 percent) were the two most common scheme types, again, due to the accessibility to financial records.

The frequency of fraud decreases as one progresses up the organizational ranks, although the median loss of fraud grows significantly the higher up the fraud occurs. For instance, roughly one-third of all frauds are committed by nonmanagerial employees, but the median loss for such frauds is lower. On the other hand, frauds committed by executives and owners are much less frequent, but the median loss for such frauds at that level is significantly higher. Many firms concentrate on fraud controls at the employee level and not necessarily at the executive level, where the material loss is happening. Surely, this does not make a great deal of sense. We see many examples where an organization will have stringent controls on the sales and cash collection process, making it very difficult for employees to commit fraud. What the company didn't realize, however, was that the chief financial offcer was taking money out of the back door because he had the power to override fraud-related controls and did so at his leisure. This is certainly something that should be considered when implementing antifraud controls.

According to the ACFE, corruption and billing schemes pose the greatest risks to organizations throughout the world, where these two scheme types comprised more than 50 percent of frauds reported. Fraud offenders were most

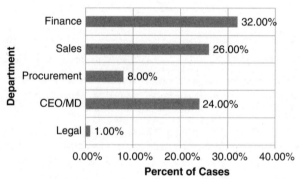

FIGURE 12.7 Department within the Organization. *Source:* KPMG, "Analysis of Global Patterns of Fraud," 2011.

likely to be found in one of six departments in an organization: accounting/finance, operations, sales, executive/upper management, customer service, and purchasing.

Access to and responsibility for organizational assets and finance and financial reporting hold the largest temptation and opportunity and are, therefore, of particular interest to fraudsters. According to the KPMG survey, 32 percent of fraudsters were employed in the finance function, followed by 26 percent in the chief executive/managing director's office. Employees in the legal department were least likely perpetrators (see Figure 12.7).

CHAPTER THIRTEEN

Profiling the Fraud Methodology or Modus Operandi

T HE ACFE HIGHLIGHTS FOUR CHARACTERISTICS that typify employee fraud:

1. The offense is undertaken in secret.
2. The perpetrators are in breach of their duty to the organization by committing the offense.
3. The motivation for the fraud is the personal benefit of the fraudster.
4. The organization, usually the employer, is the victim.

The various methods of committing the many types of fraud are generally the same or similar, for example, payroll fraud using ghost employees, accounts payable fraud with employees authorizing payment to themselves or companies they have created, or accounts receivable fraud with the falsification of bank reconciliations. It is important to include fraud methods or modus operandi when using profiling to identify fraudulent behavior in an organization. The particular modus operandi will classify the fraud risk type and enable a targeted approach in terms of implementing the best fit internal controls.

COLLUSION

When two or more individuals conspire to commit fraud against an organization, it can have an especially harmful effect, particularly when the combined efforts of the fraudsters enable them to circumvent or override antifraud controls. In the ACFE's three most recent studies, the rate of collusion has been fairly consistent; multiple perpetrators were reported in 36 percent to 42 percent of all cases (see Figure 13.1). Schemes involving collusion have also consistently resulted in much larger losses than those involving a single fraudster. As Figure 13.2 shows, the median loss in collusion schemes in the 2012 study was $250,000, which was more than twice the loss resulting from single-perpetrator schemes. Interestingly, over the last three studies, losses in single-perpetrator schemes have remained notably constant, while losses in multiple-perpetrator schemes have dropped significantly, from $500,000 in the 2008 study to $250,000 in the 2012 report.

Overall, 42 percent of the cases in the 2012 ACFE study involved multiple perpetrators, but there was a significant difference between US and non-US cases. Within the United States, only about one-third of all cases involved collusion, whereas in other regions, collusion was reported 55 percent of

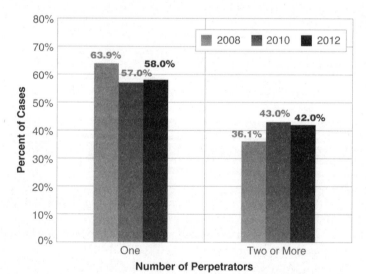

FIGURE 13.1 Number of Perpetrators—Frequency. *Source:* ACFE, *Report to the Nations,* 2012.

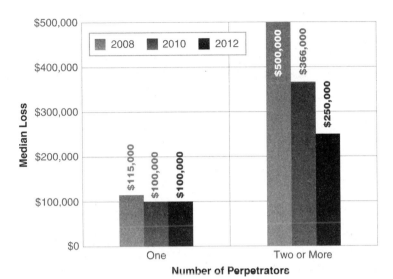

FIGURE 13.2 Number of Perpetrators—Median Loss. *Source:* ACFE, *Report to the Nations*, 2012.

the time. Also, while the median loss for single-perpetrator cases was the same ($100,000) both inside and outside the United States, collusion cases in non-US countries were almost twice as costly.

According to KPMG's 2011 "Analysis of Global Patterns of Fraud," 90 percent of fraud perpetrators were employed by the organization that they defrauded, and 61 percent of frauds involved collusion, as depicted in Figure 13.3.

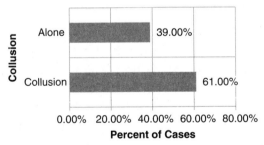

FIGURE 13.3 Fraud with Collusion. *Source:* KPMG, "Analysis of Global Patterns of Fraud," 2011.

Collusive fraud involves two or more persons circumventing the system of internal control and is more difficult to detect. Colluding parties external to the organization could be suppliers (48 percent) and customers (22 percent). Other such external parties would include consultants and subcontractors. Collusion is more prevalent in regions where there is a culture of sharing or giving gifts. Once again, this is a characteristic of the Middle East region, for example.

POSITION OF EMPLOYMENT CREATES THE OPPORTUNITY

It is interesting to note that most offenders acquire all the knowledge and skills required to commit their frauds during their normal course of employment at the organization from which they steal. The audit function is rarely perceived as a threat to them as are other methods of control. The fraudster places more emphasis on the benefits that will be gained rather than the potential cost of being caught. Whatever the reason for fraud and however it is carried out, most offenders continue, irrespective of the watchdogs, simply because the benefits of having the wealth that it creates for them are greater than the risk.

There are many fraud schemes out there and many ways to defraud an organization, many of which use a huge array of skills and innovation to perpetrate the crime. The fraudster's strategy consists of four main elements:

1. Victim selection, usually the employer but there may be easier targets.
2. Perpetration strategies, or the modus operandi.
3. Detection avoidance strategies, perhaps by using identity theft, counterfeiting, or forgery to hide his tracks.
4. Securing the gains.

Fraud is characterized by a wide range of behaviors but all include deception with the intention of personal gain. These frauds can range from internal frauds, where a previously law-abiding employee exploits an opportunity within his organization, to a variety of external attacks, often by organized crime syndicates. Common forms of external attack might be investment frauds, mass marketing scams, advance fee (419) scams, or quite simply using identity theft to deceive the organization. Whether internal or external, all frauds can be characterized by misrepresentation, failing to disclose information, and abuse of position of trust.

Investment frauds and mass marketing scams may take the form of the bombardment of literature and phone calls with an aim to get hold of any spare capital that your organization may have to invest in a "fantastic once in a lifetime investment opportunity." The schemes are exotic and make use of fake bios and spoof websites and many look very convincing. Such investments could be targeted at the organization or its employees, offering pyramid investment schemes, work from home scams, bogus products, bogus career scams with false recruitment agencies requiring advance fees, and loan scams. I have long believed that the easiest fraud to perpetrate is that of raising false invoices to organizations for goods that were not delivered and services not carried out. Some time ago, while investigating in South Africa, we carried out a prenotified fraud test as part of a vulnerability review exercise. We simply printed off 1,000 identical invoices for $1,000 each and sent them to different organizations by fax and mail. The invoices were false as no goods or services were ever carried out or delivered. In many frauds, small monetary values are lost to fraud as they simply fall below the radar and are perhaps considered as immaterial to organizations. The tactic of some fraud schemes is to secure such a small sum of money that the victim will not miss or will be less bothered about it. It did not surprise me that 40 of the 1,000 invoices were paid in full with no questions asked. This is simply because of the agency theory, with smaller invoices being sent through for payment by relatively junior and underpaid clerks whose primary objective is to get paid at the end of the month and obviously not to verify goods received notes or quality of deliverables. In the real world of fraud, I am sure the payment percentage would have been much higher due to collusion between the fraudster and the paying party. Just to clarify, all amounts were returned, and we cleverly wormed our way into these organizations to charge consulting fees in order to close the gaps and reduce the fraud opportunities.

Another common theft would be to steal IP and e-mail addresses and use these to commit further frauds, perhaps by communicating with existing clients and customers in an attempt to redirect funds to the fraudster's accounts or to undertake phishing activities.

Card-not-present fraud creates problems for organizations, particularly those in retail and operating online, whereby fraudsters can make purchases with stolen cards or card details. While on the subject of credit card fraud, skimming is a sophisticated way of copying card details for later use to either copy the magnetic details onto other stolen cards or to simply go on a spending spree on the Internet. The skimming device is about the size of a cigarette box and fits nicely into a waiter's pocket. Waiters might earn $1,000 plus tips a month from the restaurant but may earn 10 times that amount by selling skimmers full of up to 300 card swipes to a fraud syndicate. This type of fraud is being challenged by the banks with the requirement of personal identification numbers. However, this technology has not yet reached many countries.

Advance fee fraud or 419 scams are also quite popular external fraud attacks against organizations or their employees. Being the third largest income generator for Nigeria, this represents a phenomenal amount of money, although I have never been able to determine how they get to such a statistic. One advance fee fraud that we looked at used spoof websites of a bank in an attempt to convince the victim that he was in direct contact with the bank that was requiring the advance fee in return for onward transmission of the proposed monies. The spoof bank website was identical to the bank's real site, apart from one character difference in the web address, which is, of course, sent by a link in an e-mail. The fake site contained counterfeit documents pertaining to alleged transfers made and fake IDs of alleged bank officials. All very convincing to the layman, if you were to ask me. I do, however, wonder how easy it would be to create a fictitious advance fee scam against my organization and reap the rewards while blaming some external scammer.

MANY WAYS TO DEFRAUD AN ORGANIZATION

Any fraudster has to work to his own modus operandi and ensure that it is under the detection radar by concealing his actions and concealing his identity. He has to then remain concealed. One method of remaining below the radar is to steal or use someone else's identity to perpetrate his crime.

Identity fraud can be defined as unlawfully using another person's identity details for personal gain or to avoid an obligation. The Home Office in the United Kingdom describes *identity fraud* as when a false identity or someone else's identity details are used to support unlawful activity. The Home Office also includes when people avoid obligations or liabilities by falsely claiming that they, themselves, were the victim of identity fraud. Identity fraud involves the use of an individual or an organization's identity information to open accounts or obtain credit or goods or services by deception. It can also be described as the use of that stolen identity in criminal activity to obtain goods or services by deception. It is important to note that stealing an individual's identity in itself does not constitute identity fraud. It is the actual use of the stolen identity to deceive that constitutes the crime. Identity fraud is, by its nature, usually temporary as the real person whose identity has been stolen invariably finds out as their credit is turned down or they start receiving invoices for mysterious purchases.

The huge costs of fraud facilitated by identity theft is significant reason in itself for identifying and understanding identity fraud and developing fraud profiling methodologies, tools, and solutions to deter, prevent, and detect it.

Opportunities have arisen for perpetrators of identity fraud to exploit the anonymity afforded when exploiting systems that lack a proof of identity (POI) control, either by biometric (e.g., fingerprints), attributed (e.g., your full name), or biographical (e.g., education or employment history) identity attributes.

Fraudsters steal rubbish. *Dumpster diving*, as it is known, is big business. It is simply stealing an organization's trash. If that organization is a bank or insurance company or any organization with financial or personal data, then that data is of value. Bank statements, credit card details, even electricity bills all contain data of use to fraudsters. I once was asked to investigate a missing amount of money from a bank account of a customer of a prominent Parisian bank. As it happens, the customer had mailed a letter to the bank asking the bank to transfer an amount in the hundreds of thousands to "the following bank account," the details of which were in the following paragraph in the middle of the page of the letter. Unbeknownst to him and to the bank, the letter had been stolen en route, not Dumpster diving but mail diving. The fraudsters cut out the middle of the page with the depository banking details and replaced it with an insert with their bank account details thereon. A bit of tape, some whiteout, and three photocopies later and the letter was sent on its way to the Parisian bank. The transfer was made to the "following" bank account, which was, of course, the fraudsters' account. My challenge as the forensic accounting expert was to determine who was at fault and whether the customer could recover the lost funds from the bank (i.e., could I find negligence within the actions of the bank?). The answer was yes. Upon examining the bank mandate, it was apparent that photocopy customer signatures were not to be accepted as authorized instructions to transfer funds. Fortunately for me, I had traveled to Paris with the actual blue pen that had signed the original letter. The signature on the letter was most definitely light gray, after having been photocopied at least three times. Case won, as was a free weekend in Paris.

Profiling has the potential for use in identity fraud, yet it has had limited study. What is needed is the development of a conceptual framework in order to build a profile of a perpetrator that will help identify the perpetrator through the fraud he has committed after having obtained POI documentation.

There are three main POI attributes (biometric, attributed, and biographical) that are prerequisite to POI documentation requirements. These identity attributes are the underlying pieces of information that a perpetrator seeks, through identity theft or identity deception, to commit identity fraud acts against targets to secure money or assets. Biometric attributes are becoming more important and constitute inclusion on an expanding number of different POI documentation (e.g., passports), due to the underlying data being based on attributes such as fingerprints, face geometry, DNA, or voice patterns that do not change substantially over an individual's life. Past reliance on attributed and biographical attributes is waning due to the perpetrator's ability to compromise this on POI documents more easily. In a growing number of cases, perpetrators just invent identity details.

Induction and deduction are among the most pivotal theoretical and practical issues in criminal profiling and can be used for identity fraud profiling, yet they are the most poorly understood. *Induction* involves statistical correlation reasoning whereby the current offender is assessed by virtue of his or her difference or similarity to past similar offenders. *Deduction*, on the other hand, involves in-depth analysis of the current case and involves reasoning that if the evidence collected is accurate, then the conclusions that flow from that evidence must also be accurate. Inductive criminal profiling develops a profile of a suspect based on the results gathered from other crime scenes and can also draw on profiles and information from formal and informal studies of known criminals and from publicly available data sources to provide guidance.

Organizations monitor their business transactions, products, channels, employees, internal and perimeter systems, and procedures in a variety of ways. These include data matching, data mining, formal and informal information sharing about attacks of known perpetrators, employee screening, and audits.

Fraud risk management involves the use of a vast array of methods to deter, detect, and prevent perpetrators by corroborating the background, who they are undertaking business with, by validating details such as name, address, age, mother's maiden name, unique identifiers (alpha and numerical) on identity, passport, social security, tax, welfare, medical, licenses, and student documents or cards, to name but a few. Most of these documents or cards are easily replicated based on real or invented individual identities by perpetrators as they rely on attributed or biographical attributes and less on biometrics. Where biometrics are used—such as signature on a check, photo in a passport or license—perpetrators were also able to forge or replace these biometrics by bypassing those controls.

In today's electronic information security environment, organizations computerize or digitize data for profiling the underlying information. This is important because currently identity fraud perpetrators are targeting, to a greater extent, financial institutions to misappropriate funds or goods, or avoid payments or losses. Therefore, the ability to mitigate identity fraud in real time by using an information security environment rather than face-to-face interactions is critical for these organizations.

It is interesting to note for profiling that, generally speaking, fraudsters are required to have good general business skills and in particular some basic understanding of accounting systems and entries. In addition to this, reasonable organizational skills would enable the fraudster to perpetrate his act in a structured and methodical way with due consideration to the next moves of any detection mechanisms. Good networking skills would also be of benefit as collusion in some way makes it easier to not only carry out the fraud but also hide the proceeds of crime through a syndicate or network with contacts and links in banks and money exchangers.

Many fraudsters make use of the latest technology to carry out their deeds. Identity fraudsters use sophisticated software and develop unique programs and hardware to copy cards. Most use the Internet, which opens up many scams to the mass fraudster market and gives access to more victims.

In my mind the worst type of fraud is the one that uses the threat of violence. Often called intimidation, this tactic is frequently deployed as a fraud reaches its conclusion and the fraudster gets frustrated with the victim, with whom he has built a relationship. Fraudsters rarely intimidate a stranger with whom they have no relationship and ammunition. I recall working on clearing up the mess after a black dollar scam at a hotel close to an airport in South Africa in which the box full of allegedly canceled dollar bills that were supposed to be rendered uncanceled after the application of a magic chemical were covered in blood. The Chinese victims had unfortunately questioned the contents of the box and were thereafter executed when guns were pulled out in the hotel room meeting point.

The modus operandi can be complex and varied, but once analyzed, it can, through a methodology footprint, give not only insight into who is likely to have perpetrated the crime but also an antidote or applied antifraud program that is targeted to that particular way of perpetrating fraud.

CHAPTER FOURTEEN

Profiling the Victim Organization and Its Geography

N THE UNITED KINGDOM, an estimated 48 percent of the population has been targeted with a scam and 8 percent admit to being a victim of one. Clearly, either few attempts succeed or people are not admitting to having been duped. Interestingly, in the study of victimology we can analyze and profile which organizations are more likely to become victims of fraud. This data or profiling is of use not only to consulting firms in their marketing strategies but also to organizations themselves. If you are in a low-risk organization, in a low-risk industry, in a country where fraud and corruption are historically low, then you are not going to spend a great deal of time or money on expensive fraud risk management.

According to the ACFE, the industries most commonly victimized at the time of writing are the banking and financial services, government and public administration, and manufacturing sectors.

The presence of antifraud controls is notably correlated with significant decreases in the cost and duration of occupational fraud schemes. Victim organizations that have implemented common antifraud controls experience considerably lower losses and time-to-detection than organizations lacking these controls.

I lived and worked in the Middle East for many years where incidences of fraud were relatively low compared to other regions. Some of the following factors can be attributed to influencing the low fraud rate in the region:

- There is the death penalty. This is possibly the ultimate deterrent.
- It is a wealthy, oil money–fueled region and therefore, theoretically, has reduced motivational factors.
- There are high levels of regulation.
- It has a religion and culture that focus on honesty.
- There is a large footprint of experienced audit and fraud investigation professionals policing the economy.

However, it should be noted that the laws of supply and demand are also in effect in the fraud world, and there are also some factors that need to be considered as to the reasons fraud can and actually does happen in the Middle East. Put simply, where there is wealth, there is lots of money to steal. Mix this with a historical culture of giving gifts in exchange for contracts or an order as a thank-you rather than a bribe to influence a decision, and you will have fraud and corruption risk. Locals working more than one job and owning several organizations may clear the way for preference in tender fraud scenarios as they direct large contracts toward their own, often more expensive suppliers. Furthermore, the fact that most of the workforce in the region is actually expatriate and, therefore, not influenced by the local cultural and wealth reasons for not committing fraud increases fraud risk.

FRAUD VICTIM ORGANIZATIONS BY GEOGRAPHIC LOCATION

The ACFE 2012 study analyzed 1,388 cases of occupational fraud from 96 countries, providing a truly global view of and insight into occupational fraud schemes, based on the geographic region in which the frauds occurred. Figure 14.1 reflects the distribution of cases by region and the corresponding estimated median loss.

In high-growth areas of the world, fraud can be sizable and result in large losses; therefore, regulatory requirements demand effective fraud risk management not only to curb losses but to protect the reputation of the financial and stock markets in these countries. According to KPMG's 2011 analysis of fraud loss, there are significant variations by geographic region, with the Asia Pacific

Region*	Number of Cases	Percent of Cases	Median Loss (in US Dollars)
United States	778	57.2%	$120,000
Asia	204	15.0%	$195,000
Europe	134	9.9%	$250,000
Africa	112	8.2%	$134,000
Canada	58	4.3%	$87,000
Latin America and the Caribbean	38	2.8%	$325,000
Oceania	35	2.6%	$300,000

*See Appendix for a list of countries included in each multicountry region.

FIGURE 14.1 Geographic Location of Victim Organizations. *Source: ACFE, Report to the Nations, 2012.*

region showing the highest average loss per fraud of $1.4 million, followed by the Americas with $1.1 million, and Europe, the Middle East, and Africa with $900,000.

Organizations move to the Asia Pacific region to exploit larger markets and potentially cheaper labor sources and warehousing costs, despite the increased fraud risk factors. In order to overcome language barriers and get through regulatory red tape, businesses moving to this region tend to use local labor and with this comes increased fraud risk from local employees who seek opportunities to tap into large international corporate bank accounts or assets. Fraud takes much longer to detect in Asia Pacific than in other regions, on average taking 5 years, with 16 percent of frauds going undetected for 10 years or more. This may be because of the cultural sensitivities to challenging one's superior in this region, as opposed to in Europe or the United States, where such disclosures are encouraged, rewarded, and protected, and where fewer than 3 percent of frauds took 10 years or more to detect. For those regions where detection time frames are lengthy, questions need to be asked about the effectiveness of management oversight and response to red flags and the need for fraud profiling.

The ACFE study analyzed the types of fraud per geographic region in order to gain insight into likely fraud types per country. It can be clearly seen that corruption is the most significant fraud type in the study, being 51 percent of cases in Asia, 44 percent of cases in Europe, 39 percent of cases in Africa, and 25 percent of cases in the United States. At the bottom end of the scale, financial statement fraud and cash frauds were the types less prevalent in terms of number of cases across all geographies.

Region	Number of Corruption Cases	Percent of All Cases in Region	Median Loss
Asia	104	51.0%	$250,000
Latin America and the Caribbean	18	47.4%	$300,000
Europe	59	44.0%	$250,000
Oceania	14	40.0%	$300,000
Africa	44	39.3%	$350,000
Canada	17	29.3%	$200,000
United States	195	25.1%	$239,000

FIGURE 14.2   Corruption Cases by Region.   *Source:* ACFE, *Report to the Nations*, 2012.

CORRUPTION CASES BY REGION

Many organizations are concerned about the risk of corruption as they expand operations into new geographic areas. Consequently, an examination of the breakdown of reported corruption cases by region is of particular interest. The results of this analysis are presented in Figure 14.2.

TYPES OF FRAUD VICTIM ORGANIZATIONS

Nearly 40 percent of victim organizations in the ACFE study were privately owned, and 28 percent were publicly traded, meaning that more than two-thirds of the victims in the study were for-profit organizations. This distribution is consistent with previous years' reports. Not-for-profit organizations made up the smallest portion of the data set, accounting for slightly more than 10 percent of reported cases, as represented in Figure 14.3.

Privately owned and publicly traded organizations also continue to suffer the highest reported median losses, as represented in Figure 14.4.

SIZE OF FRAUD VICTIM ORGANIZATIONS

Small organizations with fewer than 100 employees continue to be the most common victims in the fraud instances reported in the ACFE survey, although the overall variation between size categories is relatively small (see Figure 14.5).

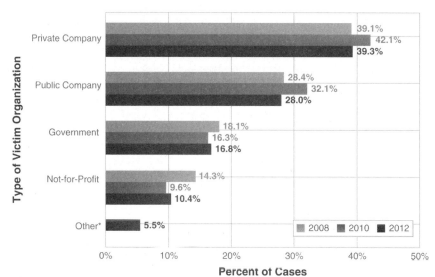

*"Other" category was not included in the prior years' reports.

FIGURE 14.3 Type of Victim Organization—Frequency. *Source:* ACFE, *Report to the Nations*, 2012.

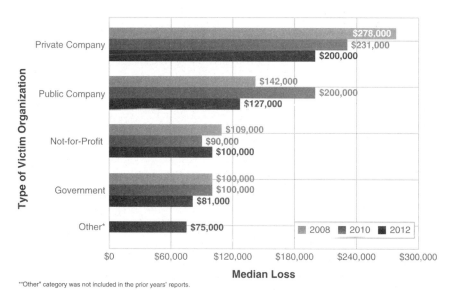

*"Other" category was not included in the prior years' reports.

FIGURE 14.4 Type of Victim Organization—Median Loss. *Source:* ACFE, *Report to the Nations*, 2012.

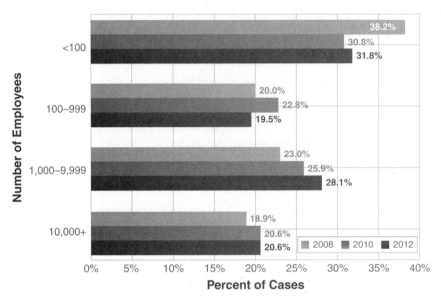

FIGURE 14.5 Size of Victim Organization—Frequency. *Source:* ACFE, *Report to the Nations*, 2012.

This can be attributed to the fact that larger organizations are more able to employ large audit departments or hire CFEs to formally investigate fraud cases. The two categories of smaller organizations with fewer than 100 employees and those with 100 to 999 employees consistently experiencing higher median losses than their larger counterparts reflect the significance of fraud in the smallest organizations, as depicted in Figure 14.6.

 ## METHODS OF FRAUD IN SMALL BUSINESSES

The ACFE research reinforces the point that the specific fraud risks faced by small organizations typically differ from those faced by larger organizations. For example, corruption was observed to be the most prevalent fraud committed in larger organizations, occurring in nearly 35 percent of reported cases in companies with more than 100 employees, compared to 28 percent of small business cases. In contrast, billing schemes were the most common fraud committed in smaller organizations. In addition, check tampering was three times as common and payroll and skimming schemes were noted almost twice as often in smaller organizations than in their larger counterparts (see Figure 14.7).

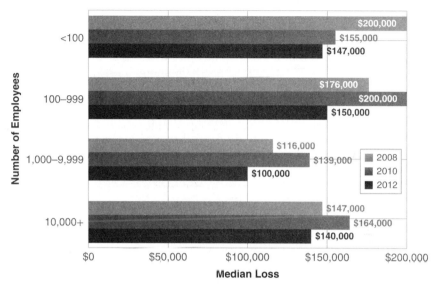

FIGURE 14.6 Size of Victim Organization—Median Loss. *Source:* ACFE, *Report to the Nations,* 2012.

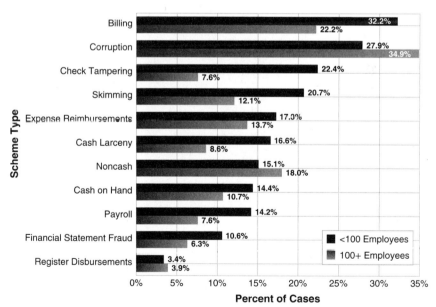

FIGURE 14.7 Scheme Type by Size of Victim Organization. *Source:* ACFE, *Report to the Nations,* 2012.

INDUSTRY OF FRAUD VICTIM ORGANIZATIONS

For a better understanding of where fraud is occurring and at what frequency, reported cases were categorized by industry. Banking and financial services, government and public administration, and manufacturing accounted for a combined 37 percent of the fraud cases reported. Overall, the distribution of cases remains fairly consistent throughout all types of industries (see Figure 14.8).

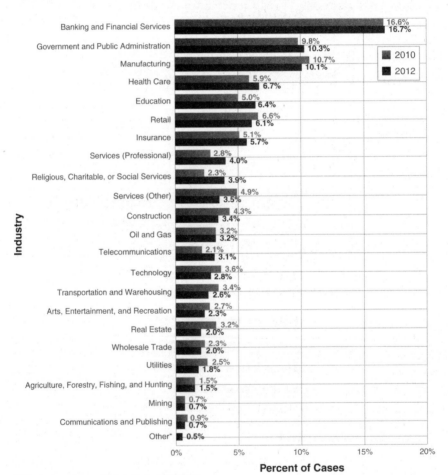

*"Other" category was not included in the 2010 report.

FIGURE 14.8 Industry of Victim Organizations. *Source: ACFE, Report to the Nations, 2012.*

Industry	Number of Cases	Percent of Cases	Median Loss
Mining	9	0.7%	$500,000
Real Estate	28	2.0%	$375,000
Construction	47	3.4%	$300,000
Oil and Gas	44	3.2%	$250,000
Banking and Financial Services	229	16.7%	$232,000
Manufacturing	139	10.1%	$200,000
Health Care	92	6.7%	$200,000
Transportation and Warehousing	36	2.6%	$180,000
Services (Other)	48	3.5%	$150,000
Communications and Publishing	9	0.7%	$150,000
Other	7	0.5%	$150,000
Telecommunications	43	3.1%	$135,000
Services (Professional)	55	4.0%	$115,000
Agriculture, Forestry, Fishing, and Hunting	20	1.5%	$104,000
Government and Public Administration	141	10.3%	$100,000
Retail	83	6.1%	$100,000
Technology	38	2.8%	$100,000
Insurance	78	5.7%	$95,000
Religious, Charitable, or Social Services	54	3.9%	$85,000
Arts, Entertainment, and Recreation	32	2.3%	$71,000
Wholesale Trade	27	2.0%	$50,000
Utilities	24	1.8%	$38,000
Education	88	6.4%	$36,000

FIGURE 14.9 Industry of Victim Organizations—Median Loss. *Source:* ACFE, *Report to the Nations, 2012.*

Figure 14.9 sorts the industries of the victim organizations by median loss. Although the banking and financial services, government and public administration, and manufacturing sectors had the highest number of fraud cases, they were not as severely impacted by the reported frauds as other industries. For example, only nine cases reported involved the mining industry, but those cases resulted in the largest median losses.

Similar findings were noted in the real estate, construction, and oil and gas industries.

For a more detailed breakdown of how fraud affects higher risk organizations, the ACFE survey examined fraud scheme types within the banking and financial services industry, having the highest number of fraud cases.

Corruption was the highest, being 36 percent of cases, and payroll fraud was the lowest at only 1 percent of cases. Other scheme types reported included cash, billing, financial statement fraud, skimming, check tampering, and expense and register disbursements. Clearly, corruption or the abuse of one's position of power or control is, once again, most prevalent in the banking and financial services industry, possibly because it is an industry where those involved are given higher levels of delegated authority and possibly responsibility.

CORRUPTION CASES BY INDUSTRY

Certain industries are often considered to be particularly susceptible to bribery and other forms of corruption. Consequently, the ACFE report provides an industry-to-industry comparison of the rates at which corruption occurred in the cases reported.

Of the cases affecting organizations in the mining, utilities, and oil and gas industries, 50 percent or more involved some form of corruption. The mining sector had a particularly high occurrence of these schemes, with seven of the nine reported cases involving corruption. Corruption cases by industry are detailed in Figure 14.10.

Upon profiling victims there is no doubt that there are many unknowing victims—those organizations and employees in those organizations who are just unaware that they have been defrauded. Perhaps their detection methods are weak or perhaps their reconciliation and reporting does not extend to fraud risk. Some victims may be in denial with an attitude of "it cannot have happened to me." This may be the case in certain cultures of privacy and embarrassment, where any such loss would be taken personally. Other victims have good detection processes in place and are aware of fraud in their organization. Some report the fraud and some do not. Again, whether fraud occurrence is in the public domain can, to a great extent, be attributable to the culture of the organization and the region in which it operates. The Middle East, for example, does have a culture of underreporting. Profiling victims by level of knowledge is depicted in Figure 14.11.

Victim organizations can be analyzed and profiled in terms of geographic location, what type of industry they are in, or the size of the industry or organization. All of these victim organization characteristics can be impacted upon by cultural issues and economic factors on a macro, worldwide stage or regionally.

Consideration of which industries are likely to be the most vulnerable to fraud and what type of fraud attaches to which industry is key to profiling.

Industry	Total Number of Cases	Number of Corruption Cases	Percent of Cases Involving Corruption
Mining	9	7	77.8%
Utilities	24	14	58.3%
Oil and Gas	44	22	50.0%
Technology	38	18	47.4%
Real Estate	28	12	42.9%
Agriculture, Forestry, Fishing, and Hunting	20	8	40.0%
Wholesale Trade	27	10	37.0%
Banking and Financial Services	229	83	36.2%
Transportation and Warehousing	36	13	36.1%
Government and Public Administration	141	50	35.5%
Construction	47	16	34.0%
Manufacturing	139	47	33.8%
Services (Other)	48	16	33.3%
Health Care	92	28	30.4%
Telecommunications	43	13	30.2%
Services (Professional)	55	15	27.3%
Insurance	78	21	26.9%
Arts, Entertainment, and Recreation	32	8	25.0%
Education	88	21	23.9%
Retail	83	19	22.9%
Religious, Charitable, or Social Services	54	12	22.2%
Communications and Publishing	9	1	11.1%

FIGURE 14.10 Corruption Cases by Industry. *Source: ACFE, Report to the Nations, 2012.*

Experience suggests that any industry type is vulnerable to fraud but that certain types of fraud are more common in particular industries such as construction, where secret commissions and corruption of the tendering process may appear, and insurance, where claims can be manipulated. Particular industries are more susceptible to fraud than others.

It can be seen from the recent 2012 ACFE report that banking and financial services is currently the industry with the highest number (16.7 percent) of fraud cases. This may be attributed to the prevalence of the recent uncovering of banking scandals attributable to the worldwide economic turmoil of late. Mining organizations are the least likely victims (0.7 percent of cases).

If we consider the geography and we look at Central and Eastern Europe, we can see that many multinationals transfer trusted employees with lengthy

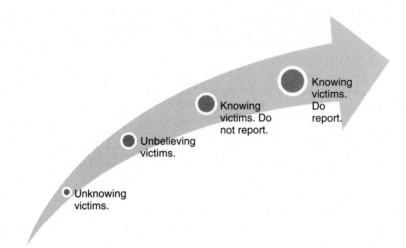

FIGURE 14.11 Profile of Victims by Knowledge. *Source:* Simon Padgett, fraud and corruption training.

tenure into key financial positions in group subsidiaries in other countries to provide the necessary experience but also to act as gatekeepers and to ensure ongoing integrity in finance functions in new operations. Key fraud risks appearing in European operations are consistent, in many respects, with fraud risk applicable to new start-ups. Such risks would be of employees reporting overinflated sales and nonexistent contracts in order to draw in further and new investment, and general managers acting with insufficient supervision, bypassing local regulatory requirements and difficulties in carrying out and obtaining reliable background information and reference checks across borders.

If we look at the United States we see a huge increase of late in the detection of fraud and corruption. Enron seems to be mentioned in every fraud and corruption conference of late, along with WorldCom and Tyco and many others, and some say that the U.S. financial system and, effectively, the discovery of financial statement fraud in the banking and mortgage market played a role in the worldwide economic slowdown and recession. This does not mean that fraud has increased in the region over the past 10 or so years, but it does mean that detection has increased. This can be attributable to antibribery and corruption initiatives that include task forces and enforcement capabilities designed to clamp down on misconduct and in particular to the introduction of the Foreign Corrupt Practices Act (FCPA). The FCPA is a federal law enacted in 1977 to prohibit companies from paying bribes to foreign government officials and political figures for the purpose of obtaining business. The FCPA applies to any person who has a certain degree of connection to the United States and engages in foreign corrupt practices. The act also applies to any act by U.S. businesses, foreign corporations trading securities in the United States, American nationals, citizens, and residents acting in furtherance of a foreign corrupt practice, whether or not they are physically present in the United States. In the case of foreign natural and legal persons, the act covers their actions if they are in the United States at the time of the corrupt conduct. Further, the act governs payments to not only foreign officials, candidates, and parties, but also any other recipient if part of the bribe is ultimately attributable to a foreign official, candidate, or party. These payments are not restricted to just monetary forms and may include anything of value.

The Dodd-Frank Act of 2010 intends to award whistleblowers a reward of between 10 percent and 30 percent of fines levied for financial misconduct. In some parts of the world whistleblower protection is legislated. In the United Kingdom, for example, the Public Interest Disclosure Act of 1998 protects employees who blow the whistle where there are reasonable grounds that a crime of fraud has been committed.

Of course, profiling forms a key part of any detection mechanism and is very timely for inclusion in robust compliance programs.

Switzerland has for a long time been the home for much worldwide money, in part due to its political neutrality and also to its attitude to confidentiality. This does, however, form an attraction to fraudsters who are forever stealing identities or are attempting to falsify authority for extracting or transferring funds with a particular focus on dormant accounts. Again, where there is money, there will be fraud, and wealth in a region is a profile in itself.

In Asia, economies are booming and so is fraud and corruption as organizations focus their efforts and money on front-end growth rather than controls. Typically, red flags are ignored and treated as one-offs or impediments to growth. When frauds come to light in this region, it is often many years later when the value has accumulated after having all the warning signs ignored. The KPMG 2011 survey reveals that fraud in the Asia Pacific region tends to take longer to detect than anywhere else in the world. Organizations in India, particularly, feel that enforcement takes up too much time and money, and many feel that fraud and corruption cost is a way of doing business that should be factored into the selling price. Profiling in this region therefore is perhaps way behind the rest of the world.

Characteristics or red flags of an organization, perhaps operating on the international stage, that leave the organization open to fraudulent activity may include the following:

- Remote overseas operation not being effectively monitored or controlled by the head office.
- Fraud not being perceived as a risk, and there is, therefore, a weak tone at the top toward fraud.
- Elsewhere in the industry, similar organizations are struggling with low or declining sales or profits, contrary to the subject organization.
- Rapid increase in revenues and profits, with little corresponding increase in cash flow.
- Difficult relationships and a resultant lack of trust between the business and the internal and external auditors.
- Complex or unusual contracts with suppliers and customers and equally complex flows of cash, deliberately set up to camouflage their true nature.
- Management who ignore irregularities.
- Dominant, egotistical leader.
- High employee turnover in a particular division or subsidiary, resulting in low morale and higher fraud risk.
- Illegal or unethical practices.
- Low training budget.
- Profit is the ultimate goal with a culture of senior managers receiving large bonuses linked to meeting targets.
- Multiple banking partners and arrangements rather than one clear provider in an attempt to reduce transparency surrounding business finances and banking.
- A particular division or overseas subsidiary is deemed to be overly complex or unusually profitable, diverting the attention of management or auditors.

15

Profiling the Consequences

A NOTHER IMPORTANT CONSIDERATION in the identification of fraud is what can be described as the impact or consequence of the fraudulent behavior.

An analysis by KPMG of fraud consequences or case results in its 2011 study found that fraud investigations had resulted in

- Disciplinary action in 40 percent of cases.
- Enforcement action, including regulatory, legal, and police involvement in 45 percent of cases.
- Civil recovery in 23 percent of cases.
- Resignation or voluntary retirement in 17 percent of cases.
- Out-of-court settlements in 6 percent of the cases.
- No action or sanction in 3 percent of cases.

To most organizations the obvious consequence of fraud is the financial loss. Some victim organizations go under and some start a slow death as credit is withdrawn or recalled due to apparent lack of controls to safeguard the lender's investment. A business may have to sell assets in order to keep its head above water. The National Institute of Justice in the United States has found that 20 percent of victims suffered severe financial loss or credit problems as a direct result of fraud.

LEGAL PROCEEDINGS AND LOSS RECOVERY

ACFE research indicates that 40 to 50 percent of victim organizations do not recover any of their fraud losses. Questions were asked in the 2012 survey about the legal proceedings and loss recovery efforts in fraud cases to help understand what happens to perpetrators and their victims in the aftermath of fraud.

As shown in Figure 15.1, in more than two-thirds of the cases reviewed, the victim organization referred the case to law enforcement authorities for criminal prosecution. The median loss in these cases was $200,000, compared to a median loss of $76,000 for cases that were not referred.

For the cases that were referred to law enforcement, survey participants were also asked about the outcome of the criminal case. In the 390 cases for which an outcome was known, approximately 16 percent of the perpetrators were convicted at trial, and 56 percent pleaded guilty or no contest to their crimes. There were only six cases in which the perpetrator was acquitted (see Figure 15.2).

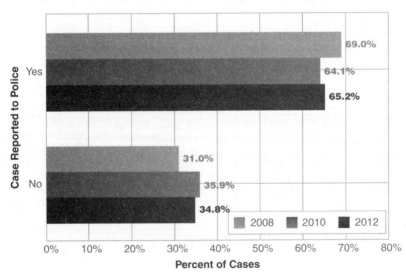

FIGURE 15.1 Cases Referred to Law Enforcement. *Source:* ACFE, *Report to the Nations*, 2012.

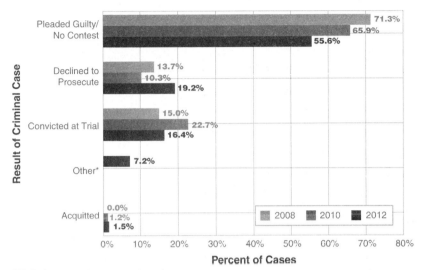

FIGURE 15.2   Results of Cases Referred to Law Enforcement. *Source:* ACFE, *Report to the Nations*, 2012.

For the 454 cases in which the victim organization did not refer the case to law enforcement, survey participants were asked to identify the reasons for this decision. As depicted in Figure 15.3, the most commonly cited factor was fear of bad publicity, followed by a determination that the organization's internal sanctions were sufficient punishment for the misconduct.

The ACFE's research shows that victim organizations are more likely to pursue criminal action against a perpetrator than they are to file a civil lawsuit. Civil suits were filed in less than one-quarter of cases in the 2012 study (see Figure 15.4). These cases tended to involve the most costly frauds; the median loss for cases resulting in a civil suit was $400,000.

When the victim organization's management did pursue a civil action against the perpetrator, they received a judgment in their favor in nearly half of the cases and settled with the perpetrator in another 31 percent of the cases. The judgment was in favor of the perpetrator in only 15 percent of the cases in which a civil suit was filed (see Figure 15.5).

LOSSES RECOVERED

Respondents were also asked about how much, if any, of the fraud losses the victim organization had recovered at the time of the survey. Survey participants

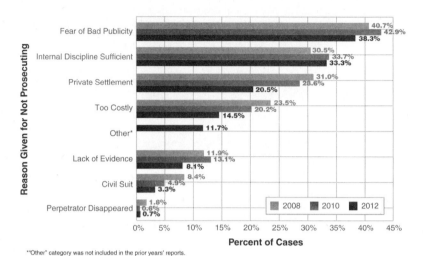

FIGURE 15.3 Reasons Case Not Referred to Law Enforcement. *Source:* ACFE, *Report to the Nations*, 2012.

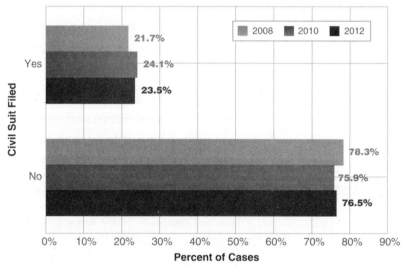

FIGURE 15.4 Cases Resulting in Civil Suits. *Source:* ACFE, *Report to the Nations*, 2012.

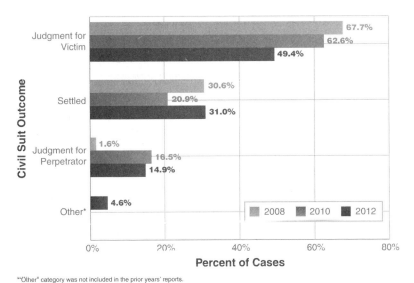

FIGURE 15.5   Results of Civil Suits. *Source:* ACFE, *Report to the Nations*, 2012.

reported that 49 percent of victims had not recovered any losses. This finding is consistent with previous research, which indicates that between 40 and 50 percent of victim organizations do not recover any of their fraud losses. In contrast, less than 16 percent of victims in the 2012 study had made a full recovery through restitution, insurance claims, or other means (see Figure 15.6).

 ## AN OFTEN UNCONSIDERED CONSEQUENCE

While the fundamental cost to the organization is the lost assets, often financial assets, the longer term reputational cost is quite often an underconsidered consequence. If a major fraud hits the front page of the newspaper, investors and bankers will not wish to pump money into a poorly controlled organization. (When I conduct my fraud training, I use the analogy of a swimming pool with holes in it. So many financiers keep pumping water into the pool and are shocked when they see it leaking out. There has to be a point when the water tap is to be stopped and the holes in the pool are actually repaired, as in repairing the weaknesses in the internal controls systems in so many organizations. Anyhow, back to that front-page headline.) Customers do not want to place deposits with an organization that lets employees steal the funds, suppliers will not supply if they fear that they will not get paid due to there being no money left after

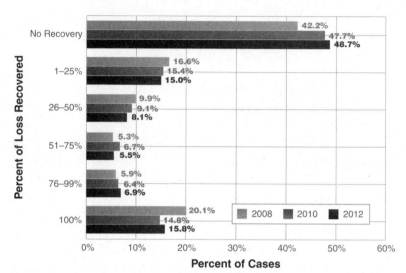

FIGURE 15.6 Recovery of Victim Organization's Losses. *Source:* ACFE, *Report to the Nations*, 2012.

the fraudster has raided the bank accounts, and employees will start to look for other jobs as a matter of longer term security. All in all one could surmise that an organization with untrusting customers and suppliers and an evacuating workforce and funders who are running away has got a serious problem with its reputation. As we know, once damaged, reputation is extremely difficult to get back or to recover from.

Consequences from the perspective of the fraudster are a little more emotive, with some fraudsters describing being caught as a relief, although being somewhat shocked. Sentences are considered to be tough among offenders. In addition to having to repay amounts stolen from pension funds and sales of homes, they consider their prison sentences to be lengthy, and to many, being banned from holding an office of director can be extremely paralyzing.

CHAPTER SIXTEEN

Using Case Studies for Profiling Fraudsters

A S WE HAVE SEEN, there are various approaches to profiling fraudsters and many angles from which we can gather and analyze data for profiling, as follows:

- Personal characteristics.
- Behavioral characteristics.
- Higher-risk industries.
- Analysis of victim organization.
- Higher-risk departments.
- Higher-risk positions.
- Modus operandi or methodology.
- Analysis of consequences.

One way of bringing all of these components together for analysis and study is to examine actual real-life cases of fraud. Using the components of fraudulent behavior—incentive/motivation, opportunity/availability of suitable target organization, and rationalization—can provide a structured approach to developing fraud profiles that can be used to formulate a focused, cost-effective response to fraud prevention and detection.

WHY REINVENT THE WHEEL?

Learning from case analysis is a long proven method of successful and innovative professional practice in solving business problems. The advantages are that real experiences, knowledge, and concepts as well as skills of critical thinking, argument, and improved decision making can be accessed and developed for the prevention of fraud and management of fraud risk.

We could study and learn from either a hypothetical fraud scenario or a real-life case. Let's say, for example, that a project manager was awarding contracts to a subcontractor in return for secret commissions. The employee would have corrupted the tendering process by including a false tender in the contract proposal at a rate higher than would be expected at normal commercial terms. Let's also assume that the employee's organization was about to undertake a major project to be managed by the employee, and the subcontractor would have secured this work, which would have meant the organization paid in excess of $2 million more than was consistent with reasonable commercial terms.

Upon further investigation into the matter, it was found that on all projects in which the employee used that particular subcontractor, the projects tended to run over budget. It was also found that invoices from the subcontractor had a pattern of being paid earlier than was normal under the organization's payment policy.

It was then discovered during the inquiry that the employee was a shareholder in a company owned by the subcontractor, and it was suspected that the employee had strong relationships at the subcontractor's business.

A number of commission payments were found to have been made to the employee by the subcontractor. When questioned on this, the employee stated that he had done some consulting work for the subcontractor. The total amount of the payments was $100,000. Neither the employee nor the subcontractor was able to provide any credible information or evidence of the consulting work alleged to have been performed. The relationship and potential conflict of interest had not been disclosed by the employee in the organization's conflict of interest declaration within its code of conduct.

In this hypothetical case we can summarize the key areas of motivation, opportunity, availability of suitable target organization, and rationalization to draw out information for profiling. We see that the motivation is quite probably some form of financial urgency but possibly an element of revenge and greed. The employee had been seen gambling, and he was known to like his alcohol.

The opportunity was that there was an existing relationship with the supplier with no pressure to disclose it and a total lack of supervision and approval over the process, along with a lack of segregation of duties in relation to the awarding of contracts. The suitable target was, as usual, the employer organization. Fraud indicators of modus operandi were there, in overpriced contracts, common in construction project awarding and close personal relationships with the supplier or contractor. All indicators passed unnoticed. The consequences of the fraud were financial loss in overpriced contracts, projects running over budget, probable early payment of the creditor, and possible reputational damage.

 ## SOME HIGH-PROFILE FRAUD CASES

There are, no doubt, great advantages in compiling hypothetical cases and calculating and examining possible outcomes and consequences to determine likely profiles, but the best advantage of case study is in examining real fraud cases, and there is possibly no better case currently than that of Bernard Madoff.

Bernie Madoff

Bernard ("Bernie") Lawrence Madoff (born in 1938) is a former stockbroker, investment adviser, financier, and nonexecutive chairman of the NASDAQ stock market and is currently a self-confessed fraudster and operator of a Ponzi scheme that is considered to be the largest financial fraud in U.S. history in today's money.

Madoff was born in Queens, New York, to Jewish parents, Sylvia and Ralph Madoff. His father was a plumber and a stockbroker, and his grandparents were emigrants from Eastern Europe.

Madoff founded the Wall Street firm Bernard L. Madoff Investment Securities LLC in 1960, and was its chairman until his arrest in 2008. The firm was one of the top market maker businesses on Wall Street, which bypassed firms by directly executing orders over the counter from retail brokers. He employed his brother, Peter, as senior managing director and chief compliance officer; Peter's daughter, Shana, as the firm's rules and compliance officer and attorney; and his sons, Andrew and Mark. Peter has since been sentenced to 10 years in prison, and Mark sadly committed suicide two years after his father's arrest.

In late 2008, Madoff's sons reported to authorities that their father had confessed to them that the asset management unit of his firm was just a huge Ponzi scheme, and quoted him as describing it was "one big lie." The following day, the FBI arrested Madoff and charged him with securities fraud. The U.S. Securities and Exchange Commission (SEC) had previously conducted investigations into Madoff's business practices, but had not uncovered the massive fraud.

On March 12, 2009, Madoff pleaded guilty to defrauding thousands of investors out of up to $65 billion, admitting that he commenced the Ponzi scheme in the early 1990s. Federal investigators, however, believe that the fraud scheme started as far back as the 1970s. On June 29, 2009, Madoff was sentenced to the maximum sentence of 150 years in prison.

Madoff's firm started as a penny stock trader with $5,000 that he had saved from working as a lifeguard, as well as a secured a loan of $50,000 from his father-in-law. In order to compete with other firms he began using innovative computer information technology to carry out his trades. Ultimately, the technology that his firm had developed became the backbone to the technology used by the NASDAQ. The firm had an investment management and advisory division, which it did not publicize. This division was to be the focus of the fraud investigation.

Concerns about Madoff's business surfaced as early as 1999, when a financial analyst, Harry Markopolos, informed the SEC that he believed it to be legally and mathematically impossible to achieve the level of gains that Madoff had been claiming to deliver, and he quickly concluded that Madoff and his activities must be fraudulent. Markopolos has since published a book, *No One Would Listen*, about the frustrating efforts that he and his team had made over a 10-year period to alert the government, the industry, and the press about the Madoff fraud.

A complaint received by the FBI stated that during early December 2008, Madoff had confided in a senior employee, identified by Bloomberg News as one of his sons, stating that he said he was struggling to meet $7 billion in redemptions. According to the sons, Madoff had told Mark Madoff on December 9 that he planned to pay out $173 million in staff bonuses two months early. Madoff said that "he had recently made profits through business operations, and that now was a good time to distribute it." Mark advised Andrew Madoff, and the next morning they asked him how he could pay the bonuses to his staff if he was having trouble paying clients. Madoff responded by telling them that he was "finished" and that he had "absolutely nothing." On June 26, 2009, Madoff was ordered to forfeit $170 million in assets. Prosecutors asked the judge to sentence Madoff to the maximum 150 years in prison. Bankruptcy trustee Irving Picard indicated that "Mr. Madoff has not provided meaningful cooperation or assistance."

In February 2009, the SEC banned Madoff from the securities industry for life.

According to the SEC indictment, two back-office workers who had worked for Madoff had created false trading reports based on the returns that Madoff had ordered for each customer. Once Madoff had determined a customer's return, one of the back-office workers would enter a false trade from a previous date and then enter a false closing trade in the amount of the required profit, according to the indictment. Prosecutors allege that the fraud involved the use of a computer program specially designed to backdate trades and manipulate account statements. In some cases returns were allegedly determined before the account was even opened.

Madoff admitted during his March 2009 guilty plea that the modus operandi of his scheme was to deposit client money into a Chase Manhattan Bank account, rather than invest it and generate steady returns as clients had been led to believe and had expected. When clients wanted their money back or their returns on investment, "I used the money in the Chase Manhattan Bank account that belonged to them or other clients to pay the requested funds," he told the court.

David Sheehan, chief counsel, stated on September 27, 2009, that about $36 billion had been invested in the scheme, returning $18 billion to investors, with $18 billion missing, although by 2011 the loss was stated as being around $65 billion.

In his plea, Madoff stated that he began his Ponzi scheme in 1991. He admitted he had never made any legitimate investments with his clients' money. Instead, he said, he simply deposited the money into his personal bank account at Chase Manhattan Bank. When his customers asked for withdrawals, he paid them out of this Chase account. It was a classic "robbing Peter to pay Paul" scenario. Chase and its successor, JPMorgan Chase, it was alleged, had earned as much as $483 million from the operations of his bank account. He was committed to satisfying his clients' expectations of high returns, despite the onslaught of an economic recession. He admitted to false trading activities and false SEC filings. He stated that he had always intended to resume legitimate trading activity, but it proved "difficult, and ultimately impossible" to reconcile his client accounts. In the end, Madoff said, he realized that his scam would eventually be exposed.

On June 29, 2009, Madoff was sentenced to a maximum sentence of 150 years in prison despite Madoff's lawyers having originally asked the judge to impose a sentence of 7 years and later requesting that the sentence be limited to 12 years, because of Madoff's life expectancy at 71.

Madoff apologized to his victims, stating that "I have left a legacy of shame, as some of my victims have pointed out, to my family and my grandchildren. This is something I will live in for the rest of my life. I'm sorry."

HBO is currently making a movie about Madoff and his fraud in which actor Robert De Niro is set to star, based on the best-selling book *The Wizard of Lies*, by Diana B. Henriques.

If we were to profile the Madoff case, we would see a male, well over 40 years of age, holding a senior position in his organization. There is no doubt that he is intelligent, possibly feels challenged by regulation, and is egotistical and inquisitive. The nature of both his trade and the fact that he committed fraud tell us that he is a risk taker, willing to bend the rules and take chances, and a rule breaker, taking shortcuts and justifying infractions of laws, rules, and regulations. Like most fraudsters, he was known for being a hard worker, being the first to arrive in the morning, last to leave at night, and taking few vacations, despite the magnificence of his vacation homes. Madoff was certainly under stress, particularly toward the end as the pyramid grew larger and larger and investors started to request their investments back. With no apparent need to satisfy a financial shortfall in his life or lifestyle, Madoff can be seen as a typical example of greed in order to keep the ball rolling, particularly as he had several family members involved who each had requirements to maintain their lifestyles. I would say that the only area of his life where he felt disgruntled or may have tried to get even was when he looked at the worldwide economic situation. He had taken in all these funds, and in 2007 the markets crashed. The timing of the economic slowdown would have made him feel unlucky, a little angry, and certainly aggrieved at the situation. Cash coming in slowed down to a trickle, requests for withdrawals and sales started to reverse the flow, and any legitimate investments that he was involved with started to show only marginal returns with underriding fears of possible liquidations. Yes, he was a big spender, possibly the most visible characteristic of a fraudster, with expensive homes and hobbies, but perhaps not necessarily living beyond his means as, since the early days, he had actually done very well for himself and had always had the means.

Frank Abagnale

Another interesting fraud case to profile would be that of Frank William Abagnale, born in 1948, an American security consultant, confidence trickster, escape artist, and convicted fraudster. He became one of the most famous impostors ever, claiming to have assumed at least eight identities, including an airline pilot, a doctor, a teacher, a prison agent, and a lawyer. He escaped from police custody twice before he was 21, once from a taxiing airliner and once from a U.S. jail. He served fewer than five years before starting to work for the federal government. He is currently a consultant and lecturer for the FBI and also runs Abagnale & Associates, a financial fraud consultancy company, turning to legal ways to make money out of fraud. Abagnale's life story provided the inspiration for the film *Catch Me If You Can*.

Frank Abagnale, one of four children, grew up in New York State. His French mother, Paulette, and father, Frank Abagnale Sr., divorced when he was 14. His first victim was, surprisingly, his father, who had given him a truck and a fuel credit card to assist him in his commute to work. Abagnale quickly devised a fraud scheme in which he would purchase vehicle spares at gas stations with the fuel card and then ask the attendants to give him cash in return for the products. His father then ultimately became liable for the cost of the goods. Abagnale was a confidence trickster, and his early confidence tricks included writing personal checks on his own overdrawn account. This would obviously only work only for a limited period of time before the bank would demand payment, so he would open other accounts at many other banks after creating different identities and committing check fraud using these accounts.

Abagnale spent much time experimenting with different fraud schemes and developed varying ways of defrauding banks and their customers. One trick that he used was to print his account number on blank bank deposit slips and then add them to the stack of blank deposit slips in the bank branch customer waiting area, resulting in the deposits written on those slips by bank customers being deposited into his own account rather than the accounts of the legitimate customers. Another of his methods was to print out his own almost-perfect copies of payroll checks. He would deposit these checks into his bank account and then persuade the banks to advance him cash on the basis of his somewhat impressive account balances. Abagnale had also noticed a location where airlines and car rental businesses would drop their daily collections of money into a drop box at the airport using a zip-up bag. Disguised as a security guard using a uniform that he had purchased at a local costume shop, he left a sign at the drop box saying, "Out of Service. Place deposits with security guard on duty." Abagnale sat there and collected the money. Later he disclosed how he could not believe that this idea had actually worked, stating with some astonishment, "How can a drop box be out of service?" Abagnale was one day passing some airline pilots in the street and was immediately impressed by their glamorous image, particularly in the eyes of the ladies. He had, for some time, wanted to fly around the world and saw the opportunity of impersonating airline pilots as a way of doing this for free. He obtained a uniform by calling Pan Am and telling the company that he was a Pan Am pilot who had lost his uniform. He obtained and used a fake employee ID and fake Federal Aviation Administration pilot's license to collect the uniform from the uniform store. Pan Am estimated that between the ages of 16 and 18, Abagnale had flown over 1 million miles on over 250 flights and that he had satisfied his ambition to travel by flying to at least 26 countries. He also found that he was able to stay at hotels for free during this time with everything from accommodations to food and laundry being billed to the airline. Abagnale showed off that he had often been invited by actual pilots to take the controls of the plane. Abagnale then worked as a sociology teaching assistant at Brigham Young University for a semester, under the alias of Frank Adams, and for almost a year he impersonated a pediatrician in a Georgia hospital under the name of Frank Conners after befriending a real doctor who lived in the same apartment complex. While he was posing as a Pan Am first officer, Abagnale passed the Louisiana Bar exam by forging a Harvard University law transcript and got a job at the Louisiana state attorney general's office.

Abagnale was eventually caught in France in 1969, and after some time was deported to the United States, where he was sentenced to 12 years in prison for multiple counts of forgery. On his return to the United States, Abagnale escaped from the airliner as it landed at New York's JFK International Airport.

After having served less than 5 years of his 12-year sentence, in 1974 the U.S. federal government made Abagnale a proposition and released him on the condition that he would assist the government in its fight against fraud by revealing how fraud is carried out from the side of the fraudster. After his release, Abagnale tried several jobs, including a grocer, cook, and movie projectionist, but he was fired from most of these after his employers discovered that he had failed to disclose any of his criminal history. He then approached a bank, explained his criminal history and deep experience of fraud, and offered to carry out fraud sensitization training to the bank's employees, effectively showing them various tricks of the trade used to defraud banks. With that, he began a legitimate life as a fraud risk security consultant, one of the few ways to legally make money out of fraud.

He later founded Abagnale & Associates, based in Oklahoma, advising companies on fraud risk. His main client is still the FBI, with whom he has now been associated for many years. He teaches at the FBI Academy and lectures to FBI field offices throughout the country. According to Abagnale's website, more than 14,000 institutions have adopted his fraud prevention programs.

We can see that Abagnale follows a similar fraudster profile, being male and intelligent; having a large ego; being inquisitive perhaps to the extent of excitement as to whether he may be caught; being a risk taker; being willing to bend the rules; taking chances; being a rule breaker; taking shortcuts; self-justifying infractions of law and rules; being a hard worker, effectively burning the midnight oil preparing his checks for the next day's banking; being under stress; being greedy after initially having a genuine financial need; being disgruntled at initially not finding work; and being a big spender. A consistent pattern in terms of Abagnale's modus operandi was identity fraud, which he used persistently to con people and organizations.

Barry Minkow

Another fraudster who has found his name on the list of educational case studies is Barry Minkow. In 1981, as an ambitious 16-year-old high school student, Minkow started a carpet cleaning business, which he named ZZZZBest (ZBest). ZBest was an immediate business failure, having few customers and quickly running into debt. Minkow ignored the day-to-day operations and cost controls required of any new organization. By the time he was 17, Minkow and his company were heavily in debt. Despite his misfortune, Minkow was determined to have ZBest bring him financial success and opened new locations.

As his expenses increased, Minkow could not meet his liabilities and turned to insurance fraud to raise money. He staged a break-in at a ZBest location and fraudulently claimed a loss on the insurance. He also reported ownership of fictitious equipment to use as security to secure loans, falsified contracts to secure loans, stole money orders for cash, and added zeros to the bills of customers who paid by credit card. Minkow was living the good life with a new sports car and condominium, but, as he said, "both the Ferrari and the house were mortgaged to the hilt."

In order to raise more cash, Minkow decided in 1986 to make ZBest a public corporation. Minkow falsified financial statements in an attempt to greatly improve the financial appearance of ZBest. On floatation he was worth around $12 million on paper, a substantial sum at that time. Minkow was continually raising money from new investors to pay off old investors. By April 1987, ZBest stock was selling for $18 a share. The company's book value was $210 million at that time. Barry Minkow was worth $109 million on paper.

As a result of numerous television appearances, Minkow became something of a media celebrity. He was featured in *Newsweek* and *American Banker* and developed a reputation as an entrepreneurial legend. However, this reputation would change after an investigative report published in the *Los Angeles*

Times in 1987. The report identified Minkow as the "whiz kid" behind a trail of false credit card billings. Minkow, the boy wonder, was now the "kid who swindled Wall Street." Within a month, ZBest stock plummeted from $18 to $6 a share.

In July 1987, Minkow resigned from ZBest at the age of 22, citing ill health. ZBest shares were selling for just pennies. Minkow was charged with bank, stock, and mail fraud; money laundering; racketeering; conspiracy; and tax evasion. ZBest, a company once purported to be worth hundreds of millions of dollars, auctioned off its entire assets for just $62,000.

ZBest was actually a front for a Ponzi scheme. When the scheme collapsed in 1987, it was deemed to be one of the largest investment frauds ever perpetrated by a single person, as well as one of the largest accounting frauds in history, costing investors and lenders, many of them major banks, over $100 million. ZBest is often used as a case study in accounting training and fraud seminars.

Minkow and 10 other ZBest insiders were charged with 54 counts of bank fraud, embezzlement, money laundering, racketeering, securities fraud, mail fraud, and tax evasion. Minkow was charged with defrauding investors and banks of millions of dollars and with systematically draining assets from his company, setting up dummy companies, and false accounting. Prosecutors estimated that as much as 90 percent of ZBest's revenue was fraudulent, originating particularly from false contracts and forged invoices. Effectively, Minkow had become a document creator and photocopying expert. Minkow was also charged with credit card fraud.

In 1989, Minkow was found guilty on all charges and was sentenced to 25 years in prison and was ordered to pay $26 million in restitution. In sentencing Minkow, the judge described him as a man without a conscience. While Minkow admitted to manipulating ZBest's share price, he claimed that he was forced into turning the company into a great Ponzi scheme while being under pressure from an organized-crime syndicate, a story that he later admitted was also false. The judge rejected Minkow's plea for a lighter sentence as "a joke" and said that it was "a slap on the wrist" for someone who had manipulated the financial system to such an extent. Minkow was also banned from ever serving as an officer or director of a public company again. He served just over seven years.

In preparing for his incarceration, Minkow became a born-again Christian and during his prison stay became involved in a Christian ministry. Following his release, he became a pastor at the Community Bible Church in San Diego and subsequently operated the Fraud Discovery Institute and spoke at schools about ethics. This all came to an end in 2011, when he admitted to manipulating share prices and was ordered back to prison.

Once again, we see that Barry Minkow had all the characteristics of a fraudster, including the following:

- Male.
- Intelligent.
- Egotistical.
- Inquisitive.
- Risk taker.
- Rule breaker.
- Hard worker.
- Under stress.
- Greedy.
- Financial need.
- Disgruntled or a complainer.
- Big spender.
- Overwhelming desire for personal gain.
- Pressured to perform.
- Close relationship with vendors, suppliers, bankers, and auditors.

■   ■   ■

The study of real-life cases provides accurate and effective support for the development of fraud profiles and for using these fraud profiles to identify the potential for fraud or existing fraud within an organization.

CHAPTER SEVENTEEN

The Use of Offender Profiling in Forensic Investigations

F ORENSIC INVESTIGATIONS can be defined as inquiries aimed at ascertaining the facts that will lead to the reconstruction of a crime, usually referring to a court-driven process for the purposes of instituting criminal and/or civil proceedings in a court of law.

 ## COLLATION OF INFORMATION

Offender profiling is a method of collating various pieces of information and data relating to an offender, with the intention of establishing the most likely offender who committed the crime. It is the identification of actual or potential offenders on the basis of behavioral or other attributes. It is used to understand why and how the crime was committed. This profiling may be carried out by retrospectively identifying an offender after a crime has taken place or it may be predictive in nature by attempting to identify and thereby inhibiting potential criminals.

The term *forensic* is derived from the Latin word *forensis* meaning "public" or "of the forum." In ancient Rome, the forum was a generic term for the meeting place where the law courts were located. The *Concise Oxford Dictionary* appears to follow this theory and describes *forensic* as being used in connection with courts of law. From this we can deduce that a forensic investigation is an inquiry aimed at ascertaining the facts that will lead to the reconstruction of a crime for presentation to a court of law. Certainly, the integrity of any evidence gathered during an investigation must be preserved and a chain of evidence maintained. Evidential integrity relies upon the acceptability of physical evidence in court, so the recording of the continuity or chain of possession or custody of evidence is therefore crucial to its admissibility in court. The successful finalization of a criminal case in a court of law is largely dependent on how evidence is initially gathered, collected, and preserved.

Edwin Sutherland coined the term *white-collar crime* in 1939 and defined it as "a crime committed by a person of respectability and high social status in the course of his occupation." In many respects, occupational fraud can be the most difficult in terms of evidence collection.

The objective of a forensic investigation is to first determine whether a crime of fraud has been committed and the materiality of it. If only $100 is determined to be at stake at the preliminary review, then a full-blown investigation is not likely. Then the investigators collect initial observations at the crime scene and conduct the gathering of evidence whereby the experience of witnesses is documented, paper trails are followed, and other physical clues and evidence is gathered. Individualization of the criminal is then undertaken by linking the fraud offender to the crime, through available information, so as to create enough evidence to justify an arrest. The arrest of the fraudster upon positive individualization and identification of the offender will require the investigator to ensure the fraudster's presence in court. The investigation will continue to the recovery of stolen property in order to return it to the victim and to present the recovered property as evidence during the trial. The investigator will also be involved in the prosecution process whereby the investigator presents the collected evidence in court.

 ## FRAUD CRIME INTELLIGENCE

Crime intelligence is defined as intelligence used in the detection or prevention of crime. It can further be defined as the product of information that has been taken from its raw state and processed, refined, verified, and evaluated. If correctly administered and applied, crime intelligence in the form of offender profiling could serve as a useful tool in the hands of the investigator in solving crime, although experienced investigators, it is argued, should be the ones to analyze the information. Fraud crime information is raw data that has to be analyzed to produce crime intelligence.

Fraud or fraudster information can emanate from any of three sources:

1. Human intelligence (employees and informants).
2. Technical intelligence (images, computers, and telephone records).
3. Data intelligence (public information databases and company records).

Anonymous reporting or whistleblowing, referred to many years ago as poison pen letters, whether from a loyal employee or vindictive ex-employee, is deemed to be an important key to the discovery of fraudulent activity. The ACFE 2012 *Report to the Nations* determines whistleblowing to be the most effective means of both detecting and preventing fraud. Crime intelligence has been developed from the investigatory arm of law enforcement where investigators collected their own intelligence and controlled their informants. The techniques and methods used by modern fraud offenders are far more sophisticated and require an equally advanced level of approach to intelligence. For example, where numerous procurement frauds were perpetrated and the suspect had always been the procurement manager, we could deduce from such intelligence that investigators should focus their attention on procurement managers in the procurement departments.

There are three types of fraud crime intelligence:

1. Prospective.
2. Retrospective.
3. Applied crime intelligence.

Prospective intelligence refers to fraud crime intelligence available for profiling before the event, such as a possible fraud that will be committed and the likely suspects who may be involved. This type of intelligence is used to plan proactive fraud risk management techniques to prevent the crime from occurring.

Retrospective intelligence refers to fraud crime intelligence obtained during or after the event. An example is when the investigator would arrest a fraud offender and profile him by requesting previous conviction records.

Applied crime intelligence refers to fraud crime intelligence that is actively used to trace a suspect (e.g., during an investigation). In the case of applied crime intelligence, there should be readily available profiles on offenders, in the form of already analyzed and processed data on, for example, motive, modus operandi, opportunity, and target organization. This type of intelligence would be able to link a suspect to a crime and to trace a suspect during an investigation.

INTELLIGENCE-LED INVESTIGATING

Intelligence-led investigating is a process where data analysis and fraud crime intelligence are central to an objective decision-making framework that facilitates fraud and corruption reduction through strategic management and effective enforcement strategies that target serious fraud offenders. This means that intelligence can be gathered before a crime is committed. In other words, investigators can use the intelligence to plan their investigations. Certain types or groups of fraudsters committing a specific type of fraud exhibit the same behavioral patterns and knowledge of these patterns can be of value during the investigation and in the combating of crime, as well as when assessing potential suspects. Indeed, fraudsters display similar patterns when committing, for example, procurement fraud or payroll fraud.

It can be said that the motive of the fraud offender is almost always the need or greed for money. A motiveless crime that results in financial loss to a company can only result in an internal disciplinary charge of negligence. If the important element of intention is lacking in such a situation, fraud cannot have been committed.

Superior intellect plays a role in white-collar criminality as the act of fraud involves persuading people to part with their money by using deception or misrepresentation through words and documents. The fraudster is characterized by deceit, concealment, or violation of trust. Fraud, by its very nature, is carefully disguised to avoid detection, and the fraudsters are generally highly trusted employees within the company, often holding management positions.

THE VALUE OF OFFENDER PROFILING

Offender profiling is a valuable tool in the investigation process. The value of offender profiling is not merely the formulation of a profile of an offender before arrest but also includes the profiling of already arrested offenders. The value of profiling already arrested offenders is immense, as it will be beneficial in investigating future cases, as well as, and more importantly, the creation and implementation of antifraud strategies into the future.

There has always been a relationship, albeit to a limited extent, between offender profiling and investigations, where the modus operandi of known perpetrators is reviewed in order to shorten the list of likely suspects in subsequent investigations. The use of offender profiling during investigations is not entirely new; however, there was, for a long time, no specific terminology for the information obtained from offenders, which was just referred to as crime information that was available to investigators for use in their investigations.

The objective of offender profiling, after arrest, is to establish the causes of criminal conduct and to generate predictions about future behavior. Offender profiling is used when the offender has already been arrested and should be regarded as an aid or investigative tool in investigations as offender profiles do not solve crimes on their own.

Criminal or offender profiling has a short history in which the past 30 years have seen accelerated development. Criminal profiling has been known by various names, such as *offender profiling, behavioral profiling, crime-personality profiling, crime scene profiling,* and *psychological profiling.* Criminal profiling was seen as an investigative medium, whereby the investigator focuses on the investigation, crime scene analysis, and geographical profiling. Offender profiling is a method of collating various pieces of information and data about an offender, with the intention of establishing the most likely individual who committed the crime. The profiling of an offender is used to understand why and how the crime was committed. Many, however, are of the opinion that profiling in general is guesswork, with as little as 10 percent being science. It can be seen that experienced and knowledgeable investigators can obtain important information from suspects, such as modus operandi, background information on suspects, financial position, previous convictions, and any other important information that can be used to profile.

Offender profiling reveals certain characteristics of those likely to commit fraud, but it is clear that offender profiling during fraud investigations should not be based only on psychological factors as a trained psychologist would be required to carry out this process. Investigators are generally not trained psychologists, but require practical guidance in order to profile fraud offenders themselves. Therefore, specific characteristics, red flags, modus operandi, and motives of fraud offenders appear to be most useful in offender profiling.

Psychological profiling of offenders, can, indeed, play a role in investigations, although an offender profile on its own does not solve a crime. It is only one of many tools at the disposal of an investigator.

Modus operandi is the methodology or action that an offender generally uses to commit a crime. An offender may be identified by the manner in which he committed the crime. Modus operandi is an offender identification technique that can speed up the investigation process by narrowing down the number of suspects and provide guidance to the investigators in identifying and tracing likely offenders. Understanding the modus operandi will also assist the investigator in refining his interrogation techniques and tracing physical evidence at the crime scene. Modus operandi information is valuable in the profiling of fraud offenders. Be aware, however, that modus operandi evolves and changes over time as offenders become more experienced and confident. It is therefore valuable to continuously update such information for offender profiling purposes.

Identifying the motive of a fraud offender is an important ingredient for compiling an offender profile, because motive forms an integral part of the commission of a crime. Investigators must identify the motive in order to assist them in solving the case by possibly linking the fraud to the money that was stolen. For example, an employee who has a gambling habit may misappropriate funds to feed the habit. Many believe that financial motives are the major cause of financial crimes such as fraud. The investigator should ascertain whether there are any red flags that will indicate the possible motive of the offender. The offender may be a lowly paid clerk who drives an expensive luxury motor vehicle. This is indicative of a change in the offender's lifestyle that will require further probing to ascertain whether the purchase of the motor vehicle was funded by the proceeds of crime or defrauded money.

It is crucial to have an interview strategy when planning to interview fraud offenders because simply profiling an offender will not provide all the answers. Investigators can glean skilled professional advice on interview strategy of both witnesses and suspects from offender profiling. When an investigator is aware of behavioral patterns of suspects, he could use this information to his advantage in preparing relevant questions for the interview as a formal part of the investigation.

 ## IMPROVED INTERNAL CONTROLS

Internal control is a process effected by the company's board of directors, management, and other personnel and is designed to provide reasonable assurance regarding the achievement of control objectives. Offender profiling assists in identifying areas of internal control gaps or weaknesses where opportunities exist to commit fraud. When a fraud offender is questioned, it is important that information about the vulnerable areas where fraud may occur is gleaned from the offender. This will guide investigators into searching for evidence about the existence of fraud in those likely areas where internal controls are weak or deficient. Knowing in which areas to search for clues and evidence would undoubtedly save time and effort during the investigation process. It is important to understand that internal financial control is a people-driven process that not only consists of policies, procedures, and manuals but involves people carrying out an array of tasks such as segregation of duty and supervision within the organization. In terms of a crime prevention perspective, the objective of internal financial controls is to ensure that assets are safeguarded against theft, as well as the prevention and detection of fraud. It is critical to identify weaknesses in internal control systems within organizations to reduce any opportunity to commit fraud. We have to be aware, however, of the limitations in internal financial controls, which may inherently manifest themselves where an employee circumvents these controls by colluding with parties outside or inside the organization to commit fraud. A further limitation of internal control is where a member of management abuses his responsibility and overrides the internal control, for example, by exceeding his signing and approving authority.

PART THREE

Building a Fraud Profiling Methodology
for Your Organization

CHAPTER EIGHTEEN

Profiling as Part of Your Sound Antifraud Program

N DEVELOPING A FRAUD PROFILING METHODOLOGY as part of a sound antifraud program, you need to develop an awareness of the following key fraud risk indicators:

- Characteristics of employees acting suspiciously and behavioral warning signs.
- Signs or indicators of the modus operandi or fraud methodology.
- The existence of high-risk departments and positions.
- Acknowledging and understanding which industries are highest risk and if the organization is in or trading with that industry.
- Indicators of consequences of fraud risk.

It is incumbent upon senior management to recognize a proactive approach, through a sound antifraud program, as an important part of their responsibility in attending to organizational and system vulnerability and managing fraud risk.

A sound antifraud program includes the following methodologies, all targeting the deviant behavior of the human being:

- Enhanced audit department.
- Forensic accounting capacity.
- Code of ethics or code of conduct to include declarations of conflict of interest and gifts.
- Fraud policy.
- Fraud training program.
- Segregation of duties for key activities.
- Appropriate recruitment procedures, selecting honest candidates.
- Policies for rotation of staff duties and forced vacations.
- Knowledge of key fraud risks and controls, and their regular monitoring.
- Whistleblowing hotline and policy.
- Fraud risk assessment process.

If we are to consider the introduction of profiling to our antifraud program toolbox, let's first take a look at the effectiveness of some of these fundamental controls and initiatives in order that we may identify how profiling can work within them.

ANTIFRAUD CONTROLS AT VICTIM ORGANIZATIONS

As part of the research in the ACFE 2012 report, the frequency and impact of common internal controls in place within organizations to prevent and detect fraud were examined. Each survey participant was asked which of 16 common antifraud controls were in place at the victim organization at the time the fraud was perpetrated.

As reflected in Figure 18.1, external audits of the financial statements were the most commonly utilized control analyzed, employed by more than 80 percent of victim organizations.

Additionally, more than two-thirds of the victims had independent audits of their internal controls over financial reporting. Many organizations are required by regulators or lenders to undergo one or both of these forms of audits, which likely contributes to the high occurrence of these controls.

Other common controls include a formal code of conduct (78 percent of victim organizations), management certification of the financial statements

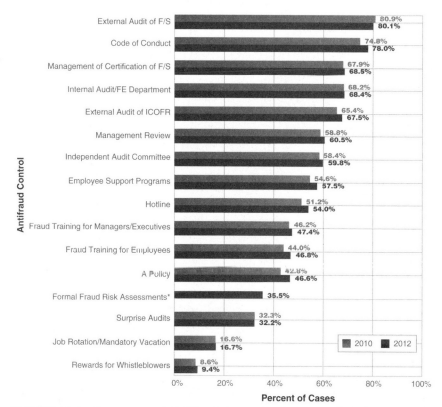

FIGURE 18.1 Frequency of Antifraud Controls. *Source:* ACFE, *Report to the Nations*, 2012.

(69 percent of victim organizations), and a dedicated internal audit or fraud examination department (68 percent of victim organizations).

Although tips are consistently the most common fraud detection method, nearly half of the victim organizations analyzed did not have a hotline mechanism in place at the time of the fraud. The ACFE data also indicates that organizations with hotlines had a larger percentage of frauds reported than did organizations without hotlines. Interestingly, less than 10 percent of the victim organizations in the study offered rewards to whistleblowers who provided tips. These low rates indicate that many organizations might not yet realize the importance of proactive efforts to support and encourage tips in order to effectively detect fraud.

ANTIFRAUD CONTROLS IN SMALL BUSINESSES

Due to their limited resources, small businesses can be especially devastated by a loss of funds to fraud. Unfortunately, however, resource restrictions in many small organizations often mean less investment in antifraud controls, which makes those organizations more susceptible to fraud. To help illustrate this problem, the ACFE broke down the frequency of antifraud controls between small companies into those with fewer than 100 employees and their larger counterparts. As shown in Figure 18.2, there is a dramatic disparity in the implementation of controls between these two groups. Admittedly, several of the controls analyzed, such as a dedicated internal audit or fraud examination department, do require a significant amount of resources that would probably not provide an appropriate cost/benefit balance for small companies. However, other antifraud measures such as a code of conduct, antifraud training programs, and formal management review of controls and processes can be

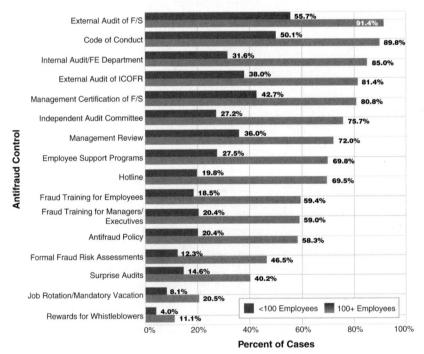

FIGURE 18.2 Frequency of Antifraud Controls by Size of Victim Organization. *Source:* ACFE, *Report to the Nations,* 2012.

implemented at a marginal cost in many small organizations and can greatly increase the ability to prevent and detect fraud.

ANTIFRAUD CONTROLS BY REGION

The ACFE also analyzed the frequency with which each of the 16 antifraud controls was implemented based on geographic region of the victim organization. The highest occurrence of antifraud controls from the survey can be seen to be the implementation of external and internal audit routines, with Asia being the region with the highest levels of implementation, with 91 percent of respondents in Asia implementing external audit and 82 percent in Asia implementing internal audit. This is closely followed by a code of conduct, with Asia again leading the field with 83 percent of respondents. Africa also was highly representative of the implementation of external and internal audits and codes of conduct as sound antifraud controls. One notable trend is that, for several controls, the implementation rate among organizations in regions containing developing countries was markedly greater than the rate in regions primarily made up of already developed nations. For example, the implementation rates of independent audits, surprise audits, antifraud policies, and rewards for whistleblowers were all greater in Africa than in other regions. This trend indicates that organizations in developing regions, many of whom are facing an uphill battle against corruption, are taking proactive and targeted steps to detect and deter fraud. It is further interesting to note that the least frequent antifraud controls across all regions are job rotation and mandatory vacations and rewards for whistleblowers, both involving cultural and regional sensitivities in the workplace. Only 5 percent of European respondents implement whistleblowing programs that offer rewards. Should we be rewarded for doing the right thing?

EFFECTIVENESS OF CONTROLS

The ACFE compared the median loss suffered by those organizations that had each antifraud control in place with the median loss in organizations lacking the control. While all controls were associated with a reduced median loss, the presence of formal management reviews, employee support programs, and hotlines was correlated with the greatest decreases in financial losses. Organizations lacking these controls experienced median fraud losses

Control	Percent of Cases Implemented	Control in Place	Control Not in Place	Percent Reduction
Management Review	60.5%	$100,000	$185,000	45.9%
Employee Support Programs	57.5%	$100,000	$180,000	44.4%
Hotline	54.0%	$100,000	$180,000	44.4%
Fraud Training for Managers/Executives	47.4%	$100,000	$158,000	36.7%
External Audit of ICOFR	67.5%	$120,000	$187,000	35.8%
Fraud Training for Employees	46.8%	$100,000	$155,000	35.5%
Antifraud Policy	46.6%	$100,000	$150,000	33.3%
Formal Fraud Risk Assessments	35.5%	$100,000	$150,000	33.3%
Internal Audit/FE Department	68.4%	$120,000	$180,000	33.3%
Job Rotation/Mandatory Vacation	16.7%	$100,000	$150,000	33.3%
Surprise Audits	32.2%	$100,000	$150,000	33.3%
Rewards for Whistleblowers	9.4%	$100,000	$145,000	31.0%
Code of Conduct	78.0%	$120,000	$164,000	26.8%
Independent Audit Committee	59.8%	$125,000	$150,000	16.7%
Management Certification of F/S	68.5%	$138,000	$164,000	15.9%
External Audit of F/S	80.1%	$140,000	$145,000	3.4%

FIGURE 18.3 Median Loss Based on Presence of Antifraud Controls. *Source: ACFE, Report to the Nations, 2012.*

approximately 45 percent larger than organizations with the controls in place. On the other end of the spectrum, external audits of financial statements, the most commonly implemented control among the victim organizations in the study, showed the least impact on the median loss suffered, with an associated reduction of less than 3 percent, as depicted in Figure 18.3.

The relationship between the presence of each control and the length of the fraud scheme was also analyzed. The controls with the greatest associated reduction in fraud duration are those often credited with increasing the perpetrator's perception of detection. Specifically, organizations that utilized job rotation and mandatory vacation policies, rewards for whistleblowers, and surprise audits detected their frauds more than twice as quickly as organizations lacking such controls. Similar to the findings regarding reductions in median losses, external audits of the financial statements were correlated with the smallest reduction in fraud duration of the antifraud mechanisms, as depicted in Figure 18.4.

Interestingly, the ACFE asked survey participants whether the victim organization had any CFEs in its employment at the time of the fraud. Approximately 45 percent of organizations had at least one CFE as an employee; these organizations experienced frauds that were 44 percent less costly based on median loss and that lasted half as long as organizations that did not have any CFEs during the fraud's occurrence.

Control	Percent of Cases Implemented	Control in Place	Control Not in Place	Percent Reduction
Job Rotation/Mandatory Vacation	16.7%	9 months	24 months	62.5%
Rewards for Whistleblowers	9.4%	9 months	22 months	59.1%
Surprise Audits	32.2%	10 months	24 months	58.3%
Code of Conduct	78.0%	14 months	30 months	53.3%
Antifraud Policy	46.6%	12 months	24 months	50.0%
External Audit of ICOFR	67.5%	12 months	24 months	50.0%
Formal Fraud Risk Assessments	35.5%	12 months	24 months	50.0%
Fraud Training for Employees	46.8%	12 months	24 months	50.0%
Fraud Training for Managers/Execs	47.4%	12 months	24 months	50.0%
Hotline	54.0%	12 months	24 months	50.0%
Mgmt Certification of F/S	60.5%	12 months	24 months	50.0%
Independent Audit Committee	59.8%	13 months	24 months	45.8%
Internal Audit/FE Department	68.4%	13 months	24 months	45.8%
Management Review	68.5%	14 months	24 months	41.7%
Employee Support Programs	57.5%	16 months	21 months	23.8%
External Audit of F/S	80.1%	17 months	24 months	29.2%

FIGURE 18.4 Duration of Fraud Based on Antifraud Controls. *Source:* ACFE, *Report to the Nations,* 2012.

CONTROL WEAKNESSES THAT CONTRIBUTED TO FRAUD

Identifying the factors that provided the opportunity for a fraud to occur is an important element of preventing similar frauds from occurring again in the future. To this end, ACFE survey participants were asked which of several common issues they considered to be the primary control weakness within the victim organization that contributed to the fraud's occurrence. An outright lack of controls was the most frequently cited factor, noted as the primary weakness in more than 35 percent of cases. This number jumps to more than 45 percent for those cases that occurred in small businesses. In 19 percent of the cases, the perpetrator overrode existing controls to carry out the fraud scheme. A similar number of respondents stated that a lack of management's review was the key control weakness that contributed to the fraud.

Interestingly, a poor tone at the top contributed to 9 percent of all the fraud cases reported but was cited as the primary factor in 18 percent of cases that resulted in a loss of $1 million or more. This reinforces the importance of a proper ethical tone from management in protecting an organization against the largest frauds—those cases that have the greatest potential to cripple the organization's finances and reputation (see Figure 18.5).

*"Other" category was not included in the 2010 report.

FIGURE 18.5 Primary Internal Control Weakness Observed by CFEs. *Source:* ACFE, *Report to the Nations*, 2012.

The ACFE has compiled a very useful fraud prevention checklist as an addendum to the 2012 report, as follows:

1. Is ongoing antifraud training provided to all employees of the organization?
   - ❑ Do employees understand what constitutes fraud?
   - ❑ Have the costs of fraud to the company and everyone in it been made clear to employees? Costs should include lost profits, adverse publicity, job loss, and decreased morale and productivity.
   - ❑ Do employees know where to seek advice when faced with uncertain ethical decisions, and do they believe that they can speak freely?
   - ❑ Has a zero tolerance for fraud policy been communicated to employees through words and actions?
2. Is an effective fraud reporting mechanism in place?
   - ❑ Have employees been taught how to communicate concerns about known or potential wrongdoing?
   - ❑ Is there an anonymous reporting channel available to employees, such as a third-party hotline?
   - ❑ Do employees trust that they can report suspicious activity anonymously and/or confidentially and without fear of reprisal?

- ❑ Has it been made clear to employees that reports of suspicious activity will be promptly and thoroughly evaluated?
- ❑ Do reporting policies and mechanisms extend to vendors, customers, and other outside parties?
3. To increase employees' perception of detection, are the following proactive measures taken and publicized to employees?
    - ❑ Is possible fraudulent conduct aggressively sought out rather than dealt with passively?
    - ❑ Does the organization send the message that it actively seeks out fraudulent conduct through fraud assessment questioning by auditors?
    - ❑ Are surprise fraud audits performed in addition to regularly scheduled audits?
    - ❑ Is continuous auditing software used to detect fraud, and if so, has the use of such software been made known throughout the organization?
4. Is the management climate and tone at the top one of honesty and integrity?
    - ❑ Are employees surveyed to determine the extent to which they believe management acts with honesty and integrity?
    - ❑ Are performance goals realistic?
    - ❑ Have fraud prevention goals been incorporated into the performance measures against which managers are evaluated and that are used to determine performance-related compensation?
    - ❑ Has the organization established, implemented, and tested a process for oversight of fraud risk by the board of directors or others charged with governance (e.g., the audit committee)?
5. Are fraud risk assessments performed to proactively identify and mitigate the company's vulnerabilities to internal and external fraud?
6. Are strong antifraud controls in place and operating effectively, including the following?
    - ❑ Proper segregation of duties.
    - ❑ Use of authorizations.
    - ❑ Physical safeguards.
    - ❑ Job rotations.
    - ❑ Mandatory vacations.
7. Does the internal audit department have adequate resources and authority to operate effectively and without undue influence from senior management?

8. Does the recruitment policy include the following (where permitted by law)?
   ❑ Previous employment verification.
   ❑ Criminal and civil background checks.
   ❑ Credit checks.
   ❑ Drug screening.
   ❑ Education verification.
   ❑ Reference checks.
9. Are employee support programs in place to assist employees struggling with addictions, mental or emotional health issues, family or financial problems?
10. Is an open-door policy in place that allows employees to speak freely about pressures, providing management the opportunity to alleviate such pressures before they become acute?
11. Are anonymous surveys conducted to assess employee morale?

The fraud risk assessment process is a fundamental part and possibly the most time-consuming of any antifraud program. It has to be analysis led and these analyses are themselves led by profiles. The methodology has to be both flexible and focused in assisting management to identify critical areas of fraud risk and assume their responsibility to proactively manage fraud risk. Fundamental to the methodology is the use of fraud profiles in determining areas of high fraud vulnerability and again through the analysis process in identifying critical areas of fraud risk or indeed fraudulent activity.

The data for analysis is derived from information from within the organization from sources such as interviews and workshops, accounting data, fraud registers, and reports. The organization extracts any knowledge of previous fraud incidents and any historically relevant information such as previously identified internal control breaches that may have given rise to fraud. It helps if any fraud registers are designed so as to include components of fraud profiles.

The profiling process then proceeds through the following stages:

1. The consolidation of information from investigations, audits and industry-specific fraud knowledge, repositories, and fraud registers.
2. Analysis, assessment, and identification of high fraud vulnerability areas using the fraud profiles and the information gathered.
3. The development of methodology to investigate these areas.

4. Analysis and assessment of findings and identification of critical fraud vulnerability areas, again using the fraud profiles and information gathered.
5. Strategies to identify if fraud is occurring through ongoing and proactive investigation using the components of the fraud profiles.

Each stage is tailored specifically to the industry and organization. The process is outlined in Figure 18.6.

The analysis process brings coherency and flexibility to the fraud prevention process, in identifying areas of high and critical fraud risk and potential fraudulent behavior. A critical fraud risk is defined as an area of high fraud risk but where there are poor risk control strategies in place or documented risk management procedures are not being followed.

Once the analysis is completed, a strategy is agreed upon. Such a strategy may include site visits and data analysis. If it is determined that fraud is being carried out, investigation can proceed. If it is concluded that fraud is not occurring, advice is provided to reduce risk and sharpen control procedures.

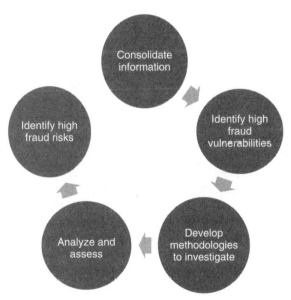

FIGURE 18.6 Staged Analysis Process. *Source:* Simon Padgett, fraud and corruption training.

In summary, qualitative data provides a means to analyze the key elements of fraud—motivation, opportunity, and target. Analysis provides an ability to identify and define fraud and ascertain its risk to organizations.

TYPES OF OFFENDER PROFILING

Behavior is exhibited at a crime scene that, when studied, allows inferences to be made about the likely offender. It has to be accepted, however, that profiles are neither a readily identifiable nor a homogeneous entity and that little has been published in academic literature on what profilers actually do and how they go about it. Of course, it does not help to have ambiguous definitions of terms such as criminal personality profiling, criminal profiling (inductive and deductive), investigative profiling, intelligence profiling, and psychological profiling.

Criminal Personality Profiling

Criminal personality profiling, for a long time referred to as psychological profiling, is a valued means of narrowing the field of the investigation as it indicates the kind of person most likely to have committed a crime by focusing on certain behavioral and personality characteristics. Criminal personality profiling has been useful to organizations when they conduct employment interviews by means of questionnaires. The objective is to identify individuals who were or may have been involved in corporate crime by narrowing down the number of potential suspects from a large group. Fraud investigators, however, do not possess the requisite skills to accurately analyze human behavior and personality and, as such, will not be able to practically implement this type of offender profiling in their daily investigations. The assistance of a qualified psychologist will be required to compile such a profile. Many police investigative psychology units compile these types of profiles to assist investigators who are responsible for criminal investigations.

Criminal Profiling

Criminal profiling attempts to determine the kind of person who committed a particular crime or series of crimes and is based on the premise that behavior reflects personality. Criminal profiling is mainly used where the culprit is a repeat or serial offender.

Inductive Criminal Profiling

Inductive criminal profiling is the process of profiling criminal behavior, crime scenes, and victims from the known behaviors and emotions suggested by other criminals and/or victims. This form of offender profiling requires the assessment of behaviors and emotions that can only be adequately carried out by qualified psychologists.

Deductive Criminal Profiling

Deductive criminal profiling is a form of offender profiling that is more specific than inductive criminal profiling. It uses the unique characteristics of the offender deduced from the behavioral reconstruction of a single offender's fraud. Once again, this type of offender profiling is best left to qualified psychologists as opposed to forensic investigators.

Intelligence Profiling

The objective of offender profiling by means of intelligence gathering is to deal with future risk and consists of the collation of information about an identified person, including information such as identity number, address, criminal record, vehicles owned, employment records, academic qualifications, cell phone records, and bank statements. This type of offender profiling requires that the offender be identified in order to gather such information.

Investigative Profiling

Investigative profiling requires the involvement of a psychologist during the investigative stage. This is where the offender is unknown and there are few leads, and the profiler provides a description of the perceived offender. Investigative profiling is a method of identifying the perpetrator of a crime based on an analysis of the nature of the offense and the manner in which it was committed. Various aspects of the criminal's personality makeup are determined from his or her choices before, during, and after the event. This information is combined with other relevant details and physical evidence and then compared with the characteristics of known personality and mental types to develop a practical working description of the offender.

Criminal personality profiling or psychological profiling may be described as a method of suspect identification that seeks to identify a person's mental, emotional, and personality characteristics (as manifested in things done or left at the crime scene). This was used in the investigation of the serial murders committed by Ted Bundy, an American serial killer from the 1970s and possibly earlier. After more than a decade of denials, he confessed shortly before his execution to 30 homicides committed in seven states between 1974 and 1978; the true total remains unknown and could be much higher. Dr. Richard B. Jarvis, a psychiatrist with expertise on the criminal mind, had predicted the age range of Bundy and his above-average intellect.

An effective offender profile should include the following:

- Modus operandi information.
- Motive for committing the fraud.
- Opportunity taken advantage of.
- Background and personal information from any publicly available information.
- Red flags or indicators of potential fraud.
- Psychological and biographical characteristics that may be used to determine what the characteristics are of people who commit fraud; may include age, race, educational qualifications, criminal record, level and type of position in the company, and employment records.
- Personal information such as identity number, address, criminal record, weapons owned, vehicles owned, employment records, verification of academic qualifications, cell phone records, and bank statements.

The objective, of course, is to avoid employing individuals who fit the profile of a fraudster in the particular industry of the organization.

By gathering relevant information to compile an offender profile, the investigator is able to prepare relevant and specific questions for the interview with the offender and to ask questions of the offender, to which the interviewer already has, to some extent, the answers. Such an approach creates the impression to the offender that the investigator knows more than he actually does about the fraud crime committed by the offender. An offender is taken by surprise when the investigator questions him about, for example, his relationship with suppliers or tenderers or other business entities implicated in the fraud. Furthermore, indicators of possible fraud or red flags also assist in narrowing down the list of likely suspects and therefore the number of interviews.

CHAPTER NINETEEN

Information Sources and the Role of Data Mining

T HERE ARE VARIOUS SOURCES available to investigators that provide valuable information that could be used to profile fraud offenders. Details such as passport or identity number, address, criminal record, vehicles owned, employment records, academic qualifications, cell phone records, and bank statements are all valuable sources of information. Access to much of this information is via databases, either run by search companies or government departments, which provide limited or full access to information to ordinary members of the public. Examples of such databases would be credit reference agencies, the Registrar of Companies, background search engines, tax authorities, and police criminal record databases.

Examples of types of information that could form the basis of data for profiling include

- Criminal history.
- Business entities where the offender has interests.
- Auditor details.
- Personal particulars, including telephone numbers and addresses.
- Passport or identity numbers.
- Spouse and children details.

- Credit history, including default judgments on bad debts.
- Previous employment history and details.
- Previous companies that conducted a vetting on the individual (This means that the name of any company that carries out a credit check on the individual will leave a footprint on the database that will reflect that the relevant named company had been approached by the individual for its service. This can be useful to know.).
- Tax details and history.
- Property ownership records.

Whistleblowing mechanisms are a great source of information that can ultimately be used in profiling. According to the ACFE, occupational fraud is more likely to be detected by a tip than by any other method. The majority of tips reporting fraud come from employees of the victim organization.

FORENSIC PROFILING AND THE USE OF DATA MINING

Forensic profiling refers to the study and discovery of historical patterns in order to draw a profile or pattern relevant to the support of fraud investigation assumptions relevant to backing or supporting the fraud investigation process. The term *forensic* in this context refers to information that is used in court as evidence.

Forensic profiling is different from offender profiling, which only refers to the identification of an offender. In particular, forensic profiling refers to the process of discovering correlations between data sets to form a profile that can be used to identify a subject as a member of a group or category.

Forensic profiling is generally conducted using data mining and analysis technology as a means by which relevant patterns are examined and profiles generated from sometimes large quantities of data.

Data mining is the computational process of discovering patterns in large data sets. The overall goal of the data mining process is to collect, extract, warehouse, and analyze information from a data set and transform it into an understandable business intelligence structure for further use. Data mining is a method of discovery.

The actual data mining task, sometimes also referred to as data analysis or data analytics, is the automatic or semiautomatic analysis of large quantities of data to extract previously unknown patterns such as groups of data records (cluster analysis), unusual records (anomaly detection), and dependencies (association rule mining). This usually involves using database techniques such as spatial indices. These patterns can then be used in further predictive analytics. The related terms *data dredging, data fishing,* and *data snooping* refer to the use of data mining methods to sample parts of a larger population data set that are too small for reliable statistical inferences to be made about the validity of any patterns discovered. These methods can, however, be used in creating new hypotheses to test against the larger data populations.

Data mining uses information from past data to analyze the outcome of a particular problem or situation that may arise in the future and is therefore of immense use as source information for profiling.

Fraud is a trillion-dollar business, and it is increasing every year, as does worldwide gross domestic product. Fraud involves one or more persons who intentionally act secretly to deprive another of something of value, for their own benefit. Fraud is as old as humanity itself and can take an unlimited variety of variety forms. However, in recent years, the development of new technologies has also provided further ways in which criminals may commit fraud. In addition to that, business reengineering, reorganization, or downsizing may weaken or eliminate internal controls, while new information systems may present additional opportunities to commit fraud.

Traditional methods of data analysis have long been used to detect fraud. They require complex and time-consuming investigations that deal with different domains of knowledge, including financial, economic, business practice, and legal. Fraud often consists of many instances or incidents involving repeated transgressions using the same method. Fraud instances can be similar in content and appearance but may not be identical.

The first industries to use data analysis techniques to prevent fraud were telephone companies, insurance companies, and banks. There are many early examples of successful implementation of data analysis techniques in the banking industry to assess fraud risk, based on neural networks.

Retail industries also suffer from fraud at the point of sale (POS). Supermarkets make use of POS data to address fraud risk among the transactions most susceptible to fraud. Internet transactions have recently raised concerns, with research showing that Internet transaction fraud is 12 times higher than in-store fraud.

Fraud that involves cell phones, insurance claims, tax return claims, credit card transactions, and so on represents a significant problem for governments and businesses, and detecting and preventing this type of fraud is far from simple. Fraud is an adaptive crime, with various methodologies, so it needs special methods of intelligent data analysis to detect and prevent it. These methods are collectively known as data mining or knowledge discovery in databases, offering applicable and successful solutions in different areas of fraud crimes.

Data analytics extends into forensic analytics, which is the procurement and analysis of electronic data to reconstruct, detect, or otherwise support a claim of financial fraud. The main steps in forensic analytics are (1) data collection, (2) data preparation, (3) data analysis, and (4) reporting. For example, forensic analytics may be used to review an employee's company credit card activity to assess whether any of the purchases were of a personal nature. Forensic analytics might also be used to review the invoicing activity for a particular vendor to identify fictitious vendors or by a franchisor to detect fraudulent or erroneous sales reports and therefore royalty payments by the franchisee in a franchising environment.

Fraud risk management is a knowledge-intensive activity. Much of this knowledge comes in the form of information stored as data. The main techniques used for extracting, examining, analyzing, and reporting this data include

- Data mining to classify, cluster, and segment the data and automatically find associations and rules in the data that may signify interesting patterns (supervised learning), including those related to fraud.
- Systems to encode expertise for detecting fraud in the form of rules.
- Pattern recognition to detect approximate classes, clusters, or patterns of suspicious behavior either automatically (unsupervised learning) or to match given inputs.
- Machine learning techniques to automatically identify characteristics of fraud.
- Neural networks that can identify and learn suspicious patterns from samples and use this information later to detect them.

 ## SUPERVISED AND UNSUPERVISED LEARNING

Machine learning and artificial intelligence solutions may be classified into two categories: *supervised* and *unsupervised* learning. In supervised learning, samples of both fraudulent and nonfraudulent records are used. This means that all the records available are labeled as *fraudulent* or *nonfraudulent*. After building a model using this training data, new cases can be classified as fraudulent or legal. This method, however, is only able to detect frauds of a type that have previously occurred. In contrast, unsupervised methods do not make use of labeled records. These methods seek accounts, customers, suppliers, and so on that behave unusually in order to output suspicious scores, rules, or visual anomalies, depending on the method used.

Whether supervised or unsupervised methods are used, note that the output given is only an indication of possible fraud. No stand-alone statistical analysis can assure that a particular object is actually a fraudulent one. It can only indicate that this object is more likely to be fraudulent than other objects.

PRIVACY AND ETHICAL CONCERNS SURROUNDING DATA MINING

Data mining is associated with the mining of information in relation to people's behavior (ethical and otherwise) or a statistical method that is applied to a set of information surrounding human behavior. There may be ethical, privacy, and legal concerns associated with the collection, storage, and use of this data. The threat to an individual's privacy only comes into play when the data, once compiled, allows the data miner or anyone who has access to the newly compiled data set to identify specific individuals, especially when the data was originally anonymous.

It is always recommended that informed consent be obtained and that a certain protocol be followed when collecting such data, disclosing such information, as follows:

- The purpose of the data collection and any known data mining projects.
- How the data will be used.
- Who will be mining the data and who will the likely users be.
- The status of security surrounding access to the data.
- How collected data can be updated.

The easy solution, of course, is that data be modified so as to become anonymous to ensure that individuals may not be readily identified.

CONTRIBUTING TO THE PROFILING MECHANISM

Electronic databases are a valuable source of information for investigators. It is important to capture information from previous investigations in a database as this will facilitate understanding of how previous frauds were committed and detected. These profiles from previous investigations have to be shared and captured. Lessons learned from successful investigations should be regularly shared with colleagues within teams as well as with clients in the consulting industry; however, in actual fact, much information is not being shared or captured onto databases, despite such databases being crucial for offender profiling purposes. This valuable information will, it could be argued, otherwise be rendered useless if left in isolated investigator's reports, working paper files, or laptops.

Public databases are valuable to investigators, as they provide vital information that can be used to profile fraud offenders.

The Association of Chief Police Officers and the Home Office in the United Kingdom recently commissioned a review to establish the fact or confirm that offender profiling is of value and that national data sets should be created to allow sufficient statistical analysis to enhance profiling. The statistical validation of offender profiling methods has been hampered, however, by a lack of data sets sufficiently large to stand up to scrutiny.

Individual fraud investigators can find little historical information or profiles on low-volume crime, despite there being a significant number of such cases. A way of developing support for these individual investigators would be to provide them with access to a pool of experience. Surely, it would benefit the fraud investigators and the victims of fraud if mechanisms were in place to collate experiences to aid future investigations. Offender profiling is a combination of two basic principles: detective experience and behavioral scientific knowledge. Furthermore, an offender profile is not an end in itself, but is purely an instrument for steering an investigation in a particular direction.

In order to maximize the benefits of the lessons that are learned from successful investigations, it is crucial, therefore, to capture relevant information about successful investigations for sharing with future investigators, and not just within their teams or with their clients, in order to enable the clients to prevent any recurrence of fraud in the workplace. Such information should be captured onto a database. Not all investigators share information about fraud offenders with their colleagues or organizations or the investigatory profession in general in any structured or formal manner. It is known that individuals seek personal or private objectives in a group, and yet this same group constrains, guides, and sustains them. The risk is that valuable information, if left unshared, can be an obstacle in the profiling of offenders. Critical crime information that is in the possession of experienced investigators is not being appropriately shared and utilized to combat fraud. Offender profiling should include capturing relevant information about previous cases that were investigated to enable other investigators to share this information and understand how previous frauds were committed and how they were detected. Investigators can exploit the benefits of the lessons learned from previous successful investigations. There is no need to reinvent the wheel, as experienced investigators have a vast amount of information readily available to them that can be used to profile future fraud offenders.

CHAPTER TWENTY

Fraud Profiling Your Organization

OFFENDER PROFILING IS A practical tool for use by investigators on a routine basis in their fraud investigations.

Compiling an offender profile will require the pooling of data and information from various sources. It should be noted that offender profiling of fraudsters involves profiling an offender who has already carried out his fraud and has been identified. The profiling process involves collating data from a myriad of sources, with the sole aim of understanding how and why the fraud was committed by the particular offender. An offender profile will prove priceless for the investigator as, for example, it provides the investigator with that extra ammunition for his questioning, forming a lever during the interrogation process and creating the impression to the offender that the investigator knows more about him than he actually does. Red flags are a warning sign that there may be fraud taking place. If those red flags are probed, it is likely that something irregular or fraudulent will be encountered.

The fundamental question is what should be included in an offender profile and how and from where should the data and information be collated. Of particular interest are personal particulars of the offender, modus operandi information, the motive of the offender, opportunity to commit the crime, indicators of possible fraud red flags, lifestyle changes, sources of information for profiling, and a summary of aspects to be included in an offender profile of a fraudster.

PERSONAL PARTICULARS OF THE OFFENDER

The profiling of a fraud offender involves an already identified offender. It is important for investigators to understand who they are dealing with and that an appropriate starting point in the investigation process would be to obtain the personal particulars of the fraud offender. Personal information such as the following should be included:

- Name of the offender.
- Home and work addresses.
- Nationality.
- Age.
- Race.
- Educational background of the offender.
- Record of the offender's previous criminal convictions.
- Identity or passport number of the offender.
- Telephone numbers.
- Bank account details.

OBTAINING MODUS OPERANDI INFORMATION

Modus operandi is derived from the Latin phrase "operational method of procedure" and is an offender identification technique. Knowledge of the modus operandi can speed up the investigation process by providing guidance to the investigators as to where to look and narrowing down the number of suspects. For example, we can look at tender fraud where the procurement manager obtains quotes from several companies that are actually owned by one individual. This procurement process would appear to be legitimate as three quotes were obtained; however, when one examines the actual modus operandi, it can be seen that only one individual actually owns all companies. Further probing by investigators and perhaps plotting all of the tendering organizations and their contact details, shareholders, and directors in forensic diagrams known as spiders' webs would more than likely lead to the visualization of these suspicious relationships and to the detection of the fraud.

There is no doubt that the types of fraud and variety of modus operandi involved in the commission of fraud are wide; a particular crime of fraud and an offender are not altogether unique, and the modus operandi for each may well have similar characteristics. If one examines the traces left at the fraud crime scene, it will offer insight into who the likely offender is due to the fact that the act of fraud leaves repeated patterns or footprints. In effect, the act of fraud is a serial offense, and capturing the repetitive pattern gives the investigator the modus operandi. In fraud a large element of the modus operandi generally lies in manipulating and misrepresenting documentary records, quite often through forgery or counterfeiting. Knowledge of this modus operandi will be beneficial to investigators, as it will serve as a useful reference point with regard to where to focus attention in the books of account.

Information about the date, time, place, tools, and methods used constitutes an important part of forming the modus operandi. Knowledge and understanding of these various modus operandi can be used by fraud investigators.

Examples of modus operandi information of use in profiling might include the following:

- Date, time, place.
- Method used to commit the fraud.
- Financial documents falsified by the offender to conceal the fraud.
- Stolen passwords and usernames used to transfer funds to fictitious suppliers or to himself.
- Bank account numbers changed and false payments effected.
- Details of suppliers overcharging for goods in collusion with employees.
- Details of payments effected with no supporting documents.
- Details of personal purchases made on the business account.
- Details of suppliers making short deliveries of goods in collusion with employees.
- Details of bid rigging whereby the buyer carries out an irregular procurement practice by obtaining three quotes from three companies that are actually owned by one individual.

 ## DETERMINE THE MOTIVE OF THE OFFENDER

The motive is a factor or circumstance that induces a person to act in a particular way. Understanding the motive of the fraud offender is a good first step in developing a profile, particularly from a proactive approach, as efforts can be made to remove that temptation. If financial need is the motive for an offender to commit fraud, then the employer can consider offering employee loans on favorable terms. If social pressure plays a role, then this is not quite so simple to alleviate in the short term. This brings into the equation the issue of socioeconomic factors such as unemployment rates and levels of fraud crime in particular geographic areas or industrial segments. We could look at certain African countries, for example, with high unemployment rates and cultural issues that have seen corruption as a norm for many years. These areas are seen as the melting pot of fraud schemes such as 419 scams or advance fee fraud.

Investigators need to create a hypothesis surrounding a fraud at the commencement of an investigation. This is assisted by the determination of the motive for the commissioning of the crime. This hypothesis will be an educated guess based on experience, the circumstances of the crime, and the clues left. Investigators need to establish up front what end state the offender desired and expected when he committed the crime; hence, knowledge of motive will lead the investigator to what the expected reward was, in the mind of the fraudster. Certain offenders will voluntarily provide the motive for committing the offense, while others will not share this information with the investigator. The investigator will then have to rely on the circumstances of the case or the background of the offender to determine his motive. Economic motives are found to be the most common among offenders who commit fraud against business, although sometimes the motive is pure greed. Greed, therefore, should be evaluated so that specific interventions can be formulated to address it. Regular fraud sensitization training within an organization, for example, sending messages that fraud is wrong and that swift action will be taken against fraudsters, is very important for fraud prevention purposes and should dampen any motive.

Understanding offender motives will lead to an understanding as to why fraudsters commit such crimes. We see from the fraud triangle that financial motives are the major cause of financial crime, ranging from an employee's inability to pay his utility bills to a senior executive who is under financial pressure because market factors have adversely affected the business.

Understanding what motivates a fraud offender to commit fraud will be helpful in the profiling process and will guide the investigator in focusing on those individuals who may have those particular motives. For example, the investigator could examine applications for employee loans or look through credit histories to determine who might have such financial pressure.

 **OPPORTUNITY**

Opportunity can be described as a chance or opening offered by circumstances for good fortune. Opportunity to commit a crime in a business or company environment is a situation where an offender circumvents internal financial controls or takes advantage of a weakness in those controls. In the opinion of Gottfredson and Hirschi, an opportunity to commit a crime has to be coupled with immediate gratification where there is little or no resistance, coupled with a limited possibility of detection of the fraud or risk of being caught.

Fraud is a misrepresentation that disguises the truth and is intended to deceive. Due to the risk involved, fraud offenders increase the amounts that they defraud over a period of time as they become comfortable that they were not being detected. They do not necessarily exploit or embark on more risky opportunities but rather increase the value of the fraudulent loot defrauded in earlier opportunities. Interestingly, employees occupying executive positions in the corporate world may choose to commit fraud because they have more opportunities available to them. Quite often, employees at the executive level are in such a position that they can actually create these weaknesses in controls, or maybe they are simply aware that there will be a certain reluctance to question them about suspicious activity.

Organizations that have well-established corporate governance structures and strong internal financial control environments will provide fewer opportunities for fraudsters at all levels and will, in all probability, deter them from committing fraud. If opportunity is a situation where a fraud offender circumvents internal financial controls, or takes advantage of a lack thereof, for a financial gain where there is little or no risk of being caught out (Gottfredson and Hirschi, 1990), then it is also important that environmental and situational factors be considered as well as individual factors of the offender and the organization.

White-collar crime or fraud occurs in private and involves an abuse of trust that is integral to the position the offender occupies. The identification and understanding of the nature of this abuse will be useful from a fraud prevention perspective so that the level of opportunities available and the likelihood of detection can be addressed.

Opportunity to commit fraud should be included as part of an offender profile. During an investigation into fraud, it is vital to understand which individuals had the opportunity to commit the fraud, or where the opportunities existed to commit fraud. This information will be useful when profiling the offender or determining in which area of the business to focus the investigation. An example may be where the offender places an order for goods and is also responsible for receiving them. In this case, with a lack of segregation of duties, there would have been no other employees available to confirm whether the goods were received, except the offender. This is an example of an opportunity existing that was exploited by a fraudster to commit fraud. It should be noted, however, that should an opportunity not exist, the offender may be in such a position in his organization that he can create the opportunity in such a way that there is limited chance of being detected. An example of an existing opportunity would be where duties are not adequately segregated, such as in the preceding case where the offender is able to execute multiple tasks such as ordering and receiving the goods. An example of a created opportunity would be where the manager was able to override an internal control in order to create an opportunity to commit fraud by exceeding his delegated authority limit and approving the purchase of goods over a predetermined value as stated in an approved authority matrix. This purchase should have gone to his superior for authorization, but the manager seized the opportunity to approve it himself. The manager would have been aware of the fact that his superior would have questioned the overpurchase and thereby uncovered the fraud, so he therefore created his own opportunity by overriding an existing system of internal financial control. Existing opportunities for fraud are an indication of internal control weaknesses in the system and a lack of compensating controls, as discussed in the fraud triangle.

In harsh economic times companies retrench employees and cut back on governance in order to curtail operational costs. This results in fewer employees carrying out more duties, with a heavy reliance being placed on the trust of these fewer employees. The duties of these employees are not segregated and the employees are quite possibly very worried about their jobs, all factors that can increase fraud risk. This is fertile ground, whereby opportunities are exploited by dishonest employees to commit fraud without being detected. It can also be said that an honest employee with a high degree of integrity may commit fraud, given a set of situational pressures and high opportunity. Conversely, an employee with low integrity may not commit fraud if he is not exposed to situational pressures and if there are strong internal financial controls that provide little or no opportunity to commit fraud.

Knowledge of an opportunity to commit a crime is a critical component in the commission of a crime and can be useful from a crime prevention perspective. It is apparent that opportunity on its own is not a catalyst for fraud to be committed. Honest and dishonest employees may commit a crime, depending on the level of opportunities available, the situational pressure at the time, and the likelihood of detection. A combination of three elements must be present for the commission of a fraud crime: a motivated offender, an opportunity, and a suitable target.

 RED FLAGS

The term *red flag* can also be described as a warning of danger. The chairman of the ACFE, J. T. Wells (2009), states that lavish spending on "outrageously ostentatious lifestyles" by employees serves as a red flag that fraud is or may be occurring. Red flags are an early warning sign that something is amiss. Living in lavish accommodations or driving luxury vehicles may be a red flag, as it may be that income does not match lifestyle. Obviously not all red flags mean fraud, but further examination will sort out the rotten fruit. There are genuinely hard-working and loyal employees who exhibit such red flags but who also are of the highest integrity. Fraud indicators or red flags should be regarded as an early warning sign and should be included in a fraud offender profile.

Examples of key red flags might include

- Lifestyle of the offender is not in line with the salary earned.
- Offender does not take leave or only takes short periods.
- Offender arrives early at work, leaves late in the evenings, and works on weekends. After all, he has two jobs to do: his fraud job and his real job.
- Offender is highly trusted.
- Offender is protective of his work environment.
- Offender is defensive when challenged.
- Documents of the offender are always locked away and not accessible to any other staff.
- Internal financial control weaknesses located within the offender's area of work responsibility.
- Offender makes significant/high expenditures on a single supplier.
- The analysis and review of financial data reveals suspicious transactions on the part of the offender.

 LIFESTYLE CHANGE

Any significant change in the lifestyle of an offender will often be openly displayed by the offender and is a form of red flag. Should the change in lifestyle be unexplained or suspicious, it should be regarded as an early warning sign that requires further probing. It is important for investigators to take note of different types of information around lifestyle changes, because it will be useful for the purposes of profiling fraudsters.

It should be noted here that lavish expenditure on luxury does not mean fraud. It is more the change in expenditure patterns that might warrant extra examination or questioning. The employee who regularly drives luxury cars could have a steady stream of other income or may have won the lottery, but the employee who has driven an older cheaper car for 10 years but suddenly buys two expensive luxury limousines perhaps warrants further probing. Call me a skeptic but, time permitting, I would run both scenarios by some extra examination procedures. Barry Minkow of ZBest, who was sent to jail for 25 years for defrauding banks to prop up his quoted business empire, famously said, "But the Ferrari and the mansion are both mortgaged to the hilt." We should also not lose sight of the fact that in some environments, there is high wealth. I lived in Abu Dhabi in the United Arab Emirates for seven years. There, you could not say that, because someone is driving a different exotic car to work every day, totally out of alignment with monthly earnings, that he or she is a fraudster. In fact, it is more likely to be the opposite, not just because of the regional covert wealth but also because of the culture, whereby fraud is a no-go area.

Examples of types of lifestyle changes that may be regarded as red flags could be sudden expenditure on

- Gambling.
- Luxury cars and jewelry.
- Private school fees.
- Large repayment.
- Property purchase.
- Overseas travel.
- Lavish lifestyle, generally.

Defrauded money is almost always used by fraud offenders for various items that enhance their lifestyle. Investigators need to ascertain how the money was spent as this may be helpful in tracking what assets were purchased and will be useful in any asset forfeiture process or recovery through civil litigation. The type of expenditure from the proceeds of crime should also be included in profiling.

By using a combination of personal particulars, red flags, lifestyle changes, and modus operandi information, it is possible for an investigator to compile a comprehensive profile of a fraud offender that will be useful when conducting the investigation and inherent interviews.

CHAPTER TWENTY-ONE

The Process of Developing a Fraud Profile

I N ORDER TO IDENTIFY SOMETHING you have to know what it looks like. If you don't know what it looks like, you may walk right past it without recognizing what it is. There are an infinite number of forms that fraud can take as there are an infinite variety of business structures, accounting systems, documentation characteristics, and so on. There are no guarantees that a fraud detection strategy will work all of the time and identify every fraud, but research indicates that most employee fraud is not sophisticated and, generally, not well concealed. All that is required, in many cases, is to identify what it would look like and it will be found. The process outlined here is not necessarily intended to provide an absolute catch-all solution to fraud detection but an incremental improvement in the odds against an organization becoming a victim of fraud.

As shown in Figure 21.1, there are three fundamental phases in the process of developing a fraud profile for your organization:

1. The first phase is the development of a *fraud risk assessment* to identify the key fraud risks and scenarios to which your business is exposed.
2. The second phase is the identification of the characteristics that these fraud exposures or hypothetical fraud scenarios would present. This is the *fraud profile*.

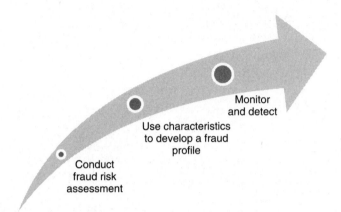

FIGURE 21.1 Process of Developing a Fraud Profile. *Source:* Simon Padgett, fraud and corruption training.

3. The final phase is the development of cost-effective monitoring to recognize, report, and react to the characteristics if they occur. This is the *detection methodology*.

 ## DEVELOPMENT OF A FRAUD RISK ASSESSMENT

The fraud risk assessment (FRA) process can be enterprise wide or specific to areas of an organization showing concerns. It is carried out not only by the examination of documentation and procedural manuals but also by a series of meetings or interviews and workshops and quite possibly by the additional use of a questionnaire-based approach. The development of an FRA involves the testing of key controls against criteria in the form of working scenarios of how fraud could be committed. As with any risk assessment, the quality of the assessment is a function of the richness of detail in the model and the relevance and completeness of the criteria against which it is tested.

It is imperative that there be a full understanding of the antifraud controls, systems, documentation, and reporting process of each material business cycle in the organization. The greater the detail, the better the profile will be. In many cases, a preliminary model will exist in one form or another, perhaps in procedure manuals, documented in internal or external audit files or ultimately in the heads of the people who operate the business. In developing the organizational model, expect that the actual way the system works is not quite in compliance with the procedure manual or as in the audit files. Ordinarily employees involved in the process will describe what should happen rather than what actually does happen. To be effective, this model needs to describe the way the business actually operates, with all of its flaws and shortcuts. Asking people to sign off on a memorandum setting out their understanding of the actual functions of the operation can be very helpful in focusing the mind on the difference between the procedural model and reality.

The next step is to identify the apparent weaknesses in the organization model that could permit errors or fraud. It is important to consider system weaknesses that could also allow errors as errors often present the same evidence or indicators as fraud with the only real differences being intent and benefit. If a system will permit an error to occur that would result in an under- or overstatement of income or irregular payments, then it will normally also permit a fraud. Many occupational frauds commence because an employee makes an honest mistake that is not detected and represents the key to the door of fraud opportunity. While the primary focus of most internal and external audit methodologies is not employee fraud, they fundamentally address error, and consequently the audit process is a valuable resource in assessing fraud risk.

The next step is to consider, develop, and document working scenarios of the ways in which employee fraud could occur in each area of the business. This involves interviews, workshops, and questionnaires and walking through the particular business processes from beginning to end to identify the junctures at which fraud could occur, who the perpetrator could be, the control weaknesses that could be exploited, and how the existing controls could be bypassed. As in most effective interviews, the value comes from listening. After all, the interviewee is the one with the knowledge of his particular area of the business. He knows his business, probably more so than the facilitator. Once again, be aware that the people assigned to develop the FRA will probably be rational, intelligent, analytical individuals, often with training in accounting and auditing and could well be employees carrying out or planning fraud. I cannot count the number of occasions on which we have been called in to conduct an investigation because there is large dollar hole somewhere with substantial sums missing, and after a number of weeks or months of investigation it is discovered that the perpetrator is a key employee in the governance and FRA process. On several occasions we found that the fraudster is actually the financial director who called us in to investigate. The purpose of the profiling exercise is to recognize and report the characteristics fraud presents just as soon as it occurs.

The output of the FRA phase is a list of fraud exposures identifying who the perpetrator could be, how the fraud would occur, and the weakness in the system that would permit the fraud to occur.

Many frauds are permitted to occur by the failure to implement or maintain the most basic of internal controls. If someone in your organization has access to cash and access to the accounting records, that person has the opportunity to commit a fraud. The failure to segregate fundamentally incompatible functions is a disturbingly frequent theme in employee fraud. If it is uneconomic to segregate functions effectively, consider other compensating controls and implement them.

It is very important in the FRA process to understand compliance. A fraud risk can exist where internal controls are not in place or are in place but are weak and where the fraud offender takes advantage of the weakness as an opportunity to commit fraud. Fraud risk is also apparent where there are controls in place but where these controls are circumvented or not complied with. Many control features rely on human beings to act as the control, for example, in any segregation of duties process or where authorizing signatories are required. If those human beings in such controlling positions are dishonest, then the controls, it must be argued, are either weak or nonexistent.

The foundations of an effective fraud risk management program are rooted in the FRA, overseen by management and the board, which identifies where fraud may occur within an organization. An FRA is performed on a systematic and recurring basis, involving appropriate personnel, considering relevant fraud scenarios, and mapping those fraud scenarios to mitigating controls. The existence of an FRA process and the fact that management is articulating its existence may even deter would-be fraud perpetrators.

The FRA is performed by identification of potential fraud scenarios at the process and activity level and ideally should be conducted on a quarterly basis.

The fraud risk origin of each fraud risk scenario is identified and categorized, distinguished by the internal or external nature of the risk, as follows:

- **Internal fraud risk.** Internal fraud refers to activities perpetrated within the organization, such as intentional misrepresentation of financial statements or financial transactions or theft, embezzlement, or improper use of the organization's resources. It comprises both employee and management fraud. The opportunities for internal fraud are under the direct control of the organization and its management.

- **External fraud risk.** External fraud refers to theft or improper use of the organization's resources perpetrated by individuals from outside the organization, that is, external service providers (e.g., strategic partners, contractors, consultants, or suppliers) or the general public. While safeguards can be put in place, effective controls against external attack can be more problematic.

In complex fraudulent activity, there may be collaboration or collusion between employees, strategic partners, contractors, and/or external service providers. In such cases, the fraud risk scenario would be classified as having both an *internal* and *external* fraud risk origin.

Each fraud scenario is further mapped into one or more of the following fraud risk categories:

- Asset misappropriation.
- Financial statement misrepresentation.
- Corruption.
- Misconduct.
- Theft of cash or assets.
- Conflict of interest, perhaps involving bribery or kickbacks.
- Fraudulent disbursements.
- Disclosure of confidential information.
- Overriding of controls.
- Disclosure/nondisclosure.
- Collusion.
- Counterfeiting/forgery.

These categories can be extended or replaced depending on the nature of the industry and potential fraud types.

The inherent fraud risk is determined by an assessment of each fraud scenario by probability (likelihood to occur) and impact (magnitude of consequence), without consideration of existing controls. This will result in the determination of inherent risk.

The residual fraud risk is determined by an assessment of each fraud scenario by probability and impact, after considering the implementation of fraud risk mitigation actions or internal controls. This will result in the determination of residual risk, assessing the fraud risk remaining after fraud risk mitigation actions have been deployed.

Inherent Fraud Risk

The method of determining the probability and impact for the inherent fraud risk rating is explained next.

Probability or likelihood is the chance that the fraud risk scenario identified will actually occur. When available, statistical data can support estimates of likelihood or probability. In practice, however, often the fraud risk champion does not have historical data. Instead, he relies on the experience of the process owners and the participants of the workshops and brainstorming sessions. Therefore, likelihood rarely implies mathematical certainty and is simply a subjective estimate (see Figure 21.2).

Impact or consequence is the severity of effect upon goals, objectives, or values. Similar to the probability rating, impact or consequence is also assessed based on statistical data or experience of process owners. The actual effect of a fraud event on an organization's finances, reputation, and operations is captured by the impact rating. The methodology for impact rating distinguishes between a direct tangible impact on the financial position and day-to-day operations and a longer-term intangible but highly significant reputational impact. The impact scale is depicted in Figure 21.3 and is illustrative only in terms of the values therein.

Probability/ Likelihood	Description
Almost Certain	The risk event is expected to occur more than 10 times per year.
Common	The risk event is expected to occur less than 10 times per year, up to once per year.
Likely	The risk event is expected to occur less than once per year, up to once in 10 years.
Rare	The risk event is expected to occur less than once in 10 years, up to once in 50 years.
Unlikely	The risk event is expected to occur less than once in 50 years, up to once in 500 years.
Remote	The risk event is not expected to occur more than once in 500 years.

FIGURE 21.2 Probability (Likelihood) Scale. *Source:* Simon Padgett, fraud and corruption training.

Impact/ Severity	Financial Impact	Operational	Employees	Health, Safety, Environment	Reputation	Regulatory/ Legal
Incidental	< $1,000 < 10% of budget	System failure up to 1 day	Negligible or isolated staff dissatisfaction	Minor effects	Minor public attention	Isolated, remedied non-compliance
Minor	$1,000 to $10,000 10% to 25% of budget	System failure 1 to 3 days	General moral problems. Under 20% staff turnover	Minor medical treatment. Rapid cleanup.	Ongoing media attention	Repeated, remedied non-compliance
Moderate	$10,000 to $100,000 25% to 50% of budget	System failure 4 to 10 days	Poor employer of choice; 20% to 40% staff turnover	Lost time injury. Cleanup by contractors.	Social criticism	Sustained non-compliance with significant fines
Major	$100,000 to $1,000,000 50% to 75% of budget	System failure 11 to 20 days	20% to 40% senior staff turnover	Single fatality or significant disability. Impaired eco-system.	Serious national social issues	Serious breaches with prosecution
Catastrophic	>$1,000,000 > 75% of budget	System failure for over 20 days	Over 40% staff and manager turnover	Multiple fatalities or disabilities. Long-term environmental recovery.	Serious regional social issues. Sustained negative outcry.	Class actions and imprisonment

FIGURE 21.3 Impact (Magnitude or Consequence) Scale. *Source:* Simon Padgett, fraud and corruption training.

	Probability					
	Remote	Unlikely	Rare	Likely	Common	Almost Certain
Catastrophic	High	High	Very High	Very High	Very High	Very High
Major	Medium	Medium	High	High	Very High	Very High
Impact **Moderate**	Medium	Medium	High	High	High	High
Minor	Low	Low	Medium	Medium	High	High
Incidental	Low	Low	Low	Medium	Medium	Medium

FIGURE 21.4   Risk Matrix or Heat Map. *Source:* Simon Padgett, fraud and corruption training.

A risk rating of *low, medium, high,* or *very high* is then assigned to the probability and impact ratings, as in Figure 21.4, to reveal the fraud risk matrix or heat map.

The inherent fraud risk rating now moves to the next level with the calculation of the combined likelihood of a fraud risk scenario and the impact on the organization if it was to occur. The rating is based on the probability multiplied by the highest of the impact category scores, therefore taking into account the worst case scenario:

$$\text{Inherent Fraud Risk Rating} = \text{Likelihood} \times \text{Worst Impact}$$

Following this methodology, the fraud risk champion determines an inherent fraud risk rating by multiplying a predefined likelihood and a predefined impact.

Identification of Controls

The fraud risk champion identifies the existing controls for each fraud risk scenario. The nature of controls can be either preventive, detective, automated, or manual. A control risk rating is applied after taking into account the existing controls in place, adjusting the inherent risk rating by the extent of the existing controls.

Residual Fraud Risk

The residual fraud risk refers to the likelihood and impact of fraud risk after taking into consideration any controls or fraud risk mitigation actions. The residual fraud risk can be defined as a combination of likelihood and impact score factoring in the mitigation effects of the antifraud controls in place. The residual fraud risk score deflates the inherent fraud risk by the mitigation controls.

The fraud risk champion assesses the residual fraud risk rating using the same methodology as illustrated for inherent FRA. In this case, he takes into account the fraud risk mitigation actions to be adopted.

All fraud risks are entered into a fraud risk register, usually one for each department and a consolidated version.

DEVELOPMENT OF THE FRAUD PROFILE

The next step is to develop the fraud profile.

The process involves the development of a set of detection controls that will identify the characteristics that fraud would present if it occurred. The characteristics exhibited by fraud fall into three general categories:

1. Behavioral.
2. Documentary.
3. Data patterning.

Behavioral Characteristics

People commit fraud. When they do so there are normally identifiable generic behavioral patterns that are consistent with fraudulent activity such as employees working long hours, not taking vacations, being protective and secretive about their work, and being generally uncooperative. They are generic by default largely because the particular personalities of individuals are not usually sufficiently well known for them to be more specific. The level at which identifiable behavioral characteristics are more specific is among coworkers, who know the individual sufficiently well to be able to identify sometimes quite subtle but very important changes in behavior. Quite often during the course of a fraud investigation and too often, in the aftermath, a coworker of the suspect will identify and comment about anomalies in the perpetrator's behavior. These behavioral anomalies observed by coworkers can be valuable indicators of fraudulent activity.

Documentary Characteristics

Documentary characteristics appear in the form of altered or missing documents or data such as changed dates or missing authorization signatures, data that is inconsistent with other characteristics such as changes to bank account details, or simply changes to the amount payable on purchase invoices. Fraudsters like to remove documentation that they have used in their fraud activities with the view that they are camouflaging the evidence by obscuring the audit trail. As a fraud investigator, there is nothing I like better than to see invoices missing from a sequential listing. It kind of draws your attention directly to the suspicious transactions, and as we all know, destroyed documents can always be re-created or copies obtained from the other party. Removing or destroying documents is rather like putting a great flashing warning sign on where the evidence lies. Activities and characteristics such as these are quite often very obvious but just as frequently overlooked or even not recognized as indicators of fraud.

Data Patterning Characteristics

Patterns in data could indicate a characteristic of fraudulent activity, particularly when those patterns are anomalies or do not follow a standard trend. These data patterns could be a key indicator of fraud and can be captured to form part of a fraud profile. For example, in a fraud involving the theft of cash by rolling accounts receivable, we will see an increasingly aging receivables in the data as cash received is not matched to the sales invoices and successive days' cash receipts will produce a time lag between receipt of cash and bank deposit. This profile of increasing debtors may be a key fraud indicator. Documentary and data patterning characteristics that exist will be particular to an individual business and will constitute the fraud profile for that business only.

With the knowledge of the documents, the people, the data patterns, the existing controls, and security and accounting systems, it is now possible to identify the characteristics that the fraud scenarios would present if they occurred in your business. The critical element of this part of the process is to identify the characteristics that individually and collectively will be of most practical value as indicators of fraudulent activity. The output is a profiling schedule that identifies the potential perpetrator or class of perpetrators, the type of behavioral characteristics, and the controls or enhanced controls that should be in place to reduce fraud risk.

This documented fraud profile can be used in conjunction with the FRA process as a methodology to focus attention on high-risk areas of the business.

Examples of likely behavioral characteristics might be

- Changes in relationships with superiors or subordinates.
- Uncharacteristic delays in producing reports.
- Unusual resistance or hostility to routine inquiries.
- Changes in the social relationships with coworkers.
- Excessive overtime or weekend work without justification.
- Sudden excessive changes in lifestyle.

There could also be documentary anomalies such as

- The absence of or delay in an authorization signature.
- The backdating of documents.
- Inconsistency in the sequence of documents.
- The absence of particular documents.
- Payment records for the same amounts to different customers.
- Bank deposit slips that have different amounts on them compared to the amounts making up the actual deposit.

Data pattern anomalies could include the following:

- Changes in the number and frequency of transactions with particular suppliers.
- The awarding of tenders to the supplier who submits the latest bid.
- An above average level of payments to one supplier.
- Excessive commissions paid to one salesman.

The value of the formalized fraud profile process in your organization is the reference framework that it provides. When documentation or other anomalies are identified in a vacuum, they can easily be rationalized away or not even recognized as anomalies. The profile is a filter that sifts out the relationships and links from a mass of otherwise unorganized information. Sometimes frauds that are actually staring us in the face can be rationalized or even categorized as errors. If they are below the radar in terms of size and materiality, they can certainly be overlooked within an audit process. In these cases, a profile of that fraud would likely have been identified it as soon as it happened.

There are, however, challenges to the development of the organization's fraud profile. As we can see, the process of developing a fraud profile requires a detailed knowledge of the people, documentation, and systems and data in the organization. Developing fraud profiles is an extremely sensitive area of risk management and requires a high level of security, not only due to the fact that it may involve and contain rather personal information, but also because the process produces a road map of how to perpetrate fraud in your organization. It also identifies where the weaknesses and vulnerabilities are. The development of the fraud profile is something that, preferably, should not be carried out or managed by someone directly involved in operations or finance. The need for this security is one reason why organizations often out-source or seek external assistance when dealing with fraud risk management. Within an organization, probably the best people to develop a fraud profile would be internal auditors. They have knowledge of the systems, documents, and people; they have relevant training; and they are not in operational, authoritative, or decision-making positions, and as we have seen, auditors are the least likely employees in any organization to commit fraud. However, there are some risks associated with using internal auditors to develop fraud risk plans. Such a process can certainly impair the independence of internal auditors. They are not going to criticize and investigate processes that they have previously advised on or implemented, and remember that you could be using someone who drew the roadmap of how to commit fraud in your business. Internal auditors have to remain independent and acknowledge that any exposure to fraud risk could, theoretically, be as a result of them not having effectively drawn attention to such fraud opportunities in previous audit reports.

 ## DEVELOPMENT OF A FRAUD DETECTION NET

The word *detect* is described in the *Concise Oxford Dictionary* as "to reveal the guilt."

The final step in the fraud profiling methodology is to develop the close monitoring procedures that will flag and report anomalies and key character-istics of fraud. These procedures can frequently be incorporated into existing processes, both computerized and manual, and control structures that have legitimate management objectives such as monitoring receivables aging and bank reconciliations. Frequently, the controls already exist. All that is required is to add a fraud dimension. If cost-effective monitoring procedures cannot be developed, reassess the preventive controls and review less effective but cheaper monitoring procedures that will at least identify the characteristics of more serious fraud.

In establishing a fraud detection methodology, let us first examine the impact of certain types of fraud detection methodologies. It is a statistical fact that frauds are much more likely to be detected by tip-offs than by any other method. The initial detection of a fraud scheme is often the most crucial moment in the fraud examination process as decisions must be made quickly to secure evidence, mitigate losses, and execute the best investigation strategy available. The method by which a fraud is uncovered can open or close several options for an organization. For instance, the outcome of a case might vary substantially if the first time management learns of an alleged fraud is through an anonymous tip-off, as opposed to a law enforcement action. Moreover, analyzing the means by which organizations detect instances of fraud gives us insight into the effectiveness of controls and other antifraud measures.

Respondents to the ACFE survey were asked to provide information about how the frauds that they had investigated were initially uncovered, allowing us to identify patterns and other interesting data regarding fraud detection methods.

Initial Detection of Occupational Frauds

Perhaps the most prevalent trend in the detection data is the ongoing importance of tip-offs or whistleblowing. I shall never forget the first day of the whistleblowing channel that we set up for an African government to deal with allegations of Social Welfare fraud in that country. There were 125,000 calls, and the call center that we had created, covering 11 official languages, simply could not cope. Of course, this tapered off as the days went on and the advertising and marketing of the hotlines was tweaked. Tip-offs are the most common method of initial detection, according to the ACFE, with management review and internal audit being the second and third most common methods of detection, respectively. Interestingly, IT controls and confessions are the two initial detection methods least prevalent, according to the survey, at 1 percent of cases for each.

Median Loss by Detection Method

Frauds that were first detected as a result of police notification cost companies the most by far, with a median loss of $1 million, perhaps due to law enforcement's focus on investigating crimes of larger amounts.

Generally, the detection categories associated with higher median losses, such as police notification ($1 million), external audit ($370,000), confession ($225,000), and accident ($166,000), are the least proactive detection methods. In other words, uncovering frauds by these methods is not generally the result of a specific internal control or antifraud measure but is reactive in nature.

Conversely, median losses from frauds that were discovered by internal audit ($81,000), document examination ($105,000), IT controls ($110,000), management review ($123,000), and account reconciliation ($124,000) were substantially lower. This latter group of detection methods reflects proactive measures within the organization to stop fraud and obviously results in lower losses.

Frauds uncovered as a result of internal audit examination were of the lowest value ($81,000). This, again, could be indicative of a sound antifraud control resulting in lower value frauds being detected. Call me skeptical, which is perhaps my nature being a forensic accountant, but could this also be because internal audits are not detecting the larger frauds?

Source of Tip-Offs

Identifying the most common source of tip-offs is essential to crafting a system and culture that encourages individuals to step forward with information. While just over half of all tips originated from employees, the ACFE research reveals that several other parties, such as customers, vendors, shareholder/owners, and competitors tip off organizations to suspected frauds. Organizations need to consider this data when deciding how to best communicate and market their reporting mechanisms, policies, and other resources to potential whistleblowers.

There are three fundamental success factors to a whistleblowing mechanism. It should allow reporting to a party outside of the organization, it should have a facility for toll free communication on the telephone element, and it should offer confidentiality and anonymity to any reporting party. There are several reasons a person might want anonymity when reporting a tip, and the data shows that a significant number of tips (12 percent) came from an anonymous source. Tools such as anonymous hotlines or web-based portals, which allow individuals to report misconduct without fear of retribution or of being identified, can help facilitate this process.

Impact of Hotlines

The presence or absence of a reporting hotline has an interesting impact on how frauds are discovered. Not surprisingly, according to the ACFE, organizations with some form of hotline in place saw a much higher likelihood that a fraud would be detected by a tip (51 percent) than organizations without such a hotline (35 percent).

Another disparity between these two classes of organizations is seen in frauds detected by accident. More than 11 percent of frauds in organizations without hotlines were caught by accident, whereas less than 3 percent of cases were detected by accident in organizations that had implemented a hotline. Similarly, external audit was the detection method for 6 percent of cases from organizations without hotlines, but only 1 percent in organizations with hotlines.

Initial Detection of Fraud in Small Businesses

Compared to large organizations, small businesses with fewer than 100 employees differ widely in organizational structure and availability of resources, with smaller organizations tending to have far fewer antifraud controls in place than larger organizations. Quite simply, smaller organizations may ordinarily be more focused on sales and expansion strategies and may not wish to be restrained (financially and with time) by focusing their attention on fraud governance structures and antifraud controls, which, in their minds would only restrain growth. Often, management within such organizations believe that they are so close to the fundamental activities and operations that they actually take on the role of watchdog. In fact, small organizations in the study were victimized by fraud more frequently than larger organizations, and they suffered a disproportionately large median loss of $147,000.

The difference in levels of control could explain some of the discrepancies between detection methods observed in small and large organizations. Smaller organizations are substantially less likely to detect fraud based on tips or internal audits, while they are more likely to uncover fraud by accident, external audit, or police notification.

Detection Method by Scheme Type

In its study, the ACFE also compared the detection method with the type of scheme reported, whether asset misappropriation, corruption, or financial statement fraud. Every organization has specific fraud risks to manage based on its profile in terms of industry, location, size, and several other factors. For instance, publicly traded organizations have specific concerns and regulatory requirements with respect to financial statement fraud, and multinational companies often have increased corruption risks to manage. Management in such organizations will find it helpful to see how different scheme types are most commonly detected.

Tips represented the most common detection method for each type of scheme, but they were significantly higher in corruption cases, at 54 percent, compared to 42 percent for both asset misappropriation and financial statement fraud schemes.

Financial statement fraud cases in the study were first uncovered by law enforcement 14 percent of the time or about three times more often than corruption cases and over five times more often than asset misappropriation schemes.

A striking similarity in the data is the consistency with which internal audit was responsible for the detection of each scheme type. In each scheme category, 14 percent of the cases were detected through internal audits.

Surveillance monitoring, confessions, and IT controls were the detection methods least responsible for the detection of each fraud scheme type, all being under 2 percent of cases.

Detection Method by Region

The ACFE also examined how frauds were detected based on the region in which they occurred. Once again tips were the most common detection method by a wide margin in each region. Africa had the highest percentage of cases detected by tip-offs, at 53 percent, and the United States, Asia, and Europe all had 43 percent of their cases in the study detected by tip-offs. Management review and internal audit consistently came in either second or third in every region. Internal audit was one of the most diverse detection methods across regions, uncovering as few as 10 percent of cases in Africa and as many as 23 percent in Europe.

Surveillance monitoring, confessions, and IT controls, once again, were the detection methods least responsible for the detection of fraud in all regions, all being under 3 percent of cases.

Information on red flags should be included in the profile of an offender, as red flags act as a trigger for investigators to become suspicious and begin a probe in order to detect any fraud. Previously profiled modus operandi would be useful in the FRA process as part of an antifraud program to identify vulnerable areas where fraud may exist. The suspected employees may be innocent, despite the red flags. Red flags are just indicators of fraud, and modus operandi information will guide the investigator in which direction to look based on previously profiled modus operandi of fraud offenders. Modus operandi information can be valuable in formulating strategies for preventing such crimes in the future. For example, an identified modus operandi of fraud offenders, such as changing the bank account numbers of suppliers in order to facilitate fraudulent payments, can be an indicator of a need to perform an FRA on the procurement and bank payments areas of the business or to conduct proactive fraud detection investigations. The investigator can review the electronic audit trails, which reveal all changes made to the bank account numbers of suppliers. As this is a known modus operandi of fraud offenders, there is a significant likelihood that fraud will be detected from such a fraud detection exercise.

The identification of how fraud is committed is inherent in the offender profiling process. Investigators, therefore, need to understand the various methods used to commit fraud to facilitate ease of detection in the future. This type of information from the profile of a fraud offender can be valuable to an investigator, serving as an early warning sign, because lavish spending on outrageously ostentatious lifestyles, for example, is a red flag that is indicative of the occurrence of fraud. Red flags are a warning sign that something is amiss, but be aware that not all red flags may be indicative of fraud.

All entities are susceptible to fraud, and no system of preventative controls can provide absolute assurance. It is therefore important to implement systems aimed at detecting fraud after it has occurred, in the event that the preventive systems fail.

A whistleblowing mechanism will provide employees and stakeholders with a platform or channel for reporting suspected fraud, either by telephone, e-mail, or Internet-based reporting. The ideal whistleblowing channel will offer anonymity and toll-free calling. It is also important that whistleblower protection is both available and evident.

Data analytics is another method of detecting fraud. By regularly running such software over data sets, anomalies in the data can be quickly identified for further examination.

A further requirement of a detection-based strategy is to develop a fraud or antifraud policy that addresses and communicates what happens when employees do find fraud. For a deterrent to be effective, clear messages are required from senior management that abuse of trust and any form of unethical behavior by anyone in the organization, regardless of their position, is unacceptable and will not be tolerated. The tone at the top must be one of zero tolerance, and senior management must walk the talk and practice what they preach.

The profile you develop is a dynamic model. It will change as people and documents change. Left unattended, over time it will become stale, less reliable, and ultimately dangerous. If reviewed frequently, however, it will improve as new insight and experience adds to its quality. Frauds identified by the profile invariably provide additional data to improve the quality of the profile. If fraud escapes the detection net, the profile will identify a set of exposures that may not have been hypothesized or a set of characteristics not contemplated. If the profile fails to identify a fraud, reassess the issues to ensure that the process covers what was overlooked and how it was overlooked. There are no more valuable experiences in this work than reviewing the circumstances of an actual fraud by treating it as a live case study. Even the experience of petty frauds is valuable. Many of the characteristics will be similar if not identical to much larger ones. It is my view that there is no such thing as an immaterial fraud—just one that hasn't had enough time to grow!

Although fraud profiling is conceptually simple, it is a rigorous, systematic process. It takes time and considerable intellectual effort to develop and implement. If it seems a daunting task, consider implementation in stages over time. While it might be desirable to have a fraud profile for all aspects of the business, any incremental improvement is a step in the right direction. Start with the areas that are most vulnerable and easiest to profile and sleep a little more easily at night.

22

The Role of the HR Recruitment Process in Profiling

THE ACFE'S 2012 *Report to the Nations on Occupational Fraud and Abuse* surmises that only 6 percent of fraudsters in the study had previous fraud convictions and that the most common behavioral red flags were living beyond one's means (36 percent of cases) and experiencing financial difficulties (27 percent of cases).

According to the ACFE, most occupational fraudsters are first-time offenders with clean employment histories. Approximately 87 percent of occupational fraudsters had never been charged or convicted of a fraud-related offense, and 84 percent had never been punished or terminated by an employer for fraud-related conduct. It is therefore not an easy task for HR departments to spot these employees and raise the alarm.

The report goes on to reveal further red flags attributable to human behavior in the workplace:

- Unusually close association with vendor or customer (19 percent of cases).
- Control issues or unwillingness to share duties (18 percent).
- Wheeler-dealer attitude (15 percent).
- Divorce or family problems (15 percent).
- Irritability, suspiciousness, or defensiveness (13 percent).

- Addiction problems (8 percent).
- Refusal to take vacations (7 percent).

PERPETRATOR'S CRIMINAL HISTORY

In 860 of the cases in the ACFE's 2012 study, the respondents were able to provide information about the fraudster's criminal history. 87 percent of fraudsters, according to the study, had never been charged or convicted of a fraud-related criminal offense. In only 5 percent of those cases the fraudster had been convicted of a fraud-related offense prior to the scheme in question. There is, however, a balance of 6 percent of cases where fraudsters had been charged but were not convicted. This is an interesting statistic that warrants further discussion, since, in the decision-making process, a fraudster might not commit his act if he knows he is likely to be caught due to the presence of strong internal controls, and he might decide to proceed if he considers his chances of getting away with it as being quite good. However, now we have the decision-making scenario whereby the fraudster feels that there is a chance that he may get caught, but he knows that if he is caught, he will not be convicted or the penalty will be very low. This can happen due to cultural sensitivities to prosecution or in regions of high corruption where the fraudster can buy his way out of a conviction. In the scenario of being caught but unlikely to be convicted, the fraudster is likely to decide to proceed with the fraud.

PERPETRATOR'S EMPLOYMENT HISTORY

There were 695 cases in which the respondents provided information on the fraudster's employment history, and their responses show that the vast majority (84 percent) of occupational fraudsters had never been punished or terminated by an employer for a fraud-related offense before the frauds in question. Only about 8 percent of fraudsters had previously been terminated by another employer for fraud, and only 8 percent had been previously punished in some other way. Once again, we are seeing that only a minority of fraudsters have a history of fraud-related activity as an indicator, making the recruitment process of vetting new employees rather challenging.

CONTROLLING HUMAN RISK

To a human resources (HR) department that is in control of its workforce with regular appraisals, monitoring, and communication with its people, such red flags should not slip below the radar, and fraud risk should be managed by stopping the event before it happens. I have been involved in many fraud assignment closeout meetings where fraud investigation reporting is carried out and a question so often asked is, how did this fraudster get through the HR recruitment processes? Indeed, HR has a fundamental role to play not only in closing the door to fraudsters or, rather, not opening it, but also in recognizing those who have slipped through the net and monitoring their activities, keeping them away from cash or assets, or removing them from the organization altogether.

The Management Assessment Risk Framework considers the different human risks that impact an organization, of which fraud risk is one. The model, taken from the European Foundation for Quality Management, is an effective framework to continuously manage human risks and is shown in Figure 22.1.

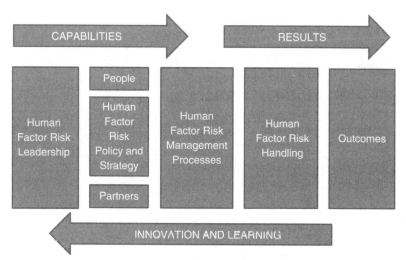

FIGURE 22.1 Human Factor Management Assessment Risk Framework. *Source:* European Foundation for Quality Management, 1999.

EFFECTIVE HUMAN PERFORMANCE

Performance indicator factors (PIFs) include any factor that can influence human performance, relating to the individual, for example, emotional state, intelligence, motivation, skill level, social factors, and stress level. PIFs can also relate to the organizational environment, for example, tone at the top on fraud, internal control systems including internal audit and fraud investigation capabilities, poor working conditions, rewards and benefits, inadequate supervision, insufficient training, organizational structure, culture, company life cycle, policies and procedures, and so on. PIFs can be described as those factors that determine the likelihood of error or effective human performance and fraudulent activity and can be divided into workplace-related factors and human-related factors. Organizational values, including integrity and honesty, should be linked to the performance of the organization to communicate values and understanding.

HR DEPARTMENTS CLOSING THE DOOR ON FRAUD

Questions are constantly being raised surrounding recruitment processes and fraud prevention through the increased vetting of new recruits and existing employees. Theorists argue that HR recruitment activities must fit the organization's stage of development or external fit as well as internal fit and that there is a need to ensure that policies be designed to fit and support each other. HR departments have to accept their role within the strategic fraud management arena with key responsibilities including that of building fraud investigation competencies internally in the long term, thereby moving toward a resource-based view of fraud risk management. This is very different from the current recruitment policies in many organizations, effectively that of outsourcing.

It is my view that in order to bring about an antifraud environment in their organizations, HR departments will have to focus on

- Recruiting the relevant skills to build fraud departments.
- Ensuring that recruitment policies address the risk of recruiting fraudsters or potential fraudsters.

The manner in which organizations utilize human resources reflects the pressure to achieve corporate strategy and to make as much profit as quickly as possible. Recruitment is all too often carried out to meet that demand with a focus on ensuring that performance management and reward hold a central place in coordinating the contribution between HR and the operational side of the business. This hire-and-fire philosophy, common in the United States, is a fraud risk in itself, as employees are insecure and become begrudged. Reducing fraud cost by introducing an antifraud program will increase the organization's competitive advantage. Indeed, it could be argued that introducing such a program is following Japanization, or the application of Japanese practices to standard HR processes. A move to an antifraud culture in organizations has to adopt professional people skills to achieve such a competitive advantage. HR strategy needs to first acquire these new forensic accounting skills and add them to their resources, and then focus on controlling the antifraud processes. On a longer-term note, to implement an antifraud program of the highest quality, organizations will have to follow Kaizen through a process of continuous improvement and learning, which follows three distinct types of learning—knowledge acquisition, habit and skill learning, and emotional conditioning—all of which will be implemented by the newly employed forensic skills. According to Kaizen, continuous improvement through learning, including fraud and corruption learning, involves everyone—employees and managers alike.

THE CURRICULUM VITAE: FACT OR FICTION?

It is commonly estimated that over 70 percent of job applications contain misleading information. The extent of occupational fraud means that HR managers have an important part to play both in ensuring the ethical development of any organization through recruiting adequate skillsets to manage fraud risk and in protecting that organization from dishonest employees through their gatekeeping recruitment processes. HR research has suggested that HR professionals have the opportunity to play a greater role in ethical stewardship and creating effective fraud risk governance that honors the obligations due to the many stakeholders by reducing fraud risk and maximizing long-term organizational wealth. The role of HR as a steward in the governance of organizations has received increasing attention in the post-Enron era. Many, myself included, advocate treating employees as owners and partners in the governance process and state that this should include sharing honest and extensive communication. It is astonishing that only 31 percent of organizations conduct background checks on existing employee promotions.

Some emphasize that conducting background checks on employees during their tenure (and particularly when elevated to positions of trust) reduces exposure to fraud.

I am a person who does not like to let go, even after an investigation is coming to closure. I recall one fraudster we nailed for insider trading at a bank some years ago, and I just happened to ask myself how such a dishonest person would have made it through the HR recruitment gatepost. Upon examining his recruitment path, I noted that both his application and curriculum vitae (CV) claimed that he had a degree from a reputable university, extensive experience in the field, and no criminal record. What he had failed to mention is that he had previously spent time in jail for theft, had a horrendous credit history, and never received the degree from the top university, which he did actually attend.

So, how much of what appears on a job application is true? Most employers are desperately seeking a qualified applicant to fill an urgent need and many in the HR department are measured on how quickly they do so. Far too often there is a failure to do a thorough background check of a CV or biography before hiring. With an increasingly competitive job market, an applicant might feel the pressure to stand out in a crowd by either exaggerating or lying about his qualifications or omitting facts that might hurt his chances of getting hired. Remember that an alarming 70 percent of applicants have lied on their job applications.

One of the more common forms of CV fraud is with regard to educational history. An applicant might fabricate a degree or change the pass grade earned. Employers can confirm education by requesting a transcript be sent directly from the university. A recent high-profile example of this form of fraud involved Scott Thompson, who was hired as a chief executive for Yahoo! in January 2012. He received his degree in accounting but also claimed to have obtained an additional degree in computer science. Being the former president of PayPal, no one questioned or verified his education. His fraud was made public once a Yahoo! shareholder exposed his lie. After investigation, it was discovered the college he attended did not offer a degree in computer science at the time that Thompson supposedly received his.

Employment history is another area that, once glorified, can increase the fraudster's chance of entering an organization. Job titles and former duties or responsibilities are sometimes manufactured or exaggerated to make the applicant more appealing. In addition, gaps in employment or a period of self-employment might be considered a red flag worth investigating. One of the most effective ways to verify employment history is by calling or e-mailing listed references or former places of employment. Through this follow-up, other issues might arise, such as the actual reason for leaving a previous job. Call me skeptical, but I would not be calling the listed references. I would actually be making contact with those who are not listed.

Applicants can also claim to possess licenses, certifications, professional memberships, or other credentials that are tailored to the position they are trying to acquire. Employers can check websites and directly contact most of these licensing institutions. The employer can also verify if the applicant has received any disciplinary action or barring related to his or her professional associations.

Job applications provide a section where applicants can list any criminal history or misdemeanors committed in the past. A common deception is omitting past offenses or lessening the degree of seriousness. Some employers now check criminal records by mandating that candidates undergo biometric or fingerprint testing. Additionally, there are several criminal background checking organizations and verification services available, from which reports on candidates can be obtained.

Depending on the position being recruited for and the level, there are other preventive actions one might consider, including checking driving records, performing credit checks, browsing the potential employee's social networking activities (e.g., Facebook, LinkedIn, Twitter, or Instagram) for any unfavorable activity, or requesting that the candidate undergo a drug test.

There are several avenues available to potential employers to confirm facts and details in one's application for employment or resume. It is in the best interest of the hiring entity to double-check facts that appear on an application before offering a job to a candidate who could cost the organization time and money should the new hire prove to be a liability rather than an asset. Of course, by profiling fraudster characteristics, it may be possible to eliminate high-risk applicants before their fraudulent and counterfeit CVs even enter the recruitment process.

HR departments have a responsibility with regard to the recruitment, training, and development of employees who will handle fraud risk in the organization and should ensure that investigators are trained to understand the importance of profiling in the investigation process. It is also advised that HR departments be involved, along with the investigators, in the compiling of a training manual for investigators on the profiling of fraud offenders. It really is a human issue. The training should include all aspects of profiling and how it interlinks with the antifraud strategies of the organization, including guidelines on the interview process and interviewing techniques to enable the investigator to use the information compiled or collected from the profiles during interviews. Combating crime not only involves investigation.

Investigators should have knowledge on identifying vulnerabilities in the internal financial control environment, and this should also form part of the training curriculum.

Theorists draw attention to areas of resistance that will have to be dealt with in introducing antifraud programs, including complacency and neglecting to anchor changes soon enough in the corporate culture. Clearly, these will have to be addressed if the antifraud initiatives are to succeed.

Bibliography

Abagnale, Frank, and Stan Redding. *Catch Me If You Can: The True Story of a Real Fake*. New York: Broadway Books, 2000.

Akst, D. *Wonder Boy: Barry Minkow, the Kid Who Swindled Wall Street*. University of Michigan: Scribner Book Company, 1990.

American Institute of Certified Public Accountants. www.aicpa.org. Accessed January 2, 2013.

Association of Certified Fraud Examiners. *Report to the Nations on Occupational Fraud and Abuse*, 2010. www.acfe.com.

Association of Certified Fraud Examiners. *Report to the Nations on Occupational Fraud and Abuse*, 2012. www.acfe.com.

Association of Chartered Certified Accountants. *Accounting and Business*, February 2012 ed.

Babbie, E. R. *The Practice of Social Research*, 7th ed. Belmont, CA: Wadsworth, 1995.

Babiak, Paul, and Robert Hare. *Snakes in Suits: When Psychopaths Go to Work*. New York: HarperCollins, 2006.

Bartol, Curt R. *Criminal Behavior: A Psychosocial Approach*, 5th ed. Englewood Cliffs, NJ: Prentice Hall, 1999.

Bartol, Curt, and Anne Bartol. *Introduction to Forensic Psychology*. Thousand Oaks, CA: Sage, 2008.

BBC News. "Fraud Levels Increased in 2011, Says BDO." January 9, 2012, www.bbc.co.uk/news/business. Accessed January 12, 2013.

Beare, Margaret. *Critical Reflections on Transnational Organized Crime, Money Laundering, and Corruption*. Toronto: University of Toronto Press, 2003.

Bekerian, D. A., and A. B. Levey. *Applied Psychology: Putting Theory into Practice*. New York: Oxford University Press, 2005.

Bennett, W. W., and K. M. Hess. *Criminal investigation*. St. Paul, MN: West Publishing Company, 1981.

Black's Law Dictionary. www.thelawdictionary.org. Accessed January 2013.

Blair, William, and Richard Brent. *Banks and Financial Crime: The International Law of Tainted Money*. Oxford: Oxford University Press, 2008.

Bolton, R., and D. Hand. "Statistical Fraud Detection: A Review." *Statistical Science* 17, no. 3 (2002): 235–255.

Burge, P., and J. Shawe-Taylor. "An Unsupervised Neural Network Approach to Profiling the Behaviour of Mobile Phone Users for Use in Fraud Detection." *Journal of Parallel and Distributed Computing* 61 (2001): 915–925.

Campbell, J. H., and D. DeNevi. *Profilers: Leading Investigators Take You Inside the Criminal Mind*. Amherst, NY: Prometheus Books, 2004.

Cardwell, Harvey. *The Logic and Language of Auditing for Fraud*. Princeton, NJ: R. T. Edwards, 1960.

Cardwell, Harvey. *Principles of Audit Surveillance*. Princeton, NJ: R.T. Edwards, 2005.

Coleman, J. M. *The Criminal Elite: Understanding White Collar Crime*, 5th ed. New York: Worth Publishers, 2002.

Comer, M. J. *Corporate Fraud*. London: McGraw-Hill, 1977.

Compliance Intelligence (formerly *Compliance Reporter*). "UK Fraud at Record Levels, KPMG," 2012.

Concise Oxford Dictionary of Current English, 8th ed. New York: Oxford University Press, 1990.

Cressey, Donald. *Other People's Money: A Study in the Social Psychology of Embezzlement*. Glencoe, IL: Free Press, 1953.

Cressey, Donald, and Edwin Sutherland. *Principles of Criminology*, 11th ed. Lanham, MD: AltaMira Press, 1992.

Croall, Helen. *Understanding White Collar Crime*. Buckingham, PA: Open University Press, 2001.

Doig, A., and H. Croall. *Fraud*. Cullompton, UK: Willan Publishing, 2006.

Domanick, Joe. *Faking It in America: Barry Minkow and the Great ZZZZ Best Scam*. Chicago: Contemporary Books, 1989.

Eichenwald, Kurt. *Conspiracy of Fools: A True Story*. New York: Broadway, 2005.

Engdahl, Oskar. "The Role of Money in Economic Crime," *British Journal of Criminology* 48, no. 2 (2008): 154–170.

Ernst & Young. "Fraud: The Unmanaged Risk." Eighth Global Survey, 2003. https://www2.eycom.ch/publications/items/fraud/en.pdf.

European Commission. *EU Anti-Corruption Report*, 2014. http://ec.europa.eu. Accessed March 15, 2014.

European Foundation for Quality Management. www.efqm.org. Accessed March 15, 2013.

Forsyth, D. R. *Group Dynamics*, 5th ed. Belmont, CA: Wadsworth, 2010.

Gottfredson, M. R., and T. A. Hirschi. *A General Theory of Crime*. Stanford, CA: Stanford University Press, 1990.

Grau, J. J., ed. *Criminal and Civil Investigation Handbook*. New York: McGraw-Hill, 1981.

Green, B., and J. Choi. "Assessing the Risk of Management Fraud through Neural Network Technology." *Auditing* 16, no. 1 (1997): 14–28.

Green, Stuart. *Lying, Cheating, and Stealing: A Moral Theory of White-Collar Crime*. Oxford: Oxford University Press, 2006.

Greenberg, J., and E. Tomlinson. "Methodological Evolution of Employee Theft Research: The DATA Cycle." In *The Dark Side of Organizational Behavior*, edited by R. W. Griffin and A. O'Leary-Kelly. New York: Pfeiffer, 2004, pp. 426–456.

Harris, Robert. *Selling Hitler*. London: Faber, 1987.

Henriques, Diana B. *Bernie Madoff, the Wizard of Lies: Inside the Infamous $65 Billion Swindle*. London: Oneworld Publications, 2011.

Hirschi, Travis, and Michael Gottfredson. "Causes of White-Collar Crime." *Criminology* 25, no. 4 (1987): 949–974.

Hollinger, Richard C., and John P. Clark. *Theft by Employees: The Hollinger Clark Study*. Lexington, MA: Lexington Books, 1983.

Holmes, R. M., and S. T. Holmes. *Profiling Violent Crimes: An Investigative Tool*, 3rd ed. Thousand Oaks, CA: Sage, 2002.

HM Treasury. "Risk Management Assessment Framework," 2003.

Institute of Internal Auditors. www.theiia.org. Accessed February 1, 2013.

Jackson, J. L., and D. A. Bekerian. *Offender Profiling: Theory, Research and Practice*. Chichester: Wiley, 1997.

Jory, Stephen. *Loadsamoney: The True Story of the World's Largest Ever Counterfeiting Ring*. London: Trafalgar Square, 2005.

Kocsis, R. N. *Criminal Profiling: International Theory, Research and Practice*. Totowa, NJ: Humana Press, 2007.

KPMG. "Analysis of Global Patterns of Fraud. Who Is the Typical Fraudster?" 2011.

Kranacher, Mary-Jo, Richard Riley, and Joseph T. Wells. *Forensic Accounting and Fraud Examination*. Hoboken, NJ: Wiley, 2010.

Langer, Walter C. *The Mind of Adolf Hitler: The Secret Wartime Report*. New York: Basic Books, 1972.

LectLaw. www.lectlaw.com. Accessed February 20, 2013.

Leeson, Nick. *Rogue Trader*. London: Little, Brown, 1996.

Levi, Michael, and John Burrows. "Measuring the Impact of Fraud in the UK: A Conceptual and Empirical Journey." *British Journal of Criminology* 48, no. 3 (2008): 293–318.

Markopolos, Harry, and David Fisher. *No One Would Listen: A True Financial Thriller*. Hoboken, NJ: Wiley, 2011.

Maxfield, M. G., and E. Babbie. *Research Methods for Criminal Justice and Criminology*. Belmont, CA: Wadsworth, 1995.

Merriam Webster. www.merriam-webster.com. Accessed May 10, 2013.

Michalski, R. S., I. Bratko, and M. Kubat. *Machine Learning and Data Mining—Methods and Applications*. Hoboken, NJ: Wiley, 1998.

National Fraud Authority. "Annual Fraud Indicator," 2011.

Nettler, Gwynn. "Embezzlement without Problems." *British Journal of Criminology* 14, no. 1 (1974): 70–77.

Newburn, Tim. *Criminology*. Cullompton, UK: Devon: Willan Publishing, 2007.

Newburn, Tim, Tom Williamson, and Alan Wright. *Handbook of Criminal Investigation*. Cullompton, UK: Devon: Willan Publishing, 2007.

Norris, James. *R G Dun & Co, 1841–1900: The Development of Credit Reporting in the Nineteenth Century*. Westport, CT: Greenwood Press, 1978.

Oxford Dictionaries. http://oxforddictionaries.com. Accessed May 10, 2013.

Palshikar, G. K. "The Hidden Truth—Frauds and Their Control: A Critical Application for Business Intelligence." *Intelligent Enterprise* 5, no. 9 (May 2002): 46–51.

Pedneault, Stephen. *Preventing and Detecting Employee Theft and Embezzlement: A Practical Guide*. Hoboken, NJ: Wiley, 2010.

Petherick, Wayne. *Serial Crime: Theoretical and Practical Issues in Behavioral Profiling*. Burlington, MA: Academic Press, 2005.

Pickett, Spencer, and Jennifer Pickett. *Financial Crime Investigation and Control*. New York: Wiley, 2002.

PricewaterhouseCoopers LLP. *Global Economic Crime Survey*, 2009.

PricewaterhouseCoopers LLP. *Global Economic Crime Survey*, 2011.

PricewaterhouseCoopers LLP. *Global Economic Crime Survey*, 2014.

Rafter, Nicole. *The Criminal Brain: Understanding Biological Theories of Crime*. New York: New York University Press, 2008.

Ratcliffe, J. *Strategic Thinking in Criminal Intelligence*. Annandale, NSW: Federation Press, 2004.

Ratcliffe, J. H. *Intelligence-Led Policing*. Cullompton: Willan Publishing, 2008.

Robb, George. *White Collar Crime in Modern England: Financial Fraud and Business Morality 1845–1929*. Cambridge: Cambridge University Press, 1992.

Robb, George. "Women and White-Collar Crime Debates on Gender, Fraud and the Corporate Economy in England and America, 1850–1930." *British Journal of Criminology* 46, no. 6 (2006): 1058–1072.

Robertson, J. C. *Fraud Examination for Managers and Auditors.* Austin, TX: Viesca Books, 2000.

Ronczkowski, M. *Terrorism and Organized Hate Crime: Intelligence Gathering, Analysis, and Investigation.* Boca Raton, FL: CRC Press, 2004.

Sackett, Paul, and Michelle Harris. "Honesty Testing for Personnel Selection: A Review and Critique." *Personnel Psychology* 37 (1984): 221–245.

Sakurai, Yuka, and Russell Smith. "Gambling as a Motivation for the Commission of Financial Crime." *Trends and Issues in Crime and Criminal Justice,* no. 256 (2005): 1–6.

Sandage, Scott. *Born Losers: A History of Failure in America.* Cambridge, MA: Harvard University Press, 2005.

Serious Fraud Office (UK). www.sfo.gov.uk. Accessed June 1, 2013.

Shone, R. *Solving Crimes through Criminal Profiling.* New York: Rosen Publishing Group, 2008.

Silverstone, H., and H. R. Davia. *Fraud 101: Techniques and Strategies for Detection,* 2nd ed. Hoboken, NJ: Wiley, 2005.

Silverstone, H., and M. Sheetz. *Forensic Accounting and Fraud Investigation for Non-Experts,* 2nd ed. Hoboken, NJ: Wiley, 2007.

Snyman, C. R. *Criminal Law.* Durban: Butterworths, 1984.

Stewart, Andrew. *Stewart's Guide to Employment Law.* Annandale, N.S.W: Leichhardt: Federation Press, 2008.

Stotland, Ezra. "White Collar Criminals." *Journal of Social Issues* 33 (1977): 179–196.

Sutherland, Edwin H. *Principles of Criminology.* Chicago: University of Chicago Press, 1924.

Sutherland, Edwin H. "White-Collar Criminality." *American Sociological Review* 10 (1940): 132–139.

Sutherland, Edwin H. *White Collar Crime.* New York: Holt, Rinehart & Winston, 1949.

Sutherland, Edwin H. *White Collar Crime: The Uncut Version.* New Haven, CT: Yale University Press, 1985.

Tonry, M., and N. Morris, eds. *Modern Policing.* Chicago: University of Chicago Press, 1992.

Transparency International. "Corruption Perceptions Index 2013." http:// cpi.transparency.org/cpi2013. Accessed February 14, 2014.

Turvey, B. "Criminal Profiling Research." Criminal Profiling, 1998. www.criminalprofiling.ch/article2.html. Accessed February 6, 2008.

Turvey, B. *Criminal Profiling: An Introduction to Behavioral Evidence Analysis.* New York: Academic Press, 2008.

Tyler, Tom. *Why People Obey the Law*. Princeton, NJ: Princeton University Press, 2006.

U.S. Department of Justice. www.justice.gov. Accessed January 10, 2013.

U.S. Legal. www.uslegal.com. Accessed January 15, 2013.

Walley, Liz, and Mike Smith. *Deception in Selection*. New York: Wiley, 1998.

Watkins, Sherron, and Mimi Swartz. *Power Failure: The Inside Story of the Collapse of Enron*. New York: Doubleday, 2003.

Weil, Joseph. *Con Man: A Master Swindler's Own Story*. New York: Broadway, 2004.

Weisburd, David, Elin Waring, and Ellen Chayet. *White-Collar Crime and Criminal Careers*. Cambridge: Cambridge University Press, 2001.

Wells, J. T. *Corporate Fraud Handbook: Prevention and Detection*, 4th ed. Hoboken, NJ: Wiley, 2013.

Wells, J. T. "Will Executive Transparency Help Curb Future Madoffs?" *Businesswire* 2009. www.businesswire.com/news/home/20090519006151/en. Accessed March 5, 2013.

Wells, J. T., and Laura Hymes, eds. *Bribery and Corruption Casebook: The View from under the Table*. Hoboken, NJ: Wiley, 2012.

Wetzell, Richard. *Inventing the Criminal: A History of German Criminology, 1880–1945*. Chapel Hill: University of North Carolina Press, 2000.

Wolfe, David T., and Dana R. Hermanson. "The Fraud Diamond: Considering the Four Elements of Fraud." *CPA Journal* 74, no. 12 (2004): 38.

Zeitz, Dorothy. *Women Who Embezzle or Defraud: A Study of Convicted Felons*. New York: Praeger, 1981.

Ziliak, Stephen, and Deirdre McCloskey. *The Cult of Statistical Significance: How the Standard Error Costs Us Jobs, Justice, and Lives*. Ann Arbor: University of Michigan Press, 2007.

Zuckoff, Mitchell. *Ponzi's Scheme: The True Story of a Financial Legend*. New York: Random House, 2005.

About the Author

S IMON PADGETT is a British qualified ACCA forensic accountant with 18-plus years of experience in fighting fraud and corruption. Simon has an MBA from Oxford Brookes University in the United Kingdom and has held director-level positions in forensic services roles, specifically carrying out fraud and corruption investigations and the provision of antifraud programs for clients and the organizations for which he has worked. Simon's career has included working and living in diverse geographical locations, such as the United Kingdom, the Caribbean region, South Africa, the United Arab Emirates, and many more locations while on assignments. He is currently the vice president of the United Arab Emirates Association of Certified Fraud Examiners chapter.

Throughout his career, Simon has spent a great deal of time and effort analyzing, designing, and implementing fraud control environments and ensuring that internal controls were adequate and sufficient enough to reduce fraud risk. This book was born out of the constant visualization that frauds are carried out by human beings who make conscious decisions to steal, often while being fundamental parts of those control environments designed to safeguard corporate assets. Having met, interviewed, questioned, and quite often been fundamental in the jailing of many of these human beings, it became obvious to Simon that further analysis and reasoning were required into the minds of human beings who turn to fraud and what makes them do so.

About the Association of Certified Fraud Examiners and the *Report to the Nations on Occupational Fraud and Abuse*

THE ACFE IS THE WORLD'S largest antifraud organization and premier provider of antifraud training and education.

Together with more than 70,000 members in over 150 countries, the ACFE is reducing business fraud worldwide and providing the training and resources needed to fight fraud more effectively.

Founded in 1988 by Dr. Joseph T. Wells, CFE, CPA, the ACFE provides educational tools and practical solutions for antifraud professionals through initiatives including

- Global conferences and seminars led by antifraud experts.
- Instructor-led, interactive professional training.
- Comprehensive resources for fighting fraud, including books, self-study courses, and articles.
- Leading antifraud periodicals including *Fraud Magazine*, *The Fraud Examiner*, and *FraudInfo*.
- Local networking and support through ACFE chapters worldwide.
- Antifraud curriculum and educational tools for colleges and universities.

The positive effects of antifraud training are far-reaching. Clearly, the best way to combat fraud is to educate anyone engaged in fighting fraud on how to effectively prevent, detect, and investigate it. By educating, uniting, and supporting the global antifraud community with the tools to fight fraud more effectively, the ACFE is reducing business fraud worldwide and inspiring public confidence in the integrity and objectivity of the profession. The ACFE offers its members the opportunity for professional certification. The CFE credential is preferred by businesses and government entities around the world and indicates expertise in fraud prevention and detection.

Immediate access to world-class antifraud knowledge and tools is a necessity in the fight against fraud. Members of the ACFE include accountants, internal auditors, fraud investigators, law enforcement officers, lawyers, business leaders, risk/compliance professionals, and educators, all of whom have access to expert training, educational tools, and resources. Members all over the world have come to depend on the ACFE for solutions to the challenges they face in their professions. Whether members have careers focused exclusively on preventing and detecting fraudulent activities or they just want to learn more about fraud, the ACFE provides the essential tools and resources necessary for antifraud professionals to accomplish their objectives.

ABOUT CERTIFIED FRAUD EXAMINERS

Certified fraud examiners are antifraud experts who have demonstrated knowledge in four critical areas: fraudulent financial transactions, fraud investigation, legal elements of fraud, and fraud prevention and deterrence. In support of CFEs and the CFE credential, the ACFE

- Provides bona fide qualifications for CFE's through administration of the Uniform CFE Examination.
- Requires CFEs to adhere to a strict code of professional conduct and ethics.
- Serves as the global representative for CFEs to business, government, and academic institutions.
- Provides leadership to inspire public confidence in the integrity, objectivity, and professionalism of CFEs.

ABOUT THE ACFE'S 2012 *REPORT TO THE NATIONS ON OCCUPATIONAL FRAUD AND ABUSE*

The 2012 *Report to the Nations on Occupational Fraud and Abuse* is based on the results of an online survey opened to 34,275 CFEs from October 2011 to December 2011. As part of the survey, respondents were asked to provide a detailed narrative of the single largest fraud case they had investigated that met the following four criteria:

1. The case must have involved occupational fraud (defined as internal fraud, or fraud committed by a person against the organization for which he or she works).
2. The investigation must have occurred between January 2010 and the time of survey participation.

3. The investigation must have been complete at the time of survey participation.
4. The CFE must have been reasonably sure that the perpetrator(s) was/were identified.

Respondents were then presented with 85 questions to answer regarding the particular details of the fraud case, including information about the perpetrator, the victim organization, and the methods of fraud employed, as well as about fraud trends in general.

The ACFE received 1,428 responses to the survey, 1,388 of which were usable for the purposes of this report. The data contained herein is based solely on the information provided in these 1,388 cases.

The Report's Analysis Methodology

In calculating the percentages discussed throughout the report, the total number of complete and relevant responses was used for the question(s) being analyzed. Specifically, any blank responses or instances where the participant indicated that he or she did not know the answer to a question were excluded. Consequently, the total number of cases included in each analysis varies. Several survey questions allowed participants to select more than one answer. Consequently, the sum of percentages in many charts and tables throughout the report exceeds 100 percent. All loss amounts discussed throughout the report are calculated using median loss rather than mean, or average, loss. Average losses were heavily skewed by a limited number of very-high-dollar frauds. Using median loss provides a more conservative and more accurate picture of the typical impact of occupational fraud schemes.

Who Provided the Data?

The survey was opened to all CFEs in good standing at the time of the survey launch. Respondents were asked to provide certain information about their professional experience and qualifications so that a fuller understanding of who was involved in investigating the frauds reported to us could be collected.

Primary Occupation of Respondents

More than half of the CFEs who participated in the 2011 survey identified themselves as either fraud examiners/investigators or internal auditors. Nearly 13 percent were accounting or finance professionals, and 7 percent worked in corporate security or loss prevention roles.

Experience of Respondents

Survey participants had a median 11 years of experience in the fraud examination profession. Of those participants who provided information on their tenure in the field, 78 percent had more than five years of antifraud experience, and nearly one-fifth of participants had worked in fraud examination for more than 20 years.

Nature of Fraud Examinations Conducted by Respondents

Of the CFEs who provided information about the nature of fraud examination engagements they conduct, more than half stated that they worked in-house at an organization for which they conducted internal fraud examinations. Twenty-nine percent identified themselves as working for a professional services firm that conducts fraud examinations on behalf of other companies or agencies, and 12 percent of respondents worked for a law enforcement agency.

To learn more, visit www.ACFE.com or call (800) 245-3321.

Index